(Continued from front flap)

distinguishing the antiquated from the permanently interesting aspects of Descartes' physiological theory. He likewise shows that Descartes' vital message endures: there is no meaningful psychosomatic medicine detached from metaphysics, physiological theory, or explicit discussion of the ultimate values by which human beings are to guide their lives. In addition to the commentary, Dr. Blom provides a conceptual index that interrelates important elements in Descartes' thought.

The letters are intrinsically interesting and inviting to the general reader. Moreover, Blom's commentary, by revealing Descartes' dependence upon classical sources, makes this volume of special value to students of French literature and history, as well as to contemporary philosophers and psychologists.

John J. Blom graduated, *magna cum laude,* from Amherst College and received his Ph.D. from Columbia University. He has taught philosophy at Columbia University, Manhattanville College and Hunter College and is the author of *René Descartes: The Essential Writings.*

D1562869

DESCARTES

His Moral Philosophy
and Psychology

DESCARTES

His Moral Philosophy and Psychology

Translated, and with Introduction and a Conceptual Index, by
John J. Blom

New York • New York University Press • 1978

Copyright © 1978 by John J. Blom

Library of Congress Cataloging in Publication Data

Descartes, René, 1596-1650.
  Descartes, his moral philosophy and psychology.

  Includes bibliographical references and index.
    1. Ethics—Collected works. 2. Psychology—Early
works to 1650—Collected works. I. Blom, John J.
II. Title.
B1837.B44   1979   194   78-55241
ISBN 0-8147-0999-0

Manufactured in the United States of America

For my Mother

PREFACE

This volume presents material, most of it for the first time in English, that is requisite for any study of Descartes' moral philosophy and psychology. Descartes' reflections on moral philosophy and psychology were largely developed in correspondence with Princess Elisabeth (of Bohemia), Queen Christina (of Sweden), and Pierre Chanut (French Ambassador to Sweden). The portion of that correspondence dealing with moral philosophy and psychology thus constitutes the core of the present volume. I have also included the Preface to the French version of Descartes' *Principles of Philosophy*. The Preface contains his views on education.

Descartes was led by this correspondence to write the *Passions of the Soul*.[1] Because the *Passions* contains antiquated physiological theory, it seems arcane to us. The correspondence, however, remains more lucid and pertinent. It shows how much Descartes hoped psychosomatic medicine would become a tool helping men to self-mastery; it likewise shows his insistence that such an instrument should subserve intelligently selected values. Of course, any serious understanding of Descartes' moral philosophy and psychology requires familiarity with his metaphysics. Therefore I have thought it best to use the bulk of my introduction to accent the continuity of Descartes' moral philosophy and psychology with his metaphysics.

The translations are based upon the original French texts presented in the standard edition of Messieurs Adam and Tannery.[2] I have aimed at fidelity in translation, trying to convey the style of the original. I also adhere quite closely to the punctuation given by Adam and Tannery and avoid recasting long sentences into short ones.

I have also added a conceptual index that divides and interrelates important elements in Descartes' moral philosophy and psychology. The significance of the major headings will be readily apparent. By reading through the index as a whole, the reader will glean some suggestions for structuring the various materials that occur in the course of the correspondence. For ease of reference, entries are made by paragraph numbers.

The reader will find important bibliographical information by consulting Gregor Sebba's *Bibliographia Cartesiana* [3] and Geneviève Rodis-Lewis' edition of *Les passions de l'âme*. [4]

In my introduction I have used some materials previously published by Harper & Row. [5]

Anne Marie Weissman has helped me over some real hurdles in translation. Dr. Charles Sherover has given me much incisive editorial advice. I am grateful to Mr. Robert Bull and Ms. Despina Papazoglou of NYU Press for their valuable suggestions regarding the organization of this volume.

Old Greenwich, Ct.   J.J.B.

CONTENTS

---

* Roman numerals indicate the listing in *Corre-
spondance, Oeuvres*, CCXXVI-CCCX in vol. III; CCCXI-
CDLXVIII in vol. IV; CDLXXIX in vol. X, *Supplément a la
Correspondance*; CDLXXXVIII–DXXXIX in vol. V.

---

* *Oeuvres,* vol. V, p 556.

BIOGRAPHICAL SKETCHES
OF CORRESPONDENTS

Pierre Chanut was French resident and then ambassador to the court of Sweden. He was brother-in-law of Descartes' translator, Clerselier. Chanut interested Queen Christina in Descartes and helped secure her invitation for the philosopher to come to Sweden. Chanut and Descartes became warm friends, and after the philosopher's death Chanut took immediate care of his papers.

Queen Christina (1626–1689) was daughter of Gustavus Adolphus and Marie-Elenora of Brandenburg. She became queen at six years of age, converted to Catholicism in 1652, and abdicated the throne in 1654. Christina was a forceful personality and powerful intellect. She was well educated and particularly talented at languages. Having persuaded Descartes to come to Sweden, she not only followed his tutoring, but had him write the statutes for a Swedish academy.

René Descartes (1596–1650) was born at La Haye in Touraine. He was the fourth child of Joachim Descartes and Jeanne Brochard. His mother died a year later after giving birth. Descartes never married but had an illegitimate daughter, Francine. He was trained at the Jesuit College of La Flèche and later studied law at Poitiers. In 1618 he went to Holland to serve in the army of Maurice of Nassau. In 1628 he retired to Holland where he remained, except for brief interludes, until he went to Sweden in 1649. It is thought that the severity of the Swedish weather and his demanding regimen in serving Queen Christina were the proximate causes of his death. Included among Descartes' correspondents were Arnauld, Balzac, Fermat, Hobbes, Huygens, and others. To the end, Descartes remained a devout Catholic.

Princess Elisabeth (1618–1680) was daughter of Elisabeth Stuart and Frederick V. On her mother's side she was descended from the House of Orange. Her father favored the Protestant cause and accepted the crown of Bohemia. As a result, the family was forced into exile in 1620 by the victory of the Spanish and Bavarian forces. Elisabeth, one of thirteen children, was raised in Holland. She was a devout Protestant and always a serious student of languages, religion, and mathematics. Elisabeth never married and was constantly concerned, but to no avail, to see her family restored. Descartes met with Elisabeth as well as corresponded with her, and to her he dedicated his *Principles of Philosophy*. Elisabeth finally accepted the post of abbess at Herford, a Lutheran monastery in Westphalia.

Alphonse de Pollot was friend to Descartes and intermediary between the philosopher and Elisabeth.

INTRODUCTION

Self-deception in the political tyrant frequently grows to the grotesque. The tyrant accordingly has become a classical symbol for that blinding universal—*ignorance*. For centuries men spoke, not only of political tyranny, but of a tyranny of their own passions. The tyranny of nature, religion, class, the unconscious, sex, motherhood, and "education," each strikes its bell with us. One thing is certain. Tyranny—or ignorance—works its mortal blow by numbing the pains intended to remind us of the requirements of health. Such a blow is never primarily physical, but rather a sedation of our powers of judgment causing us to mistake our own substance. Irrationality remains the birthright of the rational animal, and to invite a tyranny upon ourselves we need only allow ourselves to invent false enemies or become preoccupied with minor ones.

But Plato taught us we are born in a cave and must learn by imitation. First principles, at least those that are serious, cannot be proved for us straight off. Thus when theoreticians design our cave to make it less a labyrinth, our native prudence becomes apprehensive. Their blueprints are specifications of principles as yet not proved to us. The essence of great teachers—properly speaking there are no others—commands them to respect this native prudence, indeed to require it. Plato, Augustine, Descartes, Kant, intensify our problem of "faith and reason" by resisting flattery. They undoubtedly foresaw us prepared to glean from them some isolated "inspiration" for our poetry, politics, science, and religion. Yet, read them just a little, and we are embarrassed for wanting the convenience of remaining beggars. At every turn they invite us to accept or reject. We may come to decide they are in error, but we will never have grounds to charge them with a tyranny. They shun such a vulnerable paternity.

Although the intent of major philosophers remains *not* to dominate, we cannot read them without feeling we will deceive ourselves—tyrannize over ourselves—if we neglect the comprehensive experience that philosophy pursues. Philosophy indeed attempts to be comprehensive. New limits are fixed for sense, imagination, will, and intellect. As their prerogatives are changed, so are the pathologies. Reasonableness in science, politics, art, and religion do not remain the same. Our sense of humor is altered. We are tempered differently as regards the lyric mood. This philosophic comprehensiveness is no superficial conjunction of our various discoveries, no spurning of detail in favor of vague generalities. Its importance—its moral, or practical, significance—is indicated by the caution with which major philosophers try to determine the limits of particular principles. We are constantly reminded that when otherwise good principles are pushed too far, the price of one insight will be the loss of others. Philosophy promises to prevent the myopia that would cause us to mistake our own substance.

Like Socrates, Descartes assigned a perfected philosophy, and the moral autonomy it implies, only to God. Yet "to live without philosophy is to have one's eyes closed without ever trying to open them." [6] Few, he believed, are so oppressed, even by poverty or the chains that bound the less civilized, as not to have imprecisely imagined some higher good. And similarly, good fortune—as regards health, honors, wealth—only augments the ardor for philosophy, showing it to be most natural for man. Still, to partake directly in the satisfactions of philosophy, and to share in the moral self-sufficiency it holds out, a man must already be quite reasonable. For philosophy is an activity of men purely as men. Its best teachers could claim no supernatural powers.

Descartes never dared to be more than a man among men. One urgency, however, underlied his announcement of his philosophy to the learned world and to the leaders of government whose obligation it was to enhance the mores of men. That was his belief that by joining him they would speed the day of the sciences—the day when more men could share in health and wealth, not as ends in themselves, but as means to that accomplished rationality for which men are intended. Indeed, Descartes was convinced that his "method," which produced his philosophy and promised to spell progress for the sciences, was paradigmatic of rational investigation generally and should become the model whereby men developed their native powers of reasoning.

Descartes is one of the most consequential of thinkers, piloting currents of debate, research, and speculation that have brought on our modern age. From the start, his untiring efforts to cultivate his reason all aimed at responsible practice, not merely in his search for personal contentment, but in his attempt to make solid contributions to the sciences. Descartes applied himself to mathematics and physics with a view to making men masters, not usurpers, of nature. He attempted a reduction of biology to physics, hoping that medicine could be built on firm foundations.[7] He studied the human body as if it were a machine and tried to determine how its structure helps or impedes learning.[8] The details of Descartes' science are mostly antiquated. But its metaphysical foundations are more formidable and still highly influential. His views of substance, force, inertia, cannot be lightly dismissed.

Moreover, Descartes knew that the responsible *application* of the sciences requires an understanding of the metaphysical structure and purpose of man—of the causes that lay a hold on man, his powers of self-determination, the kinds of realities to which he can relate, and the solidity of the enjoyments he may take in them. Thus in addition to trying to secure the fundamentals of his mathematics and physics, Descartes used his metaphysical treatises to investigate the question of man and his place in nature. He argued for the existence of God. He attempted to establish the theory of mind-body dualism—the view that man is a composite of two different but interacting substances, mind and body. He maintained that reason suffices to determine the goods we should pursue and defended a doctrine of free will. On that metaphysical picture hinged his more detailed discussion of 'virtue', which he defined as the correct reasoning that should guide our practice. On that same picture likewise depended his conception of the humane application of the sciences. Concerning free will, Descartes held that its quality, or degree, is proportionate to one's knowledge. He also insisted that man's nervous system makes it more difficult for some to thwart their passions or even to acquire the knowledge needed for truly virtuous or voluntary action.[9] He left no doubt that without a study of the body there could be no solid moral philosophy and psychology—no finished *morale*.

It was only late in his life, at the request primarily of Princess Elisabeth of Bohemia and Queen Christina of Sweden, that Descartes discussed at length the nature of virtue, that is, the correct reasoning that should guide our practice. His letters to Elisabeth and to Christina, and the third part of his treatise, *Passions of the Soul*, contain such discussion. At the same time, Descartes also tried to lay the foundations of a psychosomatic medicine. The letters to Elisabeth, and the first two parts of the *Passions*, study the human body with regard to determining strategies whereby reason, armed with virtue or correct reasoning, can prevent the passions from becoming tyrannical. Thus the letters to Elisabeth and Christina, together with the *Passions*, constitute Descartes' *morale*. That is, they combine a consideration of what is virtuous, or right, with attention to the psychophysical conditions that bear on whether a person can realize and execute virtue.[10]

Christina wrote to Descartes only once. Normally she related her questions for Descartes to Chanut, the French ambassador to Sweden, who then wrote Descartes conveying the Queen's requests. The correspondence with Elisabeth is much more extensive than that with Christina. By the time their correspondence turned to *morale*, Elisabeth and Descartes had already corresponded about mathematics and mind-body dualism, and Elisabeth had pressed the question of how mind-body interaction is possible.[11] The turning came when Descartes' solicitations regarding Elisabeth's health led him to suggest that mental distress (melancholy) brought on her condition. She then questioned him in detail concerning the reciprocal influences of mind and body, asking him to advise strategies for gaining a mastery over the passions. Previously, in the *Discourse on Method*, Descartes noted there are illnesses of the mind that depend on the body and expressed the hope of eventually applying his physics to medicine to help cure such psychosomatic diseases. Thus Elisabeth's questioning, by leading Descartes to write the *Passions*, helped him fulfill his hope to apply science in psychosomatic medicine. The *Passions*, though touching on the topic of virtue, primarily contains an investigation of the psychophysical relation, with special emphasis on the emotions. Instead of calling the *Passions* a treatise in medicine, Descartes claimed to speak as physicist. He wished to accentuate the fact that the biological principles employed stemmed from his physics.[12]

At the same time as Elisabeth urged Descartes to explain the reciprocal influences of mind and body and recommend strategies useful in mastering the passions, she likewise insisted that indecision about desirable ends, or scruples as to whether one is pursuing them as best one can, frequently causes the discomfort that lays one open to the debilitating force of the passions. Elisabeth's concern was with the situation where the passions become debilitating. She did not wish to be relieved of such helpful "disturbances" as would keep her properly mindful of the difficulties in identifying and pursuing reasonable goals. In the *Discourse* Descartes had also touched on this crucial and primary moral question of deciding goals worthy of pursuit. There he first identified virtue with the correct reasoning whereby one determines truly desirable ends.[13] Thus, in effect, Elisabeth was also inviting Descartes to speak in the traditional vein of a moral philosopher and to elaborate upon his inchoate doctrine of virtue and value found in the *Discourse*. Failing such elaboration any strategies for redirecting the passions would remain devoid of standards for their reasonable application.

Their moral correspondence accordingly issued from Elisabeth's wanting to be counselled how to apply to daily life the philosophy Descartes had developed. She was asking him to spell out the practical consequences of his metaphysics of man. An examination of the correspondence shows that Descartes often expresses himself on moral topics with terminology familiar from the ancients—"virtue", "the sovereign good," "blessedness", "fortune". Yet the terminology acquires a new significance in Descartes' hands. He does not simply repeat old formulas. And the full import of what he does say can be gathered only when we recall his metaphysical picture of the person.

Thus, for example, rather than allow himself to be categorized with any one of the ancients, Descartes claims to reconcile what many considered three contradictory theses concerning the nature of the sovereign good— namely, the thesis of Epicurus, who held it is pleasure; that of Zeno the Stoic, who held it is virtue or honor; and that of Aristotle, who placed it in the greatest accumulation of all the goods that nature and fortune might bestow.

In trying to reconcile these theses, Descartes begins by distinguishing between the sovereign good and the blessedness that supervenes on it, and thus presupposes it. He then interprets Epicurus' 'pleasure' as comprehending all mental satisfactions, not just sensible pleasure, and he takes this epicurean pleasure as blessedness. Descartes also goes on to claim that Aristotle and Zeno are facing different concerns: Aristotle speaks of a blessedness depending partly on fortune, Zeno of a blessedness in our power. Descartes clearly endorses Zeno's existential approach, his emphasis upon a blessedness due to our actions. Thus Descartes follows Zeno in defining the sovereign good, which produces a solid blessedness or pleasure, as virtue. Descartes furthermore defines this virtue as 'correct reasoning,' maintaining he is the first to do so. Whether or not he is the first to do so explicitly, his definition nevertheless seems inspired by Zeno, for correct reasoning is *pertinent* reasoning, and nothing is more pertinent than to resist being side-tracked by good fortune and to concentrate upon such solid satisfaction as comes only from the conviction one is doing one's best.

Descartes, then, tries to reconcile the ethical formulas of the ancients. Yet until we examine his metaphysical view of human freedom and understand the realities comprising the larger whole of which he considers each man but a part, we cannot fathom the blessedness he says is consequent upon correct reasoning, that is, upon correct evaluation of one's role in that whole.

To help the reader to such a closer appreciation of Descartes' thought, I will, in Part I of my introduction, provide a preliminary sketch of the views concerning moral philosophy and psychology found in the Correspondence and *Passions*. In Part II, I will emphasize important aspects of Descartes' method, particularly as found in the *Discourse*. In Part III, I will explain the metaphysical picture on which the coherence of Descartes' views depends. Finally, in Part IV, I will give a more precise formulation of crucial elements in Descartes' moral psychology. With the preliminary sketch and this further background the reader can extract from the Correspondence itself a deeper appreciation of Descartes' position in moral philosophy.

Part I. DESCARTES' MORAL PHILOSOPHY AND PSYCHOLOGY: A PRELIMINARY SKETCH

When Descartes finally wrote the *Passions*, Elisabeth approved its manner of enumerating the various passions. And, although hesitant about the details, she clearly appreciated its emphasis upon the physiology of the passions. For her, as for Descartes, the virtuous man was obliged to study the mind-body relation as part of self-mastery and to understand others. The Stoics had conceived their sage as rational but not always as laboring under the conditions of the rational animal. Zeno had even denied that the passions are natural to man, calling them diseases.[14] Descartes and Elisabeth emerge closer to the Aristotelean position, namely, that in man the passions are natural and not an evil per se. Human rationality thus consists in not too closely likening ourselves to gods, but in recognizing the naturalness of the passions, and in studying both to prevent their becoming diseases and to cull their positive benefits. The passions, of course, operate by a kind of excess. Their force can fix our train of thought and even dispose our body to a course of action. Such force can be harmful or salutary, and we must try to direct it to beneficial ends. Following tradition, Descartes and Elisabeth will accordingly name the passions "emotions" or even "perturbations of the soul" in order to emphasize this force with which they act upon us.[15] Nonetheless, their view remains that human industry should direct the passions to their best use; it should not try to expunge them.

[1]

Chapter 1. PASSION AND VOLITION

First I will try to convey some rough idea of the relation between 'passion' and 'volition.' But before proceeding, I shall briefly explain why, not until Part III, where his metaphysics is discussed, can we fully appreciate Descartes' argument for maintaining that genuine volition, or real mental action, is possible.

1. POSSIBILITY OF VOLITION AND METAPHYSICS

'Volition' may refer to an exercise of our power to give or withhold assent from a proposition (*liberum arbitrium*). But it can also refer to any of our desires, or wants, to sustain or refrain from certain thoughts (*voluntates* or *volontés*). Sometimes these desires, or wants, will be intended to bring about an effect in the body; at other times not. It is by intelligent volitions, then, that we would normally hope to control our behavior and resist harmful passions.

Yet volition, or mental action, may easily seem a farce to anyone metaphysically committed to the wholesale materialism that views mind as nothing but mechanistically determined matter. Similarly, it will seem a farce to anyone who believes in epiphenomenalism, the doctrine that physiological occurrences rigidly determine mental ones, so that human beings have no mental spontaneity or free will. Whoever is committed to materialism or epiphenomenalism will conclude that a man's true hope for resisting harmful passions and attaining mental contentment ultimately depends, not on volition or mental action, not on anything the man can do, but on some fortunate ordering of physiological occurrences.

In our eventual examination of Descartes' metaphysics, we will see how he argues against the reducibility of mind to matter presupposed by materialism, and also against the rigid determination of mental by physiological occurrences presupposed by epiphenomenalism. We will see that Descartes *never* implies what Spinoza, for example, seems to imply: namely, that a man would reach *complete* mental contentment if only there could somehow be a correct or fortunate ordering of physiological occurrences. We shall also see that Descartes connects his metaphysical defense of free will with his metaphysical justification of values. He argues, not only for free will, but for the existence of a personal God. By admitting both free will and a personal God, his ontology thereby countenances realities and values clearly excluded by a view like Spinoza's, which denies a personal God and maintains that all mental occurrences follow from an external necessity in direct correlation with physiological occurrences. Thus the "adequate" clarification of the thoughts constituting our various passions, the tracing back of these thoughts to their grounding in genuine reality and therefore to their true and not specious value, must accordingly differ on metaphysics so different as Descartes' and Spinoza's. According to Descartes, the numerous passions that, when examined, are found to pre-suppose belief in a personal God and in human free will are accorded a legitimacy. Reason does not suggest we regard such passions as the result of some physiological quirk or piece of bad fortune.

2. PASSIONS: PRIMITIVE AND COMPLEX

Despite any bodily causes or external manifestations, the passions involve thoughts or imaginations and accordingly occur in the mind. Descartes maintains that we have six primitive passions: admiration, love, hate, desire, joy, and sorrow. These primitive passions do not occur in complete isolation even when their object is quite simple. The infant, for example, will experience, albeit confusingly, thoughts of love mixed with thoughts of desire in regard to a relatively simple object such as its nourishment. The complex passions such as pride, humility, disdain, and veneration are likewise combinations of the primitive passions. Yet rather than being simple, their object is more complicated, involving comparisons. In pride, for example, we love ourselves and desire to remain as we are; but we also compare ourselves to a certain standard. It would be an endless labor to try to label each complex passion. They are no less numerous than the vast array of objects of love, hate, and desire that we might foolishly or wisely compare in different ways.

3. PASSIONS: SOME INTERIOR; OTHERS DEPEND ON THE BODY

Although all the thoughts and imaginations experienced during the passions occur in the mind, it nevertheless seems that some passions are more interior to the mind and others more dependent on the body. Descartes maintains that an exercise of pure thought need not involve somatic accompaniments. However, where thought is also accompanied by an exercise of the imagination, the latter is often precipitated by physical stimuli and attended by bodily symptoms and motor responses. Accordingly, Descartes maintains that passions involving only pure thought seem interior to the mind, whereas those that involve thought plus imagination seem dependent on the body.

It is worth noting that an object occasionally entertained by pure thought alone is very often entertained by thought plus imagination. Thus, one can have a purely intellectual love, hate, or desire toward an object such as God, reality, evil, mankind, or one's nation, for example, when one reflects philosophically upon the nature and value of the given object. Yet, if one also imagines that same object or a symbol for that object, one adds a sensitive to the intellectual passion, for example, when, instead of thinking only of mankind or the state in general, one imagines one's neighbors or president as somehow representing them; or when, instead of using only pure thought to think of God (who has nothing intrinsically imaginable about Him), one also imagines His love for man as symbolized in the Incarnation or man's for Him as symbolized by our concernful identification with His sensible creation, that is, with nature and with neighbor.

4. INTERIOR PASSIONS AND VOLITION

To the extent, then, that we interiorize a passion, we can expect an abatement of whatever motor reactions and bodily symptoms normally attend those passions involving a use of the imagination. An interior passion can, nevertheless, be very intense, greatly occupying our thoughts and influencing our behavior. This influence will be better or worse depending on how reasonable are the thoughts constituting the passion.

When a passion seems interior to the mind, or to stem from the mind alone, one will likely consider the thoughts constituting it as becoming one's volitions if they seem either unconfused or as meriting further consideration. In the former case one will identify with the thoughts. In the latter case one will deem it foolish, even an intellectual vice, to want to neglect them. Thus, the interior passions can be useful. Indeed, to cultivate useful interior passions is, in effect, to cultivate beneficial habits of evaluation or ample powers of volition.

5. PRIORITY OF THE INTERIOR PASSIONS

We should, furthermore, strive to make the interior passions temporally and logically prior to passions involving the imagination and the human body. As indicated, the sensible realm, which, strictly speaking, is all we can "imagine," may be interpreted, sometimes as directly expressive of, sometimes as merely a symbol for, widely diverse meanings and ideas. Moreover, bodily dispositions will attend our evaluating as hateful, lovable, or desirable, the things we thus sense or imagine. These bodily dispositions will be harmful or salutary depending upon whether interpretations and evaluations are stupid or intelligent. Hence, in order to avoid harm, and to benefit as much as possible, Descartes urges that one become, as it were, an architect of the passions that affect one's body. To do that, one must first acquire intelligent interior passions or engage in the advance interior reflection that allows one to determine the bodily passions to be cultivated, including of course the interpretations and evaluations to be put on various sensible objects.

Such architecture of the passions affecting one's body is obviously an achievement; it is something to strive for. Each man is initially thrown into a world and acquires passions, he knows not how, for values he has not as yet fully examined. In order to cultivate intelligent interior passions it is important to examine first how passions that depend on the body *tend* to be formed and to note their relation to mental activity and volition.

6. FORMATION OF PASSIONS, MENTAL ACTIVITY, AND VOLITION

In the case of the numerous passions that involve the imagination and thus seem dependent on the body, physiological processes cause, or at least sustain, not only imaginations, but also exterior movements such as running or cringing, and exterior signs such as crying, pallor, or being hungry. These passions are frequently responses to an obvious external circumstance, for example, one's fear of a menacing animal or the hungry man's delight in finding nourishment. However, they are often precipitated either by some

[6]

thought or unknown internal bodily event that triggers the physiological processes that sustain one's imaginations, as when one is somehow plagued by images of a new war or cannot desist from imagining possible misuses of genetic engineering.

As mentioned, Descartes maintains that our power of pure thought seems much less intimately dependent on the body than does our power of imagination. He nonetheless assumes that, *other things being equal*, our thoughts, including thoughts of love, hate, and desire, tend to become associated with certain imaginations. Consequently they tend to become contingently connected with the often unknown underlying physiological processes that cause not only those imaginations, but also the exterior movements and signs characteristic of the passions. Hence the reoccurrence of the same thoughts will tend to be accompanied by the same imaginations and exterior movements and signs, and vice versa.

We experience near instinctive reactions. One automatically retrieves one's hand from the fire. Afterward, the thought that one shall be burned is accompanied, not only by fretful imaginations, but by a motor disposition to flee. The thoughts that come to be associated with a given stimulus can be very variable and complicated. A child may explicitly perceive the person hurting him as some or all the following: man, white man, father, professor. Other thoughts will be associated with each of these, and the child's future seeings or imaginings of such associated things may be colored by his experience of fear. Similarly, although a child may not explicitly perceive or take note of the physiognomy of the person hurting him, nevertheless his future experiences or imaginations of similar persons might, without his even realizing it, be colored by fear. Thus, one's passional life can become idiosyncratic, drifting into a complexity that defies easy labeling, even recognition. The passions, in short, can become insensible to those who undergo them and to those who would observe them. This insensibility could consist in a particular passion having no discernible object, few bodily symptoms, or both.

The complicated nature of the human passions, even those dependent on the body, thus largely derives from the complicated objects they acquire. But these, in turn, depend on two mental powers: first, that of forging and severing associations among thoughts, as in devising new propositions; and second, that of bringing about new associations between propositions and images, as in revising perceptual estimates. Without these two mental powers we could not acquire, examine, revise, or amplify the perceptions of sense and imagination or the contents of our passions.

Yet unless properly directed, these mental powers, so necessary for human thinking, can allow us to drift unaware into mistaken imaginations and passions. Descartes regards the mind as more passive, that is, less self-directive or less active, the more it fails to reflect upon and evaluate its manner of associating thought to thought and thoughts to images. The more passive the mind, the more overly dependent it is upon physiology. For, as said, *other things being equal,* thoughts tend to become associated (very often mistakenly) with particular imaginations, and these in turn become contingently connected to particular physiological occurrences. Thus if the mind remains passive, and fails to evaluate these associations or neglects to alter them when warranted, it will simply remain victim to whatever train of ill-associated thoughts and imaginations might be triggered off by physiological occurrences with which they have by chance become contingently connected.

To the contrary, as one's mind becomes active and discerning, and cultivates intelligent interior passions, reactions, even near-instinctive reactions, can be watched and modified, as when a once brutalized child, even though still disposed to imagine it or declare it, nevertheless stops inferring that any man will hurt him, or as when Joan of Arc chooses to stay at her stake. The more active one's thinking, the more voluntary will be one's thought and action. The more it will then dawn on one to notice the suggestions of passion, to evaluate them, and thus to "choose" the self, or attain to self-possession. The more one recognizes the exact good to be derived from the passions, the more voluntary one's experiences of them become—just because one is more intelligently convinced of the action one ought to take. In some cases that exact good consists in giving sway to a passion, to embracing it. In other cases it consists in resisting the passion and employing strategies to subdue it.

7. OBSTACLES POSED BY PASSIONS AND STRATEGIES FOR REDIRECTING HARMFUL PASSIONS

It depends very much on chance or fortune whether an individual has the experience—the surroundings, education, and so on—required to spur the methodical and probing thought that discerns genuine values and distinguishes passions worth cultivating from those to be eradicated. But before discussing the experience which Descartes deems requisite for ample powers of volition to emerge, we should note two general obstacles posed by passions dependent on the body, as well as certain strategies for redirecting harmful passions.

The passions that depend on the body tend to fix one's attention rigidly upon sensuous or readily imaginable goods and evils. We should accustom ourselves to weigh the suggestions of such passions against the infinitely more important mental joys and sorrows that they might impede or cause. However, the nature of these mental joys and sorrows, and their great importance, must be made plain.

Supervening upon human encounters, for example, upon loyal or unloyal friendships, rewarding or mindless conversations, genuine recognition or obsequiousness, are the more purely mental joys and sorrows that stand at the very heart of life. These mental joys and sorrows follow inevitably upon our consciousness of the values and shortcomings, or of the successes and failures, in our human encounters. One could not disregard encounters such as friendship, human communication, and human striving without walking out on life itself. The only way to avoid mental sorrow and attain solid mental pleasure is to learn forthrightly what these encounters ought to be by making explicit to oneself the objective goods and evils that conduct may involve.

The passions that operate strongly on sense and imagination will not blind one to these goods and evils provided one has cultivated worthwhile interior passions by habituating oneself to a detailed meditation upon life. Moreover, such meditation—such detailed identification and evaluation of the goods and evils that conduct may involve—will also prepare one more readily to *imagine* many concrete advantages superior to those suggested by undesirable passions. In that way one will learn to oppose beneficial to harmful imaginations—which, we will see, is a key strategy for quelling unwanted passions.

In addition, the moment of passion makes it difficult to compare even one sort of sensible pleasure or distress with others. To prepare adequately for the experience of the passions, one must remember that they often exaggerate the good or evil in the objects to whose pursuit or avoidance they incline one. Thus the imaginative anticipation of some pleasure or pain often leads one to expect better or worse than the real experience involves. What makes the objects represented in passion seem better or worse than they are stems from the fact that, when undergoing a passion, one's body is often physically disposed to pursue or avoid the object, and the nervous system inclines one to fix attention upon imagining the object even though there may well be no *rational* evidence why it should so merit concern. That is why, having evaluated, outside the moment of passion, those passions to embrace and those to resist, one can try, based on a knowledge of the nervous system, to devise strategies to subdue harmful passions.

Such strategies are discussed in the *Passions* and the Correspondence. They basically reduce to mastering the passions by indirect control of the body. Indirect control of the body has more basic applications than in the case of the passions. For example, although one may wish the pupil of one's eye to enlarge, merely wishing it without directing one's sight to a distant object is not enough. Similarly, in the case of the passions, mere wishing often cannot bring about the changes in one's nerves required to subdue unwanted imaginations or the exterior movements and signs of the passions. Yet one can try to subdue all these unwanted effects by discovering thoughts that lead to imaginations capable of inducing nervous activities opposed to those sustaining the unwanted imaginations and movements.

To develop such a technique of self-mastery fully requires background knowledge of the human body, for example, the role of the internal organs, the effects of drugs, diet, and exercise in sustaining moods and emotions, as well as careful meditation upon the relations between thoughts, imaginations, and nervous activities specific to our case. Clearly, then, such a technique is no commoner's art. Only by good fortune will a man ever have the opportunity to develop well-meditated interior passions and to furnish his imagination with valid examples. And only by an especially good fortune would he have the leisure and know-how to attend to the idiosyncrasies of his nervous system and detect the thoughts and imaginations that work particularly well for him in calming the spectrum of his passions. Thus, rather than discuss Descartes' psychophysical strategies for implementing already formed decisions as to the value of various passions, we will turn to the general conditions without which any careful insights into values could never emerge.

[11]

Chapter 2. INSIGHT INTO VALUES AND THE NEED FOR TRAINING IN THE HUMANITIES AND SCIENCES

According to Descartes, animals other than man are swept along to narrowly preordained reactions by sheer physiological mechanism and reflexivity. Passivity is their whole estate, not merely a symptom of an incompletely developed nature or lack of good fortune. Man, however, in virtue of his very capacity for reasonable loves, hates, and desires, will continue to suffer a passivity unnatural to himself until his reason learns not to misconstrue experience and begins to hit the mark in questions about values.

Man, meant for reasonable loves, hates, and desires, easily falls prey to mistaken ones. I have mentioned the power of thought whereby emotional stimuli can be perceived or misperceived in many ways, and the manifold associations to which one's thoughts and imaginations are susceptible, and by which an emotion such as love or hate can in turn be distributed, for good or for ill, over many objects. Without such powers of thought and imagination, one could never experience or share in, devise, or readapt human values and evils, such as marriage, parenthood, citizenship, competition, war, freedom, and slavery. All such values and evils are human 'institutions,' 'mores,' or 'products'—far more complicated than anything remotely similar among the animals. They are the triumphs or scandals of human reason.

If one's initial experiences of values are not correct, or sufficiently catholic, the impediments are bound to be greater to one's appreciating, even by more intellectual reflection, what others deem valuable in such experiences. To the extent one fails of the proper experiences of values, one will not be properly outfitted for empathy with others nor properly proportioned in self-esteem. In short, experience goes a long way to forming or malforming what we may call the empirical-valuing-self.

No society, moreover, any more than an individual, is

fated to hit the mark in this difficult business of avoiding "corrupt" mores and discovering and encouraging humane values and institutions. Descartes is still at home with speaking of civilized and uncivilized. More relevant perhaps is his insistence upon fostering genuine culture of which philosophy, which is at once our "sovereign good" and the highest expression of human reason, is the greatest manifestation. Thus we never find Descartes dreaming of an innocent savage. Rather, good fortune for both individual and society begins with imitating actions approved by those of higher wisdom. And the curriculum for fostering well-formed and well-informed selves requires that individual and society move toward philosophy by ascending various stages of wisdom or erudition. These stages the reader will find adumbrated in the *Discourse* and more definitively spelled out in the preface to the *Principles*. For now we need only note Descartes' view that a responsible moral education, which brings one to a philosophical insight into value, must combine training in the humanities and sciences.

Wisdom starts with the proper models, examples, and readings; it begins with humane letters, discretely taught and absorbed. Only then—after spanning time and place and becoming acquainted with what is deemed valuable in diverse mores—can one begin to judge what is truly valuable. Only then will one possess the *data* upon which to reflect about the nature of man and humane values.

Like Descartes, Cardinal Richelieu had also recognized that through the study of letters one learns to pose the question of what life is meant to be. And, like Descartes, he complained of the low state to which such studies had fallen. Richelieu recommended that only the best students be permitted to study letters. The others would simply learn to raise more doubts than they were able or patient enough to resolve. The mass of men, then, would supposedly function best if pigeonholed into the study of the commercial and technological arts.[16]

Descartes' diagnosis and prognosis were different—and

they reveal a different view of human intelligence and its products. Improperly studied, letters are, of course, a problem. However, Descartes insists that a great part of the problem in the study of letters is that men waste too much time at them and make little progress because they do not know how to reflect *methodically* on the data provided. Thus our insights into the nature of man and humane values are not advanced. Moreover, Descartes was convinced that methodical reflection on letters requires mental operations *not* essentially different from those needed to study, not only the pure sciences, but the applied arts as well. As regards discovery in the applied arts, Descartes maintained it need not be a helter-skelter matter, but that new inventions might be deduced from well-founded scientific principles.

Descartes emphasized that history would soon make it obvious that the ability to think well technologically depends on the ability to do purer scientific thinking. And in also foreseeing the enormous power of science to change the face of the earth, he warned, in a way Richelieu did not, of the great hubris of which science would be capable. For Richelieu's vision of those toiling at science and commerce constantly deferring to gentlemen of letters was an effete, not enlightened, aristocratic vision that the sheer power of science was destined to frustrate. Descartes, however, by insisting that the mental operations or strategies that make for good scientific thinking can also be applied to evaluate letters, and to resolve the questions of value and philosophy, held out the prospect of educating a modern man sufficiently willing and sufficiently able to connect questions of science and questions of value.

Descartes' emphasis on the power of science to change the face of the earth, by alerting us that the "facts" need not remain as they are, also drives home our obligation to think more responsibly, more existentially, about what ought to be. It helps create that healthy streak in the modern consciousness—the feeling that it very much depends on us whether what ought to be will in fact come to be. It makes it more difficult for us to blithely excuse what 'is' as more 'natural' than what 'ought to be'—and our theoretical and practical intelligence are accordingly less dichotomized. Indeed, according to Descartes, "true" philosophy is our "sovereign good" precisely because it teaches, and exercises us in, this unity of theoretical and practical thinking. And because Descartes' philosophy claimed to do this, his royal correspondents, Christina and Elisabeth, and that *homme d'affaires*, Chanut, naturally found its study appealing. For being political sovereigns or their deputies, they were obliged to think always with reference to the awesome questions of practice—to the making and the breaking of mores.

Chapter 3. ULTIMATE CRITERION OF VALUE, OR GOOD: THE PRINCIPLE OF BENEVOLENCE

Care with regard to judgments about mores is at once the right use of our will, or power of volition, and the mark of virtue, or correct reasoning. For when appreciable powers for moral reflection have once emerged, only one's own choosing guarantees one will do one's best, that is, take the means, or do the often arduous thinking required to make the most solid judgments about what is good. And care sets the tone, the 'virtuous' tone, of this correspondence in which Descartes tries to assist sovereigns in discovering the principles of morals: in first discovering an ultimate criterion of value or good, and then the maxims to guide application of that criterion in the process of reforming mores.

In reasoning about the ultimate criterion of value, or good, Descartes seems to embrace what we may call a metaphysical naturalism. His reasoning about man's good is based on the reality of man's place in the order of things.

That reality, as it appears to the mind of Descartes, will become clearer when we probe his metaphysical picture of man—his defense of free will and his thesis that man can learn to lead himself by reason. It suffices to say here that human society is considered natural, and there is no basic opposition between man and society. Correct, realistic, reasoning about man's good accordingly requires that we do not lose sight of the naturalness of society and of the necessity of fostering individuals who realize that to take themselves seriously they must take society even more seriously.

Of course, even the most scheming prudence will quickly see that society must be taken very seriously at least up to a point. But reason commands more. Reason commands an unconditioned devotion to the whole, not in a way that overrides the individual's right to pursue his legitimate self-interest, but precisely in a way that, by leading him to recognize and defend other people's self-interest, enables him to legitimately enjoy his own. The Correspondence, like the *Passions,* works with the idea that a man's satisfaction with himself can become greater as he identifies with, and becomes devoted to, a greater whole in whose prosperities he then shares. And, as we shall see, Descartes argues that even when such devotion calls us to great hardships, we are more than compensated by the special satisfaction of knowing we are doing what virtue dictates.

Certainly, the paradigmatic empirical-valuing-self that emerges in every society, state, or under all conditions of mores, need not be a well-formed being, empathetic and self-esteeming in the proper respects and degrees. Possibly a whole society might not be well formed or constituted. Thus Descartes is quite willing to argue that as regards value in the whole, one man may be worth more than others—worth more than a city—and should deem himself such. Nonetheless, whenever a man rightly deems his value greater than that of other individuals, it is clear that Descartes means he must put the good of the whole first. Thus, for example, prudence may tell a man, as it told Socrates, that he will do most good by remaining for an execution and becoming a powerful model; or it may tell him to flee and work under a more humane government. Nevertheless, it is clear that the man's high estimation of himself is warranted precisely by the fact that he is willing to put the good of all individuals, including his enemies', higher than his narrow self-interest—that he does what he can to help all individuals and acts under the aspect of humanity. In short, however great a man's gifts—and enormous gifts can be frightfully misused—the man can rightly, or justifiably, deem his value higher than that of others only insofar as he realizes that he, more than they, is unwilling to abuse his gifts and harm others. In the reality of human life, not harming others means not preventing them from coming to fulfillment. As the very existence of the child bespeaks an obligation upon its parents and state, so too no individual, however uncivilized or nonparticipant in any social contract, is exiled from the sphere of our respect and obligations. His existence already establishes, what he cannot yet explain, our obligation to be concerned, as much as we can, that he develop his nature.

Consider the question that sovereigns—and we now as members of sovereignties—vividly face. "How develop men's natures or decide upon the specifications according to which as yet unformed or ill-constituted empirical-valuing-selves are to be made or remade?" Descartes discusses it without reference to revealed religion and simply on the basis of reason. The implication is clear: where religion and its mores would confer less inherent dignity or social obligations on any individual than what reason determines, then we do not have true religion but only superstition. In such a case sovereigns, albeit slowly, and perhaps through "preachers", must try to change matters.

But what knowledge must the rational sovereign somehow try to impress on every individual? It has already been said. Clearly, it is the only knowledge that entitles any person, however great or limited his gifts, including the sovereign, to respect himself. Namely, the knowledge that he is a creature of a kind whose members can respect each other, and that he ought to do his best to develop his power of reasoning, not to amass with abandon the goods that science and commerce may bring, but to pursue them in a way that subordinates everything to the prime goal of fostering other selves who, not debilitated by poverty, ignorance, or cake and circus, have a degree of reason sufficient to know when they are misusing it.

Of course the differences among the social classes were enormous at the time of Elisabeth and Descartes, and the state of the sciences backward. Their correspondence accordingly contains no discussion of means for immediately improving the mores or institutions among ordinary people. Nevertheless Descartes always expresses a deep respect for human reason—for each person's having the right to have his reason come to fruition. That right is not thought of as conferred by any sovereign or derived from one's being born under any social contract, but as consequent upon one's being human. Very importantly, it entails an obligation, not only on others, but on the self who has the right. For once one gets some chance at voluntariness, or catches a glimmer of the demands of correct and pertinent reasoning, one recognizes when one is abusing thought and taking others less seriously than one ought. One perceives the obligation to cultivate one's powers of correct reasoning. Descartes makes it plain that if mores are not utterly corrupt, and the people not sadly deficient in self-esteem, they will not only see their right and obligation to enhance their reason; but even lacking the opportunity to cultivate that reason as well as others, they will nevertheless recognize why all men are of equal inherent dignity; namely, they will perceive what we noted above, that great gifts, such as intelligence, honor, and wealth, remain susceptible to great abuse, and that the only basis for meriting esteem is one's willingness to use one's gifts, whatever they be, as best one can. In short, they will see that the condition for praising anyone's gifts is that they be used in the spirit of benevolence, or good will.

[18]

Chapter 4. MAXIMS REGARDING MORES

Good will—the best use of one's reason with reference to the well-being of mankind—is called by Descartes "generosity." He uses this word to emphasize how very much the well-being of mankind—the development of good mores—depends on the virtue and dedication of those of high birth. He likewise uses this word to suggest that those of high birth might even have acquired some physiological advantage over others. Accordingly, he urges the design of good institutions and the sponsorship of medical research to help improve health and the general level of mental acumen. However, as said, Descartes was under no illusions about the backward state of the sciences, and the Correspondence contains no recipes for immediately overhauling mores. Nevertheless, if one looks closely at the Correspondence, and keeps in mind other of Descartes' works, one can, I think, extract more-or-less explicit maxims about perennial questions of moral and political education— about the rightful claims of religion, the nature of legitimate political authority and prospects for international trust and concord, and the proper organization of research.

1. RELIGION

The Thirty Years' War showed that Western Christendom was not likely to become doctrinally homogenous. It demonstrated that international alliances would not be an effective way of advancing either the Protestant or the Roman Catholic cause. Although doctrinal disputes provided the banners under which the war got off the ground, the course of the war showed how easily other kinds of motives dominated—how, when advantageous, particular Protestant and Catholic forces allied themselves with each other.

The war, however, did not drive home as vividly as it might have the need for mutual religious toleration within nations. Religious factions, by practicing social and economic exclusivity, were effectively willing to divide nations and dissolve concern for the larger public. The sectarianism of the Protestant Reformation fostered the tendency to regard the public as an imposition on the individual and to believe that the individual best discovers and expresses himself in a group very similar to himself. That line of thinking is found, for example, as late as Rousseau. Rousseau teaches us to think small. He tells us our liberty will be less encroached upon when our fellow citizens are fewer in number and homogeneous with us. Individuality goes up as our differences from others tend to zero. We are most ourselves when everyone is just like us! Cosmopolitanism is not the theme in Rousseau. We are not actively encouraged to seek out and enjoy in common those values we share with all men or large groups of men and to learn the spheres in which we and others require privacy. Rousseau betrays a frightening lack of confidence in the capacity of reason to blend men into society when he envisages his presumably enlightened citizens denying all comity to a man because he will not recite the formulas of some civil religion.

Descartes' comments about religion are not extensive. Yet, if one knows how to read, his silence has much to say. The theme is one of tolerance and cosmopolitanism. Thus Descartes tells us that even ordinary people will accept a prince of different religion provided he does not try to force a change in theirs. The same tolerance shown toward their prince could be shown toward one another, provided they are not incited to bigotry. Descartes, then, seems optimistic that all men—ordinary and educated—can combine a workable civil life with religious toleration. Reason, the common property of all men, would provide the definitive moral foundation for civil life and be the yardstick for measuring permissible forms of religion and weeding out superstition. A permissible religion would not conflict with reason on fundamental questions affecting practice. As regards the many further questions of religious faith which reason could never adjudicate, opinions will differ among the learned as well as among ordinary people, and the tenets of public morality should never touch on such questions.

Elisabeth, Christina, and Chanut appear eager to hear what philosophy, not religion, has to say about the nature of blessedness, the sovereign good, and about the question whether life is worth living, that is, the matter of suicide. They want to see whether reason alone can really discover a firm basis for morality. Their desire to see how reason fares should be understood in light of the great skepticisms about reason (about that "whore" as Luther called it) which had re-arisen in religious and other quarters. Couldn't confidence in reason be another form of superstition? Is faith in the Bible or in custom any more sectarian than faith in reason? Indeed, can reason even adjudicate among conflicting philosophical theories about the foundations of the moral life?

In discussing the *Discourse,* we will see that prior to his moral correspondence Descartes' career had been, as it were, an act of piety on behalf of reason. He had worked to reestablish the authority of reason by allaying various sorts of skepticism. His moral correspondence accordingly builds on that earlier general defense of reason. It presumes that the authority of reason has been vindicated and works within the framework of Descartes' established metaphysics. Hence the more this correspondence proceeds to establish moral principles on the basis of reason alone, without mentioning revealed religion, the more effectively it speaks in behalf of Descartes' view of permissible religion, namely, that however much religion may arrive at some realm of faith, it should depart from a grounding in common human reason sufficient to establish a solid basis for the moral life.

But how does the ultimate principle commanding benevolence relate to the propositions of Descartes' metaphysics? What is the moral-metaphysical foundation on which any permissible religion would depend? The possibility of practicing benevolence presumes that men's wills are free to recognize the legitimate interests of other rational beings and to be motivated by an unconditional respect for those interests. Skepticism had arisen as to whether free will is illusory. If the world unfolds according to some mechanical or other inexorability, the case for human freedom is threatened. Similarly, the predestination that seems implied by the thesis of a personal God also appeared to jeopardize freedom. Thus Descartes' defense of the possibility of benevolence had to turn on metaphysical reasoning. In Part III we will see the arguments by which he tried to prove the existence of a personal God and dismiss any wholesale determination of human action by physiology. We will likewise see how he tried to reconcile human freedom with God's omnipotence and omniscience. We will see how he argued that, simply in virtue of their nature as rational beings, and without requiring any special 'grace,' human beings are capable of freely respecting other persons.

God, then, plays a paramount role in the metaphysics by which Descartes tries to definitively ground the possibility of human freedom, and hence of any moral and religious virtue. Yet, according to Descartes, our moral obligations remain unconditional. He mentions the hope for the immortality of the soul, but he does not try to justify ultimately, or verify, the labors of virtue by appealing to a heaven-hell calculus. If God rewards the difficulties of our former virtue after death, that reward will be given us on the same condition as we now obtain a special moral satisfaction from being virtuous under trial, namely, because our actions have been done with a primary view to virtue. Nor does Descartes ever suggest that the labors of virtue will cease to be needed. He does not expect God to remove the toils involved in being reasonable and virtuous. Indeed, Descartes' conviction that men's wills are free means that all men will continue to be worth the labors of our virtue, and that none are to be considered predestined failures. Moreover, Descartes reminds us that the intellectual love of God soon becomes complemented by a sensuous one if only we allow generosity to lead us to identify with and serve His creatures. This generosity, although it never conveniently dismisses anyone as lost, will nevertheless be tempered with justice. It will make every reasonable demand on the free will of others and pity most, not their bad fortune, but their difficulty in facing it.

2. POLITICAL AUTHORITY AND THE PROSPECTS FOR INTERNATIONAL TRUST AND CONCORD

Elisabeth asks Descartes what maxims he would offer sovereigns for managing civil affairs. Descartes expresses his own views largely by way of explaining his disagreements with Machiavelli's *Prince*. Moreover, like Plato, Descartes writes about the sovereign *qua* sovereign. That is, he lays down maxims for a sovereign who is trying to perform the objective task of sovereignty, namely, to practice benevolence by promoting the well-being of his subjects and of mankind generally. *Pace* Thrasymachus and Machiavelli, Descartes argues that such a sovereign is possible—and that his justice can be his strength.

Descartes operates on the very natural view that to practice benevolence toward mankind requires that we be especially solicitous about smaller units, for example, when Socrates works for all mankind by being especially caring about the well-being of Athenians. Among smaller units such as family, profession, and religion the institution of the state is indeed crucial. The state is the establishment upon which the security of other institutions largely depends. But although it is easy to perceive the need for states, Descartes does not seem to share Dante's vision of the practicability of a world emperor superintending the relations among the nations. Indeed, Descartes is not very optimistic about the prospects for international peace. And to minimize these international confrontations, he advocates a policy of frankness, not dissimulation, among sovereigns.

Descartes reasons about statecraft with direct reference to monarchies. His terminology for conceptualizing political structure nevertheless has certain similarities to that familiar from republican and democratic theories. The very nature of ruling—of establishing and maintaining mores— involves common problems whoever wields the sovereignty. Absolute authority, whether of monarch, of people, or of people's deputies, is a myth. Descartes points to certain objective chores of sovereignty which, if unfulfilled, will mean the dissolution of the sovereign's authority whatever the hands in which that authority lay.

By the sovereign, or prince, Descartes means an individual person who is head of state, not the government or a theoretical entity such as the general will. He considers the government and public ministers as serving at the liege and grace of the sovereign. Subjects of the sovereign fall into two categories, the "great" and the "people".

The great are those powerful enough to form parties or factions against the sovereign and perhaps to compete for the sovereignty. The word "faction" bears a nasty connotation even in democratic theory. And to the extent that the great are really factious, that is, not acting as responsible countervailing powers, but threatening the legitimate roles and tasks of the sovereign, Descartes recommends that the sovereign think of them as enemies and extirpate them. But the mark of the wise sovereign (and Descartes gives no algorithm for this) will be to recognize the difference between *lèse majesté* and permissible recalcitrance. Indeed, the sovereign will be tested by his ability to marshall the resources of the great to a public good. And similarly, Descartes implies that, by the fact that fortune has bestowed power on the great to compete for sovereignties, they also acquire a responsibility to be on the look out for incompetent sovereigns.

The people by no means fall by the wayside in Descartes'

[24]

thinking. He attributes to them an indirect might. Their tacit consent plays a crucial role in any sovereign's ability to maintain himself. It is as though there were some unwritten constitution that a sovereign who wishes to maintain his authority with the people must not violate. In short, for the authority of the sovereign to survive, it must be grounded upon justice.

Descartes, then, keeps two ends in view when writing about statecraft. What arrangements will enable the sovereign to serve his people best and prevent the great from forming divisive factions thwarting this end? What international arrangements among sovereigns will most benefit mankind? He tries to show that if sovereigns keep these ends in view—if they think in terms of the well-being of the ruled—they will preserve themselves. However, if they follow tyrannical and despotic maxims such as Machiavelli gives, they will ruin themselves. Thus, by looking at Descartes' rejection of Machiavelli we will be naturally led to his own doctrines.

2.1. Rejection of Machiavelli

Elisabeth suggests that in advocating violent measures Machiavelli's real intent was to lay down precepts that even an honorable sovereign might have to follow when, despite being convinced in conscience of his cause, the people nevertheless regard him as a usurper. Descartes responds that it is very misleading to erect general maxims around very particular circumstances. He tries to substitute a more prudent point of departure for reasoning about statecraft. He tries to show it highly probable that any sovereign who cannot dispel from himself the aura of usurper, and therefore resorts to violence, is ill-advised to have competed for the sovereignty in the first place. This is seen as follows.

It is foolish of anyone even to try to wield a sovereignty if he is unlikely to bring about a continuing tacit consent of the people and the great. Large violence, whether inflicted by some new or well-established sovereign, often brings about a quiet—but beware the quiet before a storm! Thus, for example, Descartes warns that a sovereign who attempts to establish and maintain himself on violence cannot guard against the first person willing to risk his own life to kill him. Moreover, the violence practiced by a sovereign will only cause his subjects to seek actively or accept liberation—even from a foreign sovereign. Hence, whenever a new sovereign is indeed a liberator he will usually soon obtain consent and not bear the aura of usurper. However, whenever a new sovereign cannot dispel the aura of usurper (or whenever a well-established sovereign becomes regarded as oppressive), it is a strong sign he lacks the consent required for effective rule. This point likewise applies even to those who today dictate on behalf of the proletariat or sit on whatever other powder kegs. Walls and closed borders may contain quiet but not necessarily reconciled peoples. And the world is still filled with contingencies. Let the right factors coalesce and we might see storms.

2.2. Maxims for Instructing a Sovereign

We naturally wonder what personal happiness could be experienced by sovereigns turned tyrants—by Machiavellian characters who must be afraid of their own shadows. We recall the queasy, paranoid tyrants described by Cicero. One was so frightened that he permitted only his daughter to barber him; another was unable to enjoy even his own splendor, for as soon as Damocles admired it, he feared he aspired to it and put him to the sword. Yet such descriptions may incline us to dismiss tyrants as simply abhorrent. Abhorrent, yes; but petty, very often not. How many have reached, and will reach, such an end after sacrificing others, and ultimately perhaps their own sanity, to the illusory splendor of false idologies or the imperatives of policies that no longer distinguish means from ends?

Quis custodiet custodes? Those who are to take charge of others had better learn to take charge of themselves. And anyone giving maxims to sovereigns or might-be sovereigns ought to say something to help them preserve their vision intact. Descartes' advice is not always very explicit. Although we can infer certain things from his discussions with Elisabeth, very much has to be surmised.

The personality of the sovereign ought above all be generous, capable of becoming involved with a work bigger than himself, and capable of sacrificing for that work. As regards sacrifice, Elisabeth, for example, saw the miscarriages of politics take away not only wealth and prestige, but the life of her father, Frederick, and of her uncle, Charles I. In the case of strong natures, however, there is a basic danger that their sacrifices, both those they suffer and those they actively seek, may no longer serve their work so much as their vanity. Truly generous action—action that puts the well-being of the work first—is only possible by those who find their contentment, not in demanding success, but in doing the best they can. If one forgets that fortune can escape one, that one might *not* succeed, then there is danger that one will run down the path of self-deception, trying to tyrannize over the facts by twisting them to one's distorted vision. Launched on a path of false honor, a sovereign's sacrifices could mean protracting needless wars, seeking useless revenge, in short, establishing his illusions rather than the public good.

Moral Education of the People

Action should be a matter of applying values perceived by thought. The responsible sovereign will realize that he cannot hope to be effective in applying genuine values unless he first tries to educate men generally to a correct perception of values. Indeed, the sovereign's own perception of values may be accurate, but if he neglects educating men generally about values, he will only invite their recalcitrance. And in his frustration he might be tempted to use Machiavellian violence against them.

Now metaphysical presuppositions inevitably influence the blueprints according to which the people will be educated. Wrong presuppositions will cause men to mistake their own substance at the roots, *radically*. The people, of course, must learn first by imitation. And Descartes seems to see the job of the sovereign as educating men so that they will not be swindled out of the belief in their own freedom or in the authority of that most common of moral perceptions, the principle of benevolence.

Whenever we begin to regard human actions as pieces of destiny or as determined, we alienate our responsibility to think critically about values. Under the guise of some necessity we bestow a validity, authenticity, and naturalness upon what otherwise might seem controllable and shameful flights of passion. Ordinary moral perceptions then lose their authority. And depending on whether passion has inclined the architects of such determinisms to optimism or pessimism, we find ourselves urged to believe either that good must issue from evil, as in Marxism, or that we must inevitably live under some ogre of doom, as in the case of the Freudian death instinct.

Descartes, by contrast, investigated the more mechanical aspects of human psychology only to emphasize that they need *not* totally control or dominate us. By undercutting the spectre of human actions rigidly determined by mechanical associations, he also excluded those even more enigmatic determinisms which proclaim that somehow all our actions are inescapably shaped by covert monistic motives, either sexual, economic, or whatever.

It would certainly seem, then, that a sovereign should educate men not to believe in any debilitating determinism. He should urge them not to be distracted and prejudiced by such eschatologies. Yet Descartes does not liberate men from belief in determinism in order to give reign to a sort of Nietzschean spontaneity or creativity regarding values. He does not advocate that we try to resolve moral skepticism by some unconditional self-assertion vainly attempting to mask our finitude. What, then, is the responsible view of human finitude that a sovereign should try to inculcate? What view of human finitude leads men to recognize and submit themselves to a common source from which they can continue to derive genuine values?

Human reason is indeed finite which is the reason why the sovereign will also educate men not to allow revealed religion to become involved with the tenets of public morality. Yet, although finite, human reason can come to see its proper sphere. Descartes seems convinced that any rational being—in the very process of being released from belief in determinism and accepting that he operates on the plane of freedom with a power to conform himself to the dictates of reason—will necessarily also recognize that he can sincerely will to act reasonably in regard to other rational beings only if he constantly seeks to discover and follow the means required to practice universal benevolence. Similarly, such a rational being will recognize that this universal benevolence involves the inviolability of all persons. People are not fodder for 'progress'—not holocausts to the development of some higher type. Progress is rather to be conceived in terms of making reasonable contributions to everyone's life and preventing sheer envy from being allowed to thwart anyone's developing valuable perfections. For, if anyone could legitimately be deprived of the opportunity to develop a perfection that cost other people nothing but their envy, then we should in effect be advocating, not society, but a life geared to the lowest level of baseness— the kind of nothingness Nietzsche seems to have feared.

Advantages from Moral Education of the People

Descartes' confidence that the people are trustworthy—that they can be gradually educated to listen to reason—was not typical. Impatience with "the people" was fashionable in the seventeenth century. Such impatience flowers anytime forces fascinated by some sort of 'progress'—laissez-faire capitalism, Leninism, even mass education—meet with recalcitrance. Yet those who thus neglect, or even willingly try to blur, a peoples' moral perceptions will nurture a fickle monster. For only a people made aware of what is right, aware of the reciprocal obligations between them and the sovereign, can provide the sovereign the dependable might he needs to rule.

Descartes thinks that a sovereign who has instilled in the people the principle of benevolence, and himself follows it, has good prospects for succeeding. Unless mores are utterly corrupt, Descartes seems to think that the people will put themselves on a level of fundamental equality with the sovereign. They will perceive the inviolability of persons inherent in the principle of benevolence. This sentiment of equality is one with which it would not only be wrong, but ultimately very dangerous, for any sovereign to tamper. The people, however, also know they must be ruled. They perceive the need for stability—for *établissement*. They will accord the sovereign dignity and honors, even expect and want to do so. Nevertheless, Descartes warns against any sovereign asking of the people more than he can convince them is his due. For once they perceive him as not serving and protecting them but seeking to sack them, whatever his titles to legitimacy, they will cast off his yoke if they can. Moreover, there will always be those among the great trying to persuade the people that the sovereign is demanding too much and doing too little or doing the wrong things. Thus any sovereign who disdains trying to convince his people of his course will invite the distortions of his adversaries and augment doubts among the people.

Hence the sovereign who wishes to maintain himself has a vested interest in looking after all of the people—the whole of the people. Such a wise and prudent sovereign will find the generosity of his people rivaling his own. Descartes seems assured that once a sovereign convinces his people he merits their esteem, their sense of justice (without the need for any Machiavellian chastisements) will carry them to death if necessary to protect him. Similarly, their good sense will lead them to bear whatever hardships they think he must administer on behalf of the public good. When he administers such hardships, they will not view him as breaching the general law of benevolence which requires us to do unto others as we would have done unto ourselves.

The preservation of the sovereign's authority with the people clearly requires more than his personally forebearing from exploiting them. If he is to seem worthy of the people's support, and have them willingly bear necessary hardships, the sovereign must convince them he has a basic will to protect them from the avarice and caprice of various factions among the great—factions that would act as selfishly as would our corporate, educational, and other establishments were they not kept accountable to the public. The sovereign, in short, must superintend improvements so that they work some improvement for all and do not doom the people to an intensification of their agonies. To do that he must, of course, remind the people to ponder what their true good—the public good—requires. For there is great danger that the people, even as they become 'sophisticated', will divide into factions pitted one against the other—as when we today think no further than of the interests of our particular group associations.

This sculpting of 'a' people, the most essential and ungoing craft of a sovereign, accordingly involves fostering the research and development of the instruments of cultural advancement—such as law, science, philosophy. But the sovereign must also make every effort to see that these cultural instruments are turned to a truly public good. And we must see how this can be done.

3. THE PROPER ORGANIZATION OF RESEARCH

Chanut raises the question whether special friendships have even a permissible role in the life of men of honor, probity, and station. The question had occupied Cicero and later concerned Spinoza. The basic issue is whether special friendships among such men cause them to breach general benevolence by leading them to distribute favorable treatment on some basis other than merit. It is very natural for Chanut to raise this question. As a sovereign's deputy, he felt a particular obligation of impartiality in seeking to discover and support the work of those generous souls in the sciences, philosophy, and the arts who could benefit mankind. Thus Chanut's question is still relevant. For the sovereign must always try to be objective in the always somewhat subjective process of discovering and advancing work likely to benefit the public. Similarly, he must try to minimize lopsided emphases that rob us of other insights in the process of pinning our attention on something new.

The sovereign's task will certainly be a hopeless one if the practitioners of different disciplines cannot communicate with each other—cannot really 'go public'. Descartes was convinced that such specialists as mathematicians, physicists, and lawyers can to a very large extent explain themselves to one another, that is, to intelligent laymen. He never tires of suggesting to sovereigns that they have a right to demand accessible statements from practitioners in all the disciplines. He backed up this suggestion with action. His own work—his career—was meant to illustrate, not only to sovereigns, but to the learned themselves, that such accessible statements can indeed be produced. Descartes, then, was attempting to establish a paradigm for the modern man. For now we may confine ourselves to the outline of that paradigm, and see how he sought to commend it.

Claritas vincit omnia. Descartes believed that genuine communication is possible because clarity of expression is possible. We must try to understand this Cartesian clarity in its broadest sense. Clarity is not achieved mechanically—thoughtlessly. Special talents and labors are required to produce systematic and exoteric reasonings concerning a given subject matter. Yet Descartes insists that the greater one's understanding of a given subject matter, the more reason determines one to say something just one way and not another. Such reasonings, moreover, will appear so "natural" to the minds of others as to command their respect—as to make them want to follow them. Descartes' manner of publishing the *Meditations* also suggested a way of forcing *criticism* to be responsive and constructive. He invited objections to the treatise, and then had treatise, objections, and his replies all published together—all to be seen together. Descartes was not yet of the more frenetic world of the *Journal des Savants*.

As if to verify the force of clear reasoning, Descartes pitched his writings, even his most serious writings, to practical men who have time only to hear the best of an author's thoughts. Thus Descartes' scientific works with their lucid *prose* might still make sovereigns suspicious whenever it is maintained that technical principles are too recherché to be clearly *said*. Indeed, Elisabeth paid Descartes no higher compliment than when she admired the naturalness of his scientific reasonings and expressed her desire to make them her own.

Descartes also intended to prove by the *range* of his corpus—by mathematical, physical, metaphysical, and moral treatises—that comprehensive thinking is possible and desirable. As one reads these treatises, one recognizes that Descartes' profundity in one area is deepened by that in another. Nor does this comprehensiveness seem at all fortuitous. Rather, he makes one feel that the same human reason is at work in all the treatises. He illustrates very well that essential similarity in the techniques of sound reasoning of which he so often spoke. Although he certainly did not persuade men of all the details of his system, his paradigm of a universal knower, of a man whom all of us can at least try to *follow*, caught hold. By the time of Leibniz we find confidence that the synthesizing intellect is possible, as well as the conviction that such minds are necessary for the live, productive interrelation of the sciences.

Today, however, we forcefully question the 'modern man' of the Cartesian paradigm. We despair of attaining any near total perspective—despair of synthesis and genuine philosophy. There seems to be no standard by which a sovereign could even begin to adjudicate among various intellectual factions. We are prone to accept the fact that for men to think, in the strangest combinations, as capitalists, Marxists, Skinnerians, physicists, biologists, theists, atheists, and so on, is as natural as their being five or six feet tall. Indeed, perhaps I should say *speak* like capitalists, or Marxists, or whatever, for we are becoming profoundly skeptical of 'thinking' in the pristine sense.

Yet before succumbing to this epistemological Dadaism, we had better note how dangerous it is to lose hope in reason's competence to determine worthwhile ends, particularly now that she is so adept at furnishing the cruelest means. Moreover, there are ways of looking at our present situation, of diagnosing it, that may incline us back to a more orthodox picture of man—incline us to seek perspective again from a picture such as Descartes drew.

We have reached the point where a very deep engineering of biological nature seems feasible. From the technological point of view, the 'nature' of physical and biological nature now appears fluid indeed. Not too many years ago people still bought slaves. Who doubts that, if they could, there would be people willing to engineer obedient and not too costly or aspiring slaves? This fluid factual situation, in which man can redirect what may have seemed biologically determined, only drives home Descartes' recommendation that we learn to think of physics and biology, *qua* physics and biology, as devoid of any final causality, devoid of any sufficient basis for value.

Thus, in our search for value, the more we now look into the physical and biological world, the more adamantly does it refuse to tell us what we inevitably will do or what we ought to do. Physics and biology appear, at the very most, merely tools. Psychology too is but a tool. We can use it to help foster or impede insights. Yet psychology is not logic; it cannot decide what true insight is. We are, then, feeling the weight of our freedom. We must learn to master these tools. Our extroversion is not working. And if this is the point where we might despair of reason, it is by that very fact the point where we might learn to believe in it again. For the more reason unveils the more mechanical, more determined, aspects of our person, the more does reason appear to itself as above that passivity, as meant to ponder and superintend it. And if that conviction again takes hold we may be led to heed Descartes' and Kant's warning that reason must turn to itself to find a throne of values. We will then no longer neglect active discussion of the good to which we intend to put the lessons of history and the tools of the sciences. We will stop examining ourselves as foreign specimens and think foremost of how we *want* to form our person—of the intellectual passions we wish to nurture in ourselves with the help of whatever strategies psychology affords. In short, we will give up blithely expecting salvation from anything outside ourselves—from God or from historical necessity. We will be duly frightened of ourselves. We will learn to be affected by pride and guilt, two emotions inseparable from self-legislating rational beings.

Chapter 5. FORTUNE, THE SOVEREIGN GOOD, VIRTUE, AND BLESSEDNESS

The Correspondence, then, indicates that Descartes knew the role fortune must continue to play in human life, both personal and civil. He did not anticipate that God would ever remove the need for the labors of virtue. And since he showed no inclination to traffic with deterministic social theories, he could not thereby alleviate the frustrations of practice and settle into any easy optimism or pessimism. For all his emphasis upon developing the sciences, he remained mindful that to use nature to our advantage will continue to presuppose a theory of values and control over the passions.

Thus it seems that Descartes was reconciled to the fact that the attainment of virtue and solid contentment must always remain a demanding achievement. He knew, as did the Stoics and Augustine, that there is hardly anything that cannot be turned to evil—that misused intelligence just broadens the spectrum of the passions. The idea that life will remain a battle to put and keep the self in the order that nature intended also affects his remarks about political and moral education. Whenever he touches on his hopes that science and instruction might improve institutions, the tone is always on helping, never saving, the less fortunate. There is no indication that he ever expected man to be elevated beyond the point where new advantages could not be turned to new forms of abuse.

But despite acknowledging human fallibility and the ever-present toils of practice, Descartes' confidence in the utility of knowledge and genuine virtue did not wane. Like Plato, he warned against the attempt to rest in partial knowledge: a 'virtue' not based on the required knowledge will be false, and the greatest souls will then be capable of the greatest vices. Moreover, Descartes' discussion of a man's *summum bonum,* or sovereign good, brings to the fore the most crucial decision that forever will lie within a man's province to make, namely, the decision whether he will in fact act out of the moral motive, that is, act benevolently and with unconditional devotion to the whole, as virtue implies he ought.

Now, virtue, or correct reasoning and action as regards the whole, although demanding, nevertheless often pays. But no matter how demanding such a virtue is, it can still mask a scheming prudence if narrow self-interest predominates over the moral motive. Descartes and Elisabeth accordingly discuss how the moral motive, or virtue for virtue's sake, can suffice for man. Like Seneca, they discuss how a man can choose virtue unconditionally and yet receive his highest satisfaction, his greatest rejoicing, in the fact that when called on to do so, he acted morally.[17] Elisabeth and Descartes are not given to enthusiasms, nor would they think one is often called to do as Socrates did. Nonetheless they clearly saw the need to school oneself, and prompt oneself, and test oneself in one's duties. Thus, even our response to the tragedies of the theatre can prepare us for the tragedies of life. We discover the satisfaction the soul derives from experiencing her force to do her duties. And similarly, we discover that when she knows she has done her best, the soul can prevent the mishappenings of life from entering any more intimately into her than do the 'disasters' at which we laugh in comedies.

Descartes warns against anyone's even beginning to enter into that voluntary self-deception wherein he starts fancying, but does not examine, some supposedly superior advantage incompatible with virtue. Like the ancients, Descartes insists that all goods other than virtue remain goods for us only if sustained by virtue. Virtue alerts us to the conditions of life. It reminds us that, in respect to most goods, we have title only for a time to the fruits of their use. Youth, wealth, position, fame—virtue prepares us to give them up when we cannot have them or cannot rightly have them. By mitigating the fear of loss, virtue at once takes away the dread of acquiring goods, allows us to enjoy them when we have them, and prevents us from becoming more miserable for having had them. In respect to the goods that can come and go, we must be prepared to act like Seneca's two virtuous rich men. The first, aware of the various other goods he could effect with his riches, recognized in those who inveighed against him a knowledge of poverty but certainly not of virtue; the second, seeing his riches about to go, escorted those riches to the door and lost but one thing—his riches. Virtue, then, being the best use of every-thing at our disposal, is already blessedness. The blessed man will likewise know that he cannot demand of fortune those additions that, were they to come and were they properly used, would make his life even more blessed. But the very fact he knows this, which prevents the resentments that make one miserable and the presumption that blinds, makes him the only genuine candidate for receiving the genuinely most blessed life.

Thus, for Descartes, transgressions of virtue, or incorrect reasonings about the whole (about life), are truly arranged as we arrange self-deception. We do not examine goods thoroughly enough, but instead try to squeeze more from them than they can offer. Or refusing to examine and ac-knowledge the limitations particular to our situation, we regard goods that pertain to others as if they were stolen from us, and thus we build our life around false resent-ments. We are pained, not delighted, by the perfections we see in others. And if such self-deception brings some plea-sure, Descartes thinks it touches only the exterior of the soul, which "nonetheless feels an interior bitterness in per-ceiving that these imaginations are false." [18] In short, Des-cartes suggests we can bear the truth about ourselves, and will be dissatisfied until we hear it.

Part II. DESCARTES' METHOD, WITH PARTICULAR REFERENCE TO THE *DISCOURSE*

We now have a concise idea of the moral philosophy and psychology expressed in the *Passions* and Correspondence. Descartes' views regarding morals rest on his metaphysics, and before any further elaboration, it is worthwhile recalling certain of these metaphysical doctrines.

Chapter 6. METAPHYSICAL PRESUPPOSITIONS

Descartes not only presupposes a dualism of mind and body, but assumes that there is no wholesale determination of our mental life by physical causes. To be sure, mental habits strongly affect the mind, as when men with different customs react differently to the same physical stimuli and experience quite different emotions and values. But, according to Descartes, this capacity of the human mind to experience different emotions and values in response to the same physical stimuli testifies to the operations, although often undisciplined, of reason—not to any wholesale determination by physiology.

Physiology, then, does not ordain what values are inevitable. And however important the study of physiology is to the art of living, reason must go elsewhere to find what makes most values valuable. Similarly, Descartes shows no inclination to accept some wholesale psychological or cultural determination of values, and he is quite clear that as regards worthwhile customs a single man may be a better authority than an entire nation. The plan of a single man, for example, the legislator, may have designed and sculpted the customs of an entire nation. Thus reason cannot dispense itself of the chore of deciding what constitutes genuine values by settling into the assumption that any overwhelming determinism—physical, psychological, cultural—takes that decision out of reason's hands. However, what it is truly natural for man to be—what he ought to be—no more necessarily exists than do true beliefs about the metaphysical and physical realms. It all depends on how well reason uses, and does not forfeit, its power to think correctly and pertinently. The Correspondence provides many indications of how reason, relieved of such bogies as physical, psychological, and cultural determinism, may look confidently into itself and discern what it is truly natural for a rational being to do.

This confident tone of the Correspondence in regard to morals is, then, largely a function of Descartes' confidence that he had established a correct metaphysics. Thus we will better understand his views regarding morals if we know, not simply the metaphysical reasoning with which they are continuous, but also how Descartes originally gained confidence in such reasoning.

Chapter 7. DESCARTES' QUEST FOR A METHOD TO GROUND METAPHYSICAL AND MORAL REASONING

To the end of his life, Descartes remained convinced of what he had earlier expressed in the *Discourse:*

And finally, I would not have known how to limit my desires or rest content if I had not followed a single path by which I thought myself assured, not only of acquiring all the knowledge of which I would be capable, but also all the true goods that would be in my power . . .[19]

It is instructive to see from the *Discourse* why Descartes originally hoped a "single path" would lead to knowledge generally and all true goods, and why he believed that he had found such a path. Yet to use the information in the *Discourse* constructively, one should remember its genre. Descartes was not lacking a gift for rhetoric, nor reluctant to use it. His correspondence is testimony to the imagination with which he could adduce examples, analogies, metaphors, or even alter symbolisms, in order to encourage or discourage a point of view according as reason recommended. The intellectual autobiography in the *Discourse* is a rhetorician's example, and we must finally decide whether and how to make that *bildungsroman* exemplary for us.

Descartes' hope to find a single path leading to knowledge generally and all true goods was proportioned to his 'quantity of soul'. He obviously considered himself one of those 'larger vessels' whose fulfillment requires him to use his intellect to open up to others as many solid goods as possible. Virtue, in such a case, is particularly inseparable from comprehensive and cautious reasoning. The omission of any relevant experience or discipline would be an intellectual and moral fault. What was the young Descartes of the *Discourse* doing in so assiduously following his school curriculum, and later in travelling and studying the customs of others, except seeking out such a variety of experiences as would equip him to make solid evaluations concerning the good for man? Nor did Descartes ever repent of that curriculum or his travels. They made him realize, and realize urgently, that experience can be useful only in proportion as we know how to interpret it properly. They made him feel the need for a method that, by avoiding needless repetition and separating accidents from essentials, leads us to see the mutual bearing of our diverse learning on the question of the good for man.

Such a method is no mere formalism but a genuine logic of invention, or discovery, that helps us determine the interconnection of our subject matters and separate truths that are certain from mere probabilities. The idea of such a method is the idea of that accomplished rationality philosophy pursues. To search out such a method might, in the case of most people, be idle and pretentious. Descartes seems never to have doubted his capabilities, and he finally made the claim to have fashioned a philosophy that more than rivals those of Plato and Aristotle. Descartes, *savant et philosophe*, thought of his method as not only having general application, but as so natural to the human mind that everyone, although unable to apply it equally inventively, could nevertheless benefit from it and with practice learn to follow truths discovered by it.

Chapter 8. THE INTELLECTUAL VIRTUES AND DESCARTES' METHOD

Descartes insisted that this natural method of reasoning does not spring up automatically, but must be actively cultivated. Thus the virtue, or correct reasoning, truly natural to man must, as it were, be unearthed. We must labor to bring that natural ideal, the *Vir* of virtue, into being. The details of Descartes' method may remain subsidiary for us until we consider their role in fashioning his systematic metaphysics. Presently I will try to identify the mental habits from which Descartes' method sprang and that seem essential to its application. These habits are the virtues of the intellectually well constituted personality. They direct one's inquiries to the primary question of man's metaphysical nature; by requiring cautious reasoning, they instill confidence; and by thus laying the groundwork, they make firm moral reasoning possible.

Even if not explicitly named, these habits are expressed in the *Discourse*. As we would expect, one leads to the next. The habit of prudence organizes and directs inquiry. It requires that we cultivate the habit of pursuing rational certainty, which leads to the habit of turning away from too great a dependence upon the senses, and to learning how to bring about the correct relation between intellect and the auxiliary faculties of sense, memory, and imagination.

1. PRUDENCE

Prudence lets us see that we have not been made like the other animals which move with the rigidity of instinct. Indeed, prudence consists in a man's habitual memory that he is the animal who will always require foresight precisely because his reason, if not properly harnessed, must inevitably cause him endless vain imaginations and errors. Nothing has more clearly dawned on Descartes of the *Discourse* than the fact that the divergent customs among men proves human nature has by and large failed to reach its intended shape because human reason has not yet learned its own proper application. Descartes goes so far as to say "the single fact of diversity among states suffices to assure us that some states are imperfect." [20] As regards the basic questions of how life ought to be lived, the situation parallels that with scientific questions generally: "there cannot be more than one opinion that is true." [21]

Prudence accordingly seems to suggest that the truly natural life, and the truly natural state, can only be artificial, that is, products of correct reasoning. Yet we look in vain in the *Discourse* for any description of an ideal state or any recipes for reforming mores. These absences are also parts of Descartes' concept of prudence. First he had to tackle questions whose solutions are necessary to a basic groundwork for a rationalistic morals. Thus in the *Discourse* he seeks to remove general arguments that minimize or debunk the role of reason in the life of man. In short, he tries to defend the view mentioned above, namely, that man, unlike the other animals, possesses reason, and that his reason can properly harness and direct itself.

Descartes knew that unless he showed how reason could master itself, its very plasticity would continue to make sport with us. Reason would continue to imagine bogies that can haunt the rational life. Thus, on the one hand, the fear of some subtle physiological or other determinism could easily create an epistemological nightmare in which reason verges on reducing itself to absurdity by doubting whether it is even free to decide truths, including truths about values, on the basis of pertinent evidence. On the other hand, were differences in human beliefs and customs advanced as evidence against any such determinism, reason would still be embarrassed by lacking any definitive answer to the question how life should be lived.

Of course, Descartes' case for human reason is his metaphysical argument regarding man—the defense of dualism, the denial of determinism, and the view that rational beings most naturally determine what is right and good, not from facts as they are or have been, but from what reason says they ought to be. But since Descartes' *morale* could be no sounder than his metaphysics, prudence accordingly dictated that he be very cautious in his approach to metaphysics. In that light we can understand the habit or virtue of pursuing intellectual certainty which his method required.

2. THE PURSUIT OF CERTAINTY

Descartes' justification of his pursuit of certainty had two parts. He needed to justify the possibility of philosophical knowledge generally, and then the plausibility of his attempt to attain such knowledge.

Like Augustine, he tried to allay skepticism about reason and bestow credibility on the pursuit of philosophic knowledge by arguing that it is probable that the wise man can attain it.[22] As regards complicated questions, such as those involved in deciding reasonable customs, he argued that the 'few', not the 'many', are more likely to hit the precise mark—indeed, most people do not even know, let alone examine, their own beliefs.[23] As to why and how the few might attain to philosophical truths, Descartes seems to think, similarly to Augustine, that even the 'fool' has the notion of wisdom, so that if he uses his reason with discipline, then knowledge can be discovered or at least recognized. Thus, Descartes tried to show that disagreements among the learned testified to lack of appropriate discipline in the exercise of their reason—to a forfeiting of wisdom— rather than to a general incapacity to gain philosophical knowledge. In order to see this, we will review Descartes' condemnation of those who contented themselves with 'probabilities'. We will see the sort of preoccupation with probabilities Descartes abjured, why he thought it prevents the discovery of useful philosophical truths, and how he encouraged himself in a nobler probability, namely, that if he used his reason well, he might discover such useful philosophical truths.

In the *Discourse* Descartes presents himself as little inclined to play with ideas or use study as a *divertissement*. "I always had an extreme desire to learn to distinguish the true from the false, in order to see clearly in my actions and to walk with assurance in this life." [24] Throughout the *Discourse*, Descartes emphasizes his prevailing concern with the utility to be derived from knowledge. We see his growing awareness of the demands of knowledge and his dedication to pursuing it. Thus, he describes his poignant emotional departure from *collège* in a manner that makes it exemplary. Descartes was sixteen or eighteen years of age when he completed his schooling at the renowned *Collège La Flèche*. The young Descartes knew his school had been among the best; he thought of his instructors as men of learning; he had done well. It was natural for him to take toll of himself. But what was the effect of this reckoning? Does the *Discourse* provide any evidence of a basic change in Descartes—of any recently acquired misology? Rather than a change there seems to have been only poignant self-expression: a firm resolve not to be detoured or detained in fulfilling his extreme desire to separate the true from the false and to walk with assurance in this life. Neither the shock Descartes displayed at the magnitude of his doubts, nor the criticisms he launched at the perpetual uncertainty among the learned were accompanied by any sign of intellectual fatigue or haste. It seems that the young but prescient Descartes was determined not to exchange his passion to distinguish the true from the false for those endless pretexts for vanity awaiting a gifted mind that comes to rest its satisfactions in deftness at conjecture:

> For it seemed to me that I should be able to encounter very much more truth in the reasonings which everyone makes about things that concern them, and whose outcome, if they judge badly, would punish them, than in those reasonings a man of letters makes in his study regarding speculations that produce no effect and involve no further consequence for him— excepting perhaps that he will derive a greater vanity the more they are removed from common sense, since he will have to employ so much the more ingenuity and inventiveness to try to render them probable.[25]

Descartes often repeated his severe criticisms of those who are captivated by their ability to doubt all things by arguing for an appearance of truth (a verisimilitude, or probability) on each side of a question.[26] They forget that it is easier to devise a conjecture or counter-conjecture about any topic, however elevated, than to cast one solid judgment about a truth, however simple. Descartes was convinced that where the only procedure becomes a lack of procedure sustained by a promiscuous use of principles, the effect is to blind the natural light of reason, so that it can no longer recognize truths accessible to it. He liked to emphasize how congenial to mediocre minds would be this prospect of proving themselves in the dark cave of conjecture. A naïve opponent is lured in by the fascination of elevated debate. He takes up a position he is unable to see. Then he is shown that it is premised on quicksand. If both opponents should be habitués of such debacles, the quicksand becomes their mutual defense—every shift a new occasion for digression. Descartes' frustration, then, did not turn on the fact that innumerable things must remain less than certain, and that the most we can attain regarding them is a probability judgment. But he was unwilling to accept the view that human reason is so futile that it can, with equal legitimacy, show any opinion to be but probable. For, in effect, that would mean nothing could be shown true, not even the standard for measuring verisimilitude or probability. Thus, Descartes believed that, when people appeared to create a probability on both sides of every question, it was only because they neglected looking for a method that adequately distinguishes between facts that do and do not fall within the realm possible human certainty.

Hence Descartes portrays himself as a man determined never to appear, especially to himself, as more foolish than if he had never studied. Doubting was to be an important part of his intellectual strategy, a means of clearing the mind of prejudices. He was capable of, and prone to, intellectual deracination:

Likewise, I thought that, because we were all children before being men, and because we had to be directed for a long time by our appetites and teachers—who often contradicted one another, and who perhaps, neither one nor the other, always counselled us for the best—it is almost impossible that our judgments be so pure or so solid as they would have been if we had had the complete use of our reason from the time of our birth, and had been led only by reason . . . I was persuaded that I could not do better than to undertake, once and for all, to reject [my former opinions], in order to replace them afterward, either by better beliefs, or perhaps even by themselves, when I had made them conform to the standard of reason.[27]

Yet doubting is only part of Descartes' strategy—and much the easier part. The doubt, he insists, would be pointless without consideration of the method whereby truth can be attained:

[and] I did not wish to begin to reject entirely any of the opinions that formerly were able to slip into my belief without having been placed there by reason until I had first employed sufficient time to establish the design of the task I was undertaking, and to seek the true method for arriving at the knowledge of everything of which my wits would be capable.[28]

Descartes was neither rashly optimistic nor pessimistic about the prospects for human knowledge. Blind confidence in progress was alien to his outlook. He was convinced that some of the most robust insights of human reason had been neglected for the artificialities with which the learned had created, and undoubtedly could continue to create, their illusory daylight. By the same token, he never acted as though his own thoughts were destined to be just one more idle attempt of human reason to cast some solid judgments about the truth. His view of truth and of human reason contributed to justify his self-confidence. There is, he says, nothing older than the truth.[29] It is not man's chronological place per se that limits his access to truth. And as for human reason, its basic operations are so limited, and a sound method so essential, that neglect of method alone could explain the recurrent disagreements on fundamental points throughout the centuries. Preoccupation with method was, from Descartes' point of view, a modesty imposed upon human reason by truth itself—neglect method and human reason will drown itself in a sea of nullities of its own devising.

Descartes saw philosophers as prone to err by trying to wrest a premature and ungained comprehension of everything, but the sciences (or arts) he saw as erring by distinguishing themselves too much from each other. In their haste for immediate results, the sciences ignore principles governing their interdependence—principles that, if properly understood, would lead to more fruitful results than the most hide-bound practitioner could anticipate. By means of mathematics Descartes was convinced he could represent the highly unified nature of the objects dealt with by physics, chemistry, biology, and medicine and thus help reveal the structure and interdependence of these disciplines. His initial attention to mathematics in his attempt to achieve something solid in the sciences was not, from Descartes' point of view, a breach of his resolve never to study without a method. It was not a case of practice prior to method, for Descartes was convinced that mathematics is the best training ground for human reason, that it most manifestly involves and exercises the mental operations by which the human mind is constrained to begin the acquisition of solid cognitions. Thus it was natural for him to expect that the general method for which he sought would be best discerned in conjunction with his mathematical studies. For all his criticism of the philosophers, Descartes always knew he could not complete science, and certainly not morals, without a metaphysics. To approach philosophy, however, reason must first be trained. Before the human mind is prepared to push forward to metaphysical knowledge, it must cultivate the general method for asking questions properly and for recognizing the presuppositions of answers.

Having thus tried to establish as probable that human reason, if properly used, can attain to metaphysical truth, Descartes proceeded to test his own abilities, approaching metaphysical matters only after he 'proved' himself in mathematics and other sciences. We will now consider in a preliminary way the habit or virtue of 'turning away from the senses' that metaphysical and moral reasoning presupposes.

3. TURNING AWAY FROM THE SENSES

The nature of the human mind—the role of intellect and the auxiliary powers of sense, memory, and imagination—is not immediately apparent. We must, as it were, discover ourselves; otherwise we shall never really recognize or feel at home with the procedures of valid reasoning. According to Descartes, the habit of turning away from the senses, which is part and parcel of mathematical reasoning, helps us discover our mental powers and alerts us to their proper general use. In order to discuss this habit of turning away from the senses, it is helpful to know something further concerning Descartes' general view of the nature of the human mind.

3.1. The Nature of the Human Mind

According to Descartes, thoughts, or 'ideas' properly so called, exist only in the intellect. By such ideas he means those used in chains of mathematical and geometrical reasoning; or in chains of metaphysical and logical reasoning, as when we think of the interrelations of substance, attributes, and modes, or of the forms of causality; or in chains of moral reasoning, as when we try to consistently define justice, equality, fairness. Such ideas must be distinguished from sensuous qualities, images, and feelings that accompany our thinking of them, and to which we may at times refer or apply them.[30] For example, the same sensuous quality—say of red—might be thought of as something seemingly extended and divisible; as caused by particles in motion with complicated shapes and angular velocities; and as a mode of mental substance, that is, as an affection of one's mind. All these ideas by means of which we think about that same red must be distinguished from that sensuous quality. Indeed, only because we are able to interpret or cognize a sensuous quality through such ideas can it be experienced by us in diverse ways.

Thus, unless we were able to understand the relations of ideas to each other, we could not understand even the propositions that are referred to sense quality. Indeed, unless we could forge and sever associations among ideas, we could not devise and interpret new propositions, and thus we would be unable to study and judge the true relations among ideas. According to Descartes, our ability to devise and interpret fitting language is a sign of the mind's inherent power to forge and sever associations among ideas and thus to study and judge their true relations.[31]

There clearly are many reasons why a given idea or proposition can originally have become associated with certain sensuous examples. Thus the idea 'point' may have become associated with the *minimum visibile* or the moon; or the idea 'efficient causality' with the observation of one ball hitting upon another; or the idea 'courage' with the behavior read about in some novel. Yet such associations need not stick. Indeed, according to Descartes, the mind has a power to forge an association of certain propositions or ideas with many sensuous examples, such as associating the idea 'triangle' with images of right, isosceles, and scalene triangles. Moreover, the mind has a power of severing habits of association it finds misleading, such as the habit of associating the idea 'figure of 180°' uniquely with the image of a semicircle. Unless the mind had a power to change the associations between sensible examples and ideas or propositions, it would be unable to think intelligently, being determined instead to accept what very often would be false sensuous examples of its ideas or propositions.

3.2. Practices Involved in 'Turning Away from the Senses'

This explanation of Descartes' view of mind suffices to allow us to make our preliminary review of the habit of 'turning away from the senses'. As said, mathematical thinking supposedly fosters this habit which leads us to discover our mental powers and alerts us to their proper *general* use, that is, to their role in metaphysical and moral thinking.

Actually, 'turning away from the senses' comprehends a number of interrelated practices associated with meditation: caution as regards language; expecting certitude only from the intellect and not going back to the senses when they are no longer of help in settling a question; remembering the steps in one's argumentation; and not being misled by analogies, symbols, and so on. The application of these practices, which we here indicate only briefly, will become more apparent in Parts III & IV, where we more exhaustively treat Descartes' metaphysics and moral psychology.

Language

'Turning away from the senses' goes hand in hand with a heightened consciousness as regards the snares of linguistic habits. Language may mislead either by implying errors or by causing us to deem as obvious what is far from obvious to us. Thus language must be examined for falsities. For example, whatever the etymology of 'virtue' (*vir* = man), we are not to assume the moral quality pertains only, or most naturally, to men. Just as importantly, language must be examined with a view to isolating questions that demand further reflection. Even though the normal use of the word "cause" suggests that a cause is something different from its effect and not identical with it, it is still worthwhile to ask whether anything can be its own cause and sustain itself in existence. We typically assume that 'happiness' is our highest good, but, as Descartes points out, the French for "happiness," *bonheur,* is etymologically linked to the word for luck, *l'heur.* Thus we should think twice whether our highest good could lie in something that can escape us and is therefore bound to trouble us either because we lack it or fear losing it. Descartes argues that we should rather seek the blessedness or contentment deriving from knowing one has done one's best—that only if such blessedness is the highest object of our concern can we be benefited rather than harmed by the additional "goods" that fortune may bring. Similarly, the word "love," Descartes points out, is often used in referring to our willing identification with objects of sense. Such objects easily arouse in us the physical movements and signs typical of the passion of love. Nevertheless, Descartes maintains that we should not be blinded to the fact that there can be even stronger identifications with objects known in a more or purely intellectual way, such as our love of pursuing truth, our love of virtue, our love of mankind, our love of God.

But perhaps the best way of guarding against all deceits of language is to realize that, even in supposedly true propositions, we should seek to determine exactly how subject is connected to predicate. Indeed, until we know the steps connecting subject and predicate we will likely remain uncertain whether a proposition represents an impossibility, necessity, or contingency. Our acceptance or rejection of the proposition would not represent any genuine reasoning, but merely substitute for such. For example, propositions, such as 'A square has 360°', 'moral values attach only to rational beings', and 'moral responsibility implies knowledge of that responsibility', certainly demand a careful analysis of how subject and predicate are connected. Similarly, until we know the steps connecting the subject and predicate, we might continue, as a matter of habit, to make erroneous evaluations of what we 'observe' or find 'exemplified' in sense experience. Thus, we might see that, in our society, moral responsibility is attributed only to those with a knowledge of that responsibility. Yet unless we understand why that principle is a necessary one, we might mistakenly think it to be contingent. Thus, when we find other peoples breaching the principle, we might deem our mistaken inference confirmed by experience instead of realizing that such peoples' actions only exemplify either their erroneous belief about the status of the principle or their intentional violation of the moral law.

Expecting Certitude Only from the Intellect

Mathematical thinking clearly trains us in the practice of not going back to the senses when they are no longer of help in settling a question. Even the simplest elements of geometrical reasoning, such as infinitely divisible lines or indivisible points, cannot be perspicuously represented in sense. Similarly, sensible imagery cannot perspicuously represent either the indefinite extension in which real geometrical bodies would reside nor the complicated figures that such bodies might possess—figures more easily thought of with the help of devices such as mathematical notations rather than diagrams or images. Thus mathematical thinking alerts us to the general fact that, even as regards distinctions referred or applied to sensible things, that is, to so-called material or physical objects, the ideas and propositions required to think these distinctions and to judge their relations to one another are nonsensuous and exist in the intellect. Moreover, by alerting us to the fact that sense does not perspicuously represent even the simplest or elementary geometrical distinctions we apply to it, mathematical thinking shows us that certitude concerning the ideas and propositions referred to sense can only be attained by the intellect—not by seeing, touching, smelling, or tasting.

[54]

Thus mathematical thinking, by bringing the intellect to recognize its own nonsensuous nature as well as that of its ideas, prepares the way for metaphysical and moral thinking about the nature of man. For beyond showing us that our minds certainly cannot be exhaustively described on the basis of the senses, it also prepares us to realize that any distinction between mind and matter must be conceived and validated, not by the senses, but by reason itself.

Memory

Mathematical thinking develops one's memory. It clearly accustoms us to review and keep in mind the steps whereby we seek to validate conclusions, as in going from axioms to theorems. For Descartes, the making of reviews, and the accustoming of oneself to trust to well-reasoned conclusions, is an essential part of mastering metaphysical argumentation. Similarly, intelligent moral preparedness presupposes careful advance consideration of moral maxims, for that alone develops such interior conviction as will prevent our becoming irresolute in moments of passion.

Analogies, Symbols, and So On

As regards the need to be cautious lest we be misled by analogies, symbols, and so on, we easily see how this general topic is continuous with those discussed above. Whether words are being used analogically rather than literally can have serious ontological consequences. For example, consider the proposition 'all colors are extended.' Unless we intend the word "extended" in some analogical sense, it would follow that even the colors we see during dreams or imaginations will necessitate the indefinite extension in which they exist. Thus, simply given the existence of any such color, there could not be any reasonable grounds for doubt concerning the existence of an 'external' world. Descartes, however, would hardly think skepticism so easily thwarted.

Moreover, as regards symbols, we must master them and not let them acquire undue authority. Even the symbols that art and custom devise to outfit intellectual things with sensuous appeal should not be allowed to divert us from the goods they were meant to enhance. Thus, for example, the finitude of the world had been taken as a symbol of God's concern for man—of his arranging things for man. Descartes clearly denies any necessary connection between the symbol and the thesis of God's special providence. On the contrary, he argues that the sublimity of an infinite world is an even more fitting symbol of that providence.

Part III. DESCARTES' METAPHYSICS: THE BACKGROUND FOR HIS MORAL PHILOSOPHY AND PSYCHOLOGY

Descartes' concern with mind-body dualism is crucial to his moral philosophy and psychology. It also demonstrates the close relationship between his moral philosophy and psychology and the metaphysics on which he grounds them.

Chapter 9. Moral Significance of Dualism

Descartes' theory of mind-body dualism asserts that man is a composite of two different but interacting substances, nonextended mind and extended matter. By means of this theory Descartes tries to establish that physiological causes do not rob the mind of a power of self-determination. Dualism, he argues, makes possible self-control and moral improvement.

The attempt to secure such power, or agency, for mind is very old—nor were the theories that assigned a special status to mind always dualistic. In the *Phaedo*, for example, we find Socrates defending the agency of mind against the rigid physical determinism of Anaxagoras, and against the Pythagorean attunement argument which holds that thinking is a mere effect of the body, as causally unspontaneous and as thoroughly necessitated as the music heard on a lyre. Socrates, in arguing for the possibility of self-control and moral improvement against such morally discouraging doctrines, suggested a view that, in one form or another, has dominated philosophic and scientific discussion. He suggested that things are multifarious yet ordered; that forces, or spiritual natures, are agents over material or more material natures; and that, in particular, the human mind does have a power over that complex called the human body and is not completely dominated by it.

Descartes' theory of mind-body dualism explicitly limits the hierarchy of ordered finite substances to two: nonextended mind, and a single physical substance, extended matter. Moreover, any failure to appreciate how seriously Descartes took physiological theory will pose a great obstacle to understanding mind-body dualism and how it secures a power of self-determination for mind. Thus behaviorists have been influenced by Descartes' characterization of the human body as a machine. Yet they rebel heartily against mind-body dualism. Behaviorists, however, are often less inclined than was Descartes to probe the inner workings of the bodily machine. But once we remember that by the human body, or the material aspect of man, Descartes means a complicated congeries of particles that can be adequately treated only through refined physiological theory, we will begin to see questions we must pursue before mind-body dualism can be understood or evaluated. Indeed, attention to physiological theory immediately helps to put into perspective two grounds often advanced for dismissing mind-body dualism: that it would be obviously simpler to reduce mind to matter; and that an interaction between nonextended mind and extended matter is either inconceivable or unlikely.

Now, physiological theory must be interpreted with reference to the more basic physical laws it presupposes. Descartes limits the physical world to particles in motion, with the only force operating between particles being that of collision. Thus, for Descartes, the machine of the human body, like every other material assemblage, consists solely of particles undergoing collision. In short, he excludes all other kinds of *physical* substances and forces that might dominate, or be agents over, a more basic matter. Descartes, however, had to construct an elaborate argument to defend this monism in respect to the physical world. There is reason to believe he would view the later theories of Newton, Leibniz, and others, which introduce powers such as attraction, cohesion and repulsion, as reinstating the proliferated hierarchy of physical substances he tried to expunge. Thus, unless we were willing to espouse the severe limitations of Descartes' monism in respect to the physical world, we cannot, in any enthusiasm to 'simplify' matters by reducing mind to the physical, cavalierly dismiss mind-body dualism on the grounds that any dualism is excessive per se. For, if ever we come to think the evidence points to a physicalistic reduction, we may well wish to identify mind with a complex made from different kinds of physical substances, so that our ontological commitments would in fact range well beyond a dualism.

Some object that an interaction between nonextended mind and extended matter is either inconceivable or unlikely, so that mind should be considered as physical. Again, unless one is willing, in rejecting mind-body dualism, to explain mind in terms of Descartes' limited physical ontology of matter in motion, one would have to make reference to physical substances or forces that dominate, or influence, extended matter. Yet such substances or forces might very likely appear nonextended themselves. That is, the relation between them and matter would be similar to the relation Descartes says holds between mind and matter. For example, a force that makes an extended body cohere or a force that causes one extended body to attract another does not itself seem to be extended. Indeed, Descartes maintained that such forces, which he tried to expunge from physics, were unnecessary fictions conceived in analogy to the relation whereby one's nonextended mind is experienced as influencing one's body. Thus, for Descartes, the conceivability of such fictitious forces is testimony to the fact that we can conceive the interaction between nonextended mind and extended matter.

Chapter 10. THE ARGUMENT FOR DUALISM, INTERACTION, AND FREEDOM CONNECTED TO THE ARGUMENT FOR GOD'S EXISTENCE

Descartes thought his argument for mind-body dualism, interaction, and human freedom attained the highest certitude—metaphysical certitude—only because he proved the existence of a good, all-powerful, God who guarantees such reasoning. His metaphysical argument for dualism, interaction, and freedom is accordingly interconnected with the proof of God.

1. PROCEDURES IN METAPHYSICAL DEMONSTRATION

For Descartes, metaphysical arguments are demonstrations. He does not use the word "demonstration" lightly. He means to suggest that the reasons by which he claims to prove the existence of God, and the distinction between mind and matter, are absolutely conclusive. Descartes distinguishes two modes of demonstration, analysis and synthesis.[32]

"Analysis" refers to the process of teaching someone, possibly oneself, to recognize first principles. First principles, or those a priori truths that are the starting points for all other knowledge, are clearly not proved by reference to other truths. However, we are likely to be blinded to these first principles by confusing prejudices that are psychologically more familiar than the first principles themselves. An analysis proceeds by exposing the dubious character of more familiar beliefs in order to aid the mind to discover what is truly a first principle or an a priori. "Synthesis" refers to the process of proceeding from first principles by necessary deduction to other truths that follow from them, or are a posteriori. Analysis leads Descartes to make God the very first principle of knowledge, so that only by reference to that knowledge of God can we, by synthesis, come to a knowledge of other metaphysical truths, such as the substantial distinction between mind and matter.

Analysis, by pushing forward to the first principles of reality, and synthesis, by carefully deducing conclusions only from such well founded premises, together demand all the practices involved in 'turning away from the senses'.

2. STEPS IN DESCARTES' DEMONSTRATION

Descartes argues, first, that although the nature and existence of material things can be doubted, the existence of mind can be known with assurance. Second, the substantial distinction between mind and matter can be known with high probability—but not with a metaphysical certitude until God's nature and existence are proved. Third, God's nature as a mind, and his existence, can be proved. Fourth, all other knowledge, including knowledge of the substantial distinction of mind and matter, and mind-body interaction, depends on our knowledge of God.

2.1. Material Things Can Be Doubted but the Existence of Mind Can Be Known with Assurance

Consonant with the reductive character of analysis, Descartes treats any belief that is not certain and indubitable as if it were false. In this way he denies these beliefs the status of first principles and recognizes that if ever they are to be known, they must be retrieved from theoretical doubt by

[61]

being deduced with necessity from the first principle or principles that emerge at the end of the process of reductive analysis.

Descartes sets out to show that sense experience provides no clear basis for construing even the notion of a material thing, or substance. It provides no principles for its own interpretation. We surely depend upon the senses and a well-functioning motor apparatus to anticipate imaginatively, discern, and react physically to the behavior of familiar objects, such as plants, ducks, lions, wax. This competence, although clearly affected by impairments of the senses or motor apparatus, such as deafness and blindness, can be exercised without any great reflection upon the nature, or essence, of material things. Hence, our task still remains, namely, to state precisely what constitutes the nature of a material thing or substance. Sense qualities themselves—colors, smells, feelings—often seem to be affections of our mind. In any case, they do not obviously reveal their purported material causes, for example, the particles, rays, and brain movements that supposedly occasion them. Thus we must definitely look further than sense to find the principles by which to construe the notion of a material thing or substance. Descartes certainly does not take the principles of Aristotle—form, matter, efficient cause, and telos—as obvious. As we will see, by also challenging mathematics, he raises a doubt as to whether the notion of a material thing can be clarified even by reference to its being something spatial, that is, something extended.

Now, Descartes says: "And because there are men who make a mistake in reasoning even regarding the most simple matters of geometry, and form paralogisms, I, judging myself subject to error as much as any other man, rejected as false all the reasons I had previously taken as demonstrations." [33] A paralogism is a contradiction, and whatever implies a contradiction is itself contradictory. Mathematics has its starting points in simple things or natures and rules of

[62]

derivation that may at first seem certain and indubitable. Not even these simple things, such as points and lines, can be perspicuously represented in, let alone validated by, sense. And no matter how certain and indubitable these simple things or natures and rules of derivation may at first seem, we cannot be sure that they are true unless we also know that no contradiction is implied by them. However, Descartes maintains that (prior to knowing God) we cannot know beyond a shadow of doubt that mathematics is not contradictory. And since geometry and arithmetic enter into our representations of the nature of material things, and since we can doubt arithmetic and geometry, we ipso facto call into doubt not merely the existence, but also the nature of material things. There is always the possibility that in representing matter by means of mathematics we are in effect representing something that is contradictory and hence impossible.

Thus reductive analysis leads Descartes to the point where no beliefs about the once-so-familiar world remain certain and indubitable. He is left with sense qualities that do not reveal their causes. But then—as it were at the terminus of reductive analysis—there emerges what he takes as his first principle· *I think, therefore I am.* From this he will somehow have to deduce with necessity whatever else he can know.

Just because the mind can be known to exist without yet knowing whether any material things exist, we cannot conclusively say the mind is *not* a material 'thing', or material 'substance'. First we must explain what constitutes a 'thing', or 'substance', and validate the truth of our conception. After we do that, we will be better able to judge whether mind and matter could be the same 'thing', or 'substance'. Nevertheless, although we are not yet in a position to say anything about the truth of so technical a conception as that of 'thing', or 'substance', still, in a less formal sense of the word 'thing', the reductive analysis has shown that the mind can recognize itself as a single thing having various aspects related in special ways. Thus we discern in ourselves sense qualities and images as related to the intellect that is aware of them by means of its 'ideas'. Similarly, willing, or our power of assent, stands in a certain relation to the intellect, as it is always ideas in the intellect that are either affirmed or not affirmed by us. Moreover, the fact that the mind can attain assurance of its own existence as a single thing having aspects in relation and at the same time remain uncertain even of the basic axioms of geometry shows that the unity of consciousness can be known better than the perhaps more psychologically familiar unities typically ascribed to geometrical and material objects, for example, when we think of 'one' divisible line as somehow constituted from a relation among indivisible points; or of 'one' triangle as a thing constituted from certain relations among lines. Thus the doubts concerning mathematics also help the mind to rid itself of a prejudice that may have inclined it to think that all things—all unities—have to be analogous to, or indeed the same as, geometrical or spatial unities. The removal of such a prejudice makes us more keenly aware of the difficulties in identifying mind, or consciousness, with matter. It accordingly better prepares us to accept the distinction of mind from matter *if* subsequent reflection upon the technical conception of 'thing', or 'substance', proves mind and matter to be different things, or substances.

2.2. The Substantial Distinction Between Mind and Matter Known with High Probability—but Not with Metaphysical Certitude Until God's Nature and Existence Are Proved

By a "substance" Descartes means a thing that is presupposed by the particular features that inhere in it, but that itself does not inhere in something further.[34] The essential meaning, then, is that two substances, despite their causal relations to each other, are distinct things, that is, not identical with each other. By examining Descartes' manner of reasoning about substance, we will see why he thinks it highly probable that, just because one can know that the mind exists without yet knowing whether the body or anything material exists, it thereby follows that the mind is a different substance from the body and thus not identical with the body even if the body does exist and interacts with it.

To shed light on this we have to consider further Descartes' manner of reasoning about substances. When the human mind conceives the thing, or substance, in which properties have to inhere in order to exist, it conceives this thing or substance through some property essential to it; and all other properties that presuppose the thing or substance are referred to the thing or substance through an essential property. Since the only way the human mind has of conceiving a thing or substance in which certain properties inhere or can inhere is by an essential property presupposed by inessential properties of the thing or substance, it follows that we would lose our conception or understanding of the thing or substance if we did not consider it as always bound to have its essential property.[35] For example, we would lose our conception or understanding of a material thing or substance if we did not consider it as bound to have the essential property that enables us to conceive or understand a material thing or substance, namely, the property of extension. From that it follows that the same thing or substance cannot be conceived to have two essential properties, that is two properties neither of which would necessarily involve the other or any third common property (excluding 'being,' 'unity', and the 'good'). For, to say that the same substance could have two essential properties is equivalent to saying that we could conceive the substance as not having a property that is essential to it. Thus every thing or substance can have only one essential property that is presupposed by the other properties that can be in it.[36] It therefore follows that the substance that thinks cannot be conceived as identical with the substance

[65]

that is extended in space, that is, with material substance. Thinking substance and material substance are not identical because, as we have seen, we can conceive and know that thinking exists without knowing whether any material thing exists and, moreover, we can conceive the nature of body—that is, extension—without attributing thinking to it.

One might still question whether it is correct to employ a notion of substance whereby we reason about substance only on the basis of properties. Should we, perhaps, introduce a notion of substance such that no human reasoning on the basis of properties could tell us which property or properties are essential to a particular thing or substance? The introduction of such a notion of substance would certainly have the result that no matter how much it seemed to us that mind and matter were capable of distinct existence we would never know it as certain. Such a notion of substance would, however, saddle us with something we do not understand. For, since we can reason only on the basis of what we discern as necessarily connected or not necessarily connected, and if we should proceed to say that such reasoning has no relevance to judging which things can exist independently, we would in effect have said that reasoning is not reasoning at all, and our intelligence would seem a farce.

The substantial distinction between mind and matter accordingly seems highly probable. Nevertheless, the lingering doubt may still remain as to whether we can unconditionally trust reasoning about substances on the basis of properties just because it is the only way we can hope to have a criterion for definitively distinguishing substances. Descartes seeks a justification for such reasoning in the *Meditations.* There he looks for metaphysical certitude. He refuses to infer immediately the distinctness of the sub stance of mind and the substance of matter simply on the basis that thinking can be known to exist while the existence and nature of matter is in doubt.[37] Yet neither does he hastily assume that there is one substance in which thinking and extension could co-inhere. Rather than immediately concerning himself with the notion of substance or with other difficult matters such as the correctness of mathematical reasoning, he proceeds to a more primary question, namely, the grounds that human reason has for trusting any of its ideas. He claims no metaphysical certitude about the substantial distinction of mind and matter, or about the possibility of mind-body interaction, until he thinks he has proved God's power, goodness, and existence.

2.3. Proof of God's Nature and Existence

Having placed into doubt both the existence and the nature of matter, having affirmed the truth of the *I think, therefore I am,** and having pointed out the general rule that whatever one perceives very clearly and very distinctly is true, Descartes proceeds to say that the existence of God—the existence of an infinite, eternal, immutable, all-knowing, all-powerful, and all-perfect being—is manifestly true. His assertion that God exists seems like a very bold forward step, and I will try to explain why I think he believed himself entitled to make so sudden and bold an advance.

Whatever can be immediately known, based on the first principle, *I think, therefore I am,* must be perceived as necessarily implied in that first principle by an immediate inference. Thus we cannot expect Descartes to prove an immediate consequence of the *I think, therefore I am* by first proving other things on which it depends, for if such had to be done it would not be an immediate consequence. However, what we can expect of him—and this he tries to do—is to remove certain prejudices that may blind us to perceiving an immediate consequence of the *I think, therefore I am.*

The problem Descartes poses is to determine whether

---

* In the *Meditations* Descartes uses the formula *I am, I exist.*

any ideas are true in addition to those that represent what we immediately discern in ourselves when perceiving the *I think, therefore I am.* It is obvious that any idea representing something about whose nature or existence we are in doubt cannot be said to be a true idea. Any such idea provides us with no firm basis for determining why we have that idea in the first place—in short, it provides no firm basis for reasoning about causality. For example, since we can doubt the nature and existence of matter, it follows that our idea of the nature of matter cannot persuade us that matter exists and causes our idea of it, nor can our idea of matter tell us what else other than matter does cause our idea of matter. Thus any idea whose truth is in doubt provides no basis for knowing what, if anything, exists outside ourselves as immediately known in the *I think, therefore I am.* By contrast, any idea so representatively perfect as to assure us that what it represents truly exists will also provide us with a reliable notion of causation by reference to which we can show that we would not have the idea unless it were caused in us by an object such as it represents. Thus, the determination of the real representative perfection of ideas, the determination of the truth of ideas, and the determination of the metaphysically valid notion of causation must be established concurrently.

Accordingly, when Descartes says that he sees no reason why those ideas that he doubts, for example, the idea of matter, may not arise from himself, he is simply emphasizing that they do not indicate with certainty and evidence that they proceed from what they represent. He is not affirming that he knows those ideas are caused by himself so much as emphasizing that he is unable, on the basis of what they represent, to determine conclusively what causes them to be in him.[38]

However, this manner of leading each of us to focus in on his own self (because we have been unable to find familiar causes for our ideas) removes an important obstacle to intuiting the true nature of causation. It vividly reminds each of us that there is no prospect for discerning the true nature of causation except on the basis of things clear and evident to us. Since what thus far has been clear and evident is only the immediately known nature of oneself as a thinking thing, one wonders whether one might indeed cause oneself and one's ideas and thus be self-sufficient and alone in the world.

Yet, since we have doubts about our own causal self-sufficiency, we are made to realize that the most essential problem is to determine both what makes something self-sufficient be self-sufficient and what makes something dependent (or an effect) be something dependent (or an effect). Clearly, our existence, or the existence of anything whatever, has some explanation, for whatever exists either is self-sufficient or depends on the self-sufficient.[39] Thus, by determining what makes the self-sufficient be self-sufficient and what makes an effect be an effect, we shall finally have the standard whereby we may know whether we explain our own existence or whether, by contrast, we depend on some self-sufficient thing whose nature we understand but recognize to be different from our own.

Before proceeding any further in our attempt to determine what constitutes the nature of self-sufficiency and what constitutes the nature of an effect, it is important to note that we cannot know what makes an effect be an effect without knowing what makes the self-sufficient on which the effect depends be self-sufficient. In the language of Descartes' *Rules,* cause and effect are not correlative, but the cause is absolute.[40] To know what effects are possible it is first necessary to know what the cause is. This is so because were it not in the nature of an effect to be necessarily dependent on its self-sufficient cause, we could conceive everything in the nature of an effect as capable of existing without its self-sufficient cause. If this were so, what we called an effect would actually be represented as having a self-sufficient nature itself. Thus we may infer that every effect is *necessarily* dependent on the self-sufficient nature on which it depends. Moreover, it becomes clearer that the self-sufficient nature, or cause, is at most one 'thing.' This is so because the self-sufficient nature cannot be multiplied in instances on whose individual features it would then depend. In short, the self-sufficient nature cannot be a universal like "man" that so depends on the matter of particulars that various causes can make it exist in some particulars and cease to exist in others. If one needs an analogy for the self-sufficient nature—and it is only an analogy—it is more like "space," which could not be in one place without being everywhere and which is always of one nature throughout.

Since one cannot know whether one is effect or self-sufficient without understanding the nature of an effect and the nature of self-sufficiency, and since one can know the nature of an effect only by first recognizing the nature of self-sufficiency that is necessarily presupposed by the nature of an effect, and since the only things known with certainty and evidence are those things immediately discerned in oneself as a thinking thing, the best procedure for each of us is to consider whether he himself could be self-sufficient by virtue of what is certain and evident about himself, namely, thinking and willing.

Now, by analyzing this provisional possibility and by seeing if I can reduce it to absurdity, I have the best prospect that the true nature of self-sufficiency, and consequently the true nature of an effect, will present itself to my intuitive grasp. What I must constantly bear in mind throughout this procedure is that there is no prospect of intuiting the true nature of self-sufficiency, and consequently the true nature of an effect, among those natures I have called into doubt, that is, among mathematical and material natures, and among any secret or obscure powers or capacities I may fancy to lie within 'regions' of the self that I do not immediately know in the *I think, therefore I am.* To go to any of these dubious terrains to look for an intuition of the true nature of self-sufficiency, and hence for the true nature of an effect, would be as silly as going back to the nature of a square in order to understand it once I have already realized that it cannot be understood except by first understanding simple things on which it must somehow depend, such as lines, angles, and so on.

Hence, realizing that my self-sufficiency, if indeed I am self-sufficient, can consist only in things known to me, I in turn must realize that the nature of self-sufficiency will have to consist in intellect and will, which is what is immediately known to me in the *I think, therefore I am*. In short, self-sufficiency can be clearly and evidently thought of by me only if I represent it through intellect and will.

However, as has been said, the self-sufficient is perfect inasmuch as all else depends on it and nothing can limit it. Thus, since I can think self-sufficiency only through intellect and will, and since the self-sufficient is perfect and unlimited, the self-sufficient nature will have to be conceived as an intellect and will that is perfect and unlimited. But to be such is to be God—it is to be omnipotent and omniscient. Therefore I can only think self-sufficiency, and hence the nature of an effect, through omnipotence and omniscience. However, my doubt informs me that I myself am not omnipotent and omniscient. Hence I know that I am not the self-sufficient but that I have the nature of an effect and must depend on this self-sufficient being who is God.

2.4. All Other Knowledge Depends on the Knowledge of God

The idea of the self-sufficient, by reference to which the idea of an effect must be clarified, is now seen to be the idea of God. Thus God's existence is shown to be an immediately necessary presupposition of the *I think, therefore I am* even if it did not seem so at first. Moreover, reference to God's nature must become the grounds whereby to assign the true, and not the seeming, representative value to the ideas that have been called into metaphysical doubt.

Review of Those Things That Have Been Doubted

Essences, not just the existence of things bearing them, have been doubted. We have called into doubt what normally are considered "necessities" presupposed for the "possibility" of other things. For example, in doubting whether we can reason about substances, or "things," on the basis of properties, we called into question whether substances, and *a fortiori*, whether distinct substances, are even possible. Similarly, in doubting the elementary conceptions of geometry, such as the point and the line, we called into question whether space is even possible. And by calling into question something so fundamental as space, we likewise called into question notions of efficient causality that presuppose the production of effects by contact. Likewise, by doubting finite substance, we called into question the efficient causality supposedly found between finite things, such as between the human mind and matter.

Moreover, the notions of mathematics and substance (no matter how highly probable and even "necessary" they had seemed) were nevertheless doubted for reasons inherent to mathematics or for reasons inherent to the conception of substance. For example, the fact that we had no proof that contradictions could not be deduced in our system of mathematics showed that even basic statements in our system of mathematics, such as $2 + 2 = 4$, are not known to be absolutely "necessary." Thus, even if some system of mathematics is true—which we were not able to know for sure—we did not have conclusive proof that it is one in which $2 + 2 = 4$, $2 + 7 = 9$, and so on are necessary. Similarly, it did not seem absolutely certain that, just because the only way we could ever hope to distinguish definitively between finite substances is on the basis of properties, that therefore substances must exist or admit of being distinguished on that basis. In other words, even if substances could exist—which we were not able to know for sure—we did not have conclusive proof that our way of attempting to know them hit the mark.

God's Goodness Provides a Basis for Retrieving Things from Doubt

Now that God's existence has been proved (which certainly happened without our knowing the truth of anything in doubt, such as the "necessities" of mathematics or of finite substance) we still do not find, by probing our idea of God's nature, any hitherto unnoticed mathematical reasons or reasons having to do with finite substance, sufficient to show us that our former doubts about mathematical "necessities" or the "necessities" concerning finite substance were wrong or rationally unsustainable on mathematical grounds or grounds having to do with substance. In other words, *if* the mathematical "necessities" we are strongly inclined to accept, or *if* the "necessities" about finite substance we are strongly inclined to accept, are true, the truth of such "necessities" does not flow from God's nature—who nevertheless must be responsible for their truth—on any grounds of mathematical "necessity" or because of any recognized "necessities" having to do with substance. From the point of view of such normal, but now questioned notions of "necessity," God's production of any such "necessities", *if* he has produced them, is not "necessary." It seems completely contingent that God produces any mathematical "necessities" or "necessities" about substance; that is, even if he has produced some such "necessities" he could have produced different ones. Moreover, *if* God has produced these mathematical "necessities" or "necessities" about substance that we are strongly inclined to accept, we obviously ought not try to conceive his manner of producing them on the basis of normal notions of efficient causality, since these normal notions, as mentioned above, already presuppose the validity of mathematics and finite substance.

Is there any way, then, to show that, even if God in no way necessarily had to use his power to render true our familiar "necessities" concerning mathematics and substance, he nevertheless has in fact rendered them true? Although we can see nothing in God's nature showing that he must necessarily have created any mathematical truths or truths about substance, nevertheless the goodness that is necessary to God's nature prevents him from tricking us by giving us misleading ideas.

According to Descartes, even our initial doubts about mathematics and substance confirm this view that God does not mislead us. For those doubts prodded us to push back, by analysis, to recognize him as the first principle of created truths, including the "necessities" of mathematics and substance. Thus, in allowing us such doubts, God's aim was obviously to instruct, not fool, us. But after such doubts have once played their role in letting us discover God, then, since he is not a deceiver, we can infer that the notions of mathematics and finite substance must be true. For inasmuch as such notions still appear highly certain to us, if God nevertheless allowed us to be mistaken about them, he would be what we have said he cannot be, a deceiver. Moreover, this inability of God to be a deceiver is no limitation upon him. On the contrary, the very wish to deceive or trick testifies to weakness—to envy or fear. Thus the goodness of God is indeed necessarily connected to his being a self-sufficient or infinite mind.[41] If there is any necessity for God to create, it is a necessity to bring about as much good or perfection as possible, which does not mean necessarily creating a world in which one mathematics rather than another is true, but rather in creating a world in which rational beings are not misled.

To summarize: Convinced of God's goodness, Descartes is assured God will not allow human intelligence to be a farce. Yet our intelligence would be a farce if we could not definitively distinguish between different finite substances—between things distinct from one another that remain capable of independent existence even if they never actually exist one without the other. Moreover, we can reason about a substance only on the basis of properties. Thus, we may now assume that, if we do so in the only way that promises us any definitive criterion for distinguishing substances, then God will guarantee such reasoning. We have already discussed at some length how to carry out such reasoning. We may tersely review and amplify what we have said.

Substantial Distinction Between Mind and Matter Is Logically Prior to Proof Matter Exists. Properties appear to us to be of two kinds, essential (attributes) and nonessential (modes). Thus reasoning about substances must be on the basis of such properties. Inessential properties seem to presuppose only one essential property. Thus, the inessential properties of figure, instantaneous velocity, and local motion all seem to presuppose only the one essential property, extension. That becomes more obvious when we realize that, while we cannot conceive any of these inessential properties without admitting they presuppose extension, we can conceive them as existing without attributing any thinking to them. Moreover, the inessential properties of sensing, imagining, and willing seem to presuppose only the one essential property, understanding (or intellect, or thought). That becomes obvious when we realize that, while we can well know that we are a being who understands, wills, imagines, and senses, we nevertheless can doubt whether extension, or matter, exists. While inessential properties seem to presuppose no more than one essential property, essential properties clearly do not seem to necessarily involve one another or any third common property (excluding 'being', 'unity', and the 'good'). Thus, as we have said, extension does not seem to necessarily involve thinking or vice versa.

Since inessential properties can be completely conceived only through essential ones, our only hope of distinguishing a particular substance is on the basis of reasoning from essential properties. But, as we have said, no essential property seems necessarily to involve another. Thus each essential property must be definitive of a distinct substance. For if two essential properties, that is, two properties neither of which seemed necessarily to involve the other, nonetheless required the same substance, we could never definitively tell anything about what is capable of independent existence from what. But, since God guarantees our intelligence, we infer that two such essential properties not only seem, but are in fact, indicative of different substances, that is, indicative of things capable of separate existence.

Moreover, we must infer that inessential properties not merely seem, but necessarily, presuppose only one essential property. This can be seen as follows. An inessential property is not a relation between substances but always exists as a mode of a particular substance the nature of which we are trying to determine. However, if an inessential property presupposed more than one essential property, we could never infer from the fact that essential properties do not seem to necessarily involve one another that they are therefore indicative of different substances. In short, we would lose what we have just shown to be our only basis for distinguishing different substances and our intelligence would be, what it is not, a farce. Therefore, we rightly infer that an inessential property not merely seems but necessarily presupposes only one essential property.

This fact that an inessential property presupposes only one essential property helps resolve whatever question might remain about the status of sense quality. Sense quality, such as color or feeling, seemed to presuppose only the one essential property, namely, thought, and not to presuppose extension. For, while we were experiencing sense quality, including color, we were able to doubt whether any extension exists, but certainly we were not able to doubt that we were thinking. However, until we had our present guarantee that inessential properties not merely seem but necessarily presuppose only one essential property, we might have had a lingering doubt that in some unnoticed way sense quality also presupposes extension. Thus from the fact we conceived thinking without extension and vice versa we could not have inferred that the substance which thinks and senses is a different substance from that which is extended. But now that we know sense quality can presuppose only one essential property, thought, we can infer that it is to be predicated only of mind, not of matter. Hence, we also now realize that in describing color as extended, the word "extended" is indeed being used analogously. Of course, nothing we have said prevents sense quality from being caused to occur in the mind by physiological activities in the body, which, as we will see, is Descartes' view.

Descartes' criterion for distinguishing substances is, therefore, logically prior even to any determination that a certain kind of substance does in fact exist. We need not know that matter exists in order to be certain that it is a different substance from thinking substance. For the very fact that we can conceive thinking substance through its essential property of thought, and yet still not recognize any necessary connection between thought and the essential property of matter, extension, shows that extension and all the modes presupposed by it, such as figure, instantaneous velocity, or motion, must, if they exist, reside in a different substance from thinking substance. Moreover, when Descartes claims there are only two finite substances, thinking substance and material substance, he does not, it seems, mean to eliminate the possibility of other finite substances. It is just that he claims not to recognize any property beyond thinking and extension (excluding 'being', 'unity', and the 'good') that is not a mode of just one of these two.

Possibility of Mind-Body Interaction Is Logically Prior to Proof Matter Exists. Just as the proof of the substantial distinction between mind and matter is logically prior even to knowledge that matter exists, so is the proof of the possibility of mind-matter interaction logically prior to the knowledge that such interaction does occur. Basically, mind-body interaction is possible because a contingent causal relation between two substances is possible. Before proceeding we should say something further about this contingent causal relation which Descartes will presuppose when he explains sensation, imagination, and the passions by reference to physiology.

Being nonextended, the mind does not have 'contact' with the body. Nonetheless, Descartes thought that for the body to cause an effect in the mind, a particular part of the brain (the pineal gland) would have to be affected first. In other words, a disturbance in any of the other parts of the body could affect the mind only by first affecting a part of the brain. Similarly, he thought the mind could cause effects in the body only by first affecting the brain (the pineal gland) whence the effect is transmitted to other parts of the body. As said, the effects of the body upon the mind and mind upon the body are brought about by a raw contingent causal relation, without anything to serve as a medium. Now it might seem that the effect of mind upon matter would be impossible for the following reason, which does not turn on the general conceivability of a contingent causal relation but on the particular nature of matter. It might seem that the movement of physical particles (and hence the behavior of macroscopic bodies such as the pineal gland) would be rigidly determined by mechanical causes or laws governing the conservation of motion, so that the mind could never manage to introduce changes into the quantity of motion of these particles nor even into their direction alone. Although we cannot pursue Descartes' reasoning here, suffice it to say he argues that the laws of the conservation of motion and inertia are not so necessary—so a priori—as to rule out such changes.

Proof of Existence of Matter. Having thus validated the metaphysical claim that mind and matter are distinct substances capable of interaction, Descartes proceeded to allay the metaphysical doubt about the actual existence of matter. He argued that sensation, imagination, and the passions seemed adequately explicable only by reference to physiological causes—and knowing that God is not a deceiver, Descartes accordingly inferred the existence of matter. Nonetheless, he claimed the existence of matter to be less certain than the proofs of God, the substantial distinction between mind and matter, and the possibility of interaction.[42]

Freedom of the Will. It seems that Descartes tries to reconcile free will with divine omnipotence and prescience by distinguishing, as it were, 'orders' of truth. Even the "necessities" concerning mathematics and finite substances are somehow produced by God and could have been different. Thus, although the denial of one mathematical "necessity" might *seem* incompatible with the assertion of another, nevertheless we cannot say such incompatibility is absolute. Similarly, although free will may *seem* incompatible with its complete dependence upon God, nevertheless we cannot say such incompatibility is absolute.

Descartes also argued that mind and body are distinct substances capable of interaction. Now although God may have established a 'harmony' between mind and body such that all our sense qualities are determined by physiological causes he clearly has not arranged things such that the material world inevitably determines us to have only true *ideas*, for we obviously can make mistakes and feel the need to make a proper use of our reason. Thus our power of free deciding (*libertas arbitrii*) would be insignificant unless it were also really in our power to properly investigate our ideas and gather the evidence required to draw a reasonable conclusion on a topic. Genuine freedom—the conviction that we are genuinely able to investigate the truth—presupposes that our wanting (*voluntas* or *volonté*) to research our ideas can direct them in a productive manner. Genuine freedom presupposes that our voluntary thinking is not so determined by physiology as to be the mere illusion of voluntariness. And if we began metaphysical reflection with only a faith in our freedom, and *then* have the divine guarantee, that faith on which the search for knowledge rests is elevated to knowledge, for God, not

[79]

being a deceiver, would not mislead us into thinking that it is in our power to attain knowledge if we have not the power to do so.

We may also indicate some of the reasons why physiological considerations themselves might show it unlikely that the body determines all our mental life. The same raw sense quality—colors, smells, feels—can be experienced, or reasoned about, correctly or incorrectly, in innumerable ways. Thus it is clear that the very same physiological occurrences that cause the raw sense quality could not *suffice* to explain our use of the myriad ideas and propositions by which the same raw sense quality is variously cognized and rendered into diverse experiences—that is, into different sensations, memories, and imaginations. In short, were these ideas and propositions to have any physiological causes, such causes would accordingly be different from those that explain only raw sense quality and motor responses.

However, since we cannot understand one idea without being able to reason about others and form innumerable propositions (reason seems to be one and indivisible), it seems that, if reason had a physiological foundation, the brain would be capable of causing each of our mathematical, metaphysical, and moral ideas, as well as our ability, at almost any moment, and whatever our sense qualities, to devise and understand new propositions.

It is, of course, easier to suppose that the brain could do this than to prove it. Suffice it to say that a closer study (which cannot be made here) of Descartes' clearly antiquated physiological model would enable us to see better why *he* thought it unlikely that the brain is able to cause all our reasonings. Descartes' particular physiological theory seems to imply rather severe limitations to the brain. Thus his physiological theory is consonant with, but not necessary to, his metaphysical, or philosophical, defense of human freedom. His metaphysical defense of freedom could be compatible with certain more modern physiological theories.

Part IV. CRUCIAL ELEMENTS IN DESCARTES' MORAL PSYCHOLOGY

Descartes, then, believed sense quality, whether present during actual sensation, imagination, or the passions, is to be explained, at least in part, by physiology. But he in no way thought that the intellect is rigidly determined by physiology in regard to its use of the 'ideas' by which it interprets or cognizes the sensuous data that is present during sensation, imagination, and the passions. And, although a highly controlled use of its ideas, such as its mathematical, metaphysical, and moral ideas, might be harder to exercise during the experience of the passions caused by the body, Descartes thought the intellect could nevertheless exercise such control if it had prepared itself by thinking out in advance worthwhile rules. Indeed, he considered such advance devising of worthwhile rules necessary even for intelligent sensing and imagining. Thus the concern to master the passions is continuous with that of learning how to sense and imagine intelligently. This advance working out of rules is, in effect, the exercise of volition.

Chapter 11. 'PASSION' AND 'VOLITION' IN THEIR BROADEST SENSE

In the broadest sense "passion" is not restricted to meaning an emotion, such as fear, desire, and so on. Rather, any occurrence caused in a given substance is a passion of that substance.[43] For example, when events in one's nervous

[81]

system cause effects in the brain that, in turn, cause the color red to occur in one's mind, the sensation of red is a passion of mental substance due to the action of the body. Similarly, when my wish to raise my hand affects my brain, which, in turn, makes my hand go up, my hand's rising is a passion of material substance wrought by the action of mental substance. Or, again, when I choose to think of an algebraic problem, my thought of it is at once a passion of my mind and an action of my mind. It is customary, however, to call such thoughts actions rather than passions. And all such voluntary thoughts are also called "volitions." [44]

In calling such thoughts volitions in this broadest sense, it is merely implied that we are *consenting* to think them, not that we are necessarily clear about their subject matters, convinced of a resolution, or even gratified by the topic. One can think willingly, but blunderingly, about a portion of logic one knows only by hearsay; one can think methodically without yet having resolved a problem in geometry; one can think dutifully on an unpleasant topic because of some necessity, for example, of the order in which employees might have to be fired. Moreover, our volitions can be confused either because we are not gifted enough to think well on a topic, because we have not yet devised a method for approaching a topic, or because we have not yet solved particular problems. Similarly, our volitions can remain stupid or confused due to our fault, when, although we choose to think on something, we nevertheless neglect to determine the merits of considering the topic in the first place, neglect to search out a method for approaching the topic, or fail to trace out sufficiently the implications of the topic to determine if what we are tending to conclude is in fact actually possible, true, and desirable.

Chapter 12. VOLITION, VIRTUE, AND VICE

In its broadest sense, then, volition can characterize thinking about any subject matter—not just 'moral' reflections. Whatever the subject matter, we can choose to conduct our reasonings with care so that, within the range of our intellectual talents, they will possess the 'virtue' of being correct. Or we might be careless and neglectful, thus guilty of intellectual vice. Hence, 'virtuous' and 'viceful' describe styles of volition. They distinguish reasoning we are choosing to conduct well from reasoning we are choosing not to conduct well. We therefore have as many opportunities for cultivating virtue or falling into vice as the occasions on which we may attempt or fail to attempt to reason correctly and pertinently. Something is undoubtedly to be learned from wisely classifying the 'virtues' by means of their subject matters or by means of rules for evaluating them. Nevertheless, Descartes thinks that, by defining virtue generally as correct or pertinent reasoning, we are best put in mind of what is most important: the need not to forget ourselves. Our thinking, then, should always strive for the *scientia vitae*, the knowledge of life. We are not to seek some merely parochial accuracy for our thoughts, such as expertise at accounting or shrewdness at winning lawsuits. Rather we are always to try as well as we can to think with reference to achieving those comprehensive insights into human nature that allow us to see man's true good.

Chapter 13. VIRTUE, PASSIONS CAUSED BY THE BODY, AND THE INTERIOR PASSIONS

Virtue is the intelligent volition that devises worthwhile rules. It *prepares* us to resist whatever harmful suggestions we experience during passions, or emotions, caused by the body—such as fear, love, or desire. Obviously, then, virtue is most ordinarily and most primarily required when there is *not yet* any passion caused by the body. Similarly, vice displays itself in our neglect of duty, or correct reasoning, even when we are not being inclined to such neglect because of a passion caused by the body.

Descartes, we noted in Part I, refers to the interior passions, that is, the emotions not due to the action of the body nor necessarily having any marked bodily effects as their consequence. Such interior joys or sadnesses supervene on thoughts we are entertaining and can be false if founded on false thoughts. Thus, they are not merely passions of the mind, but soon become its actions inasmuch as it is we who are choosing whether or not to examine the truth of the thoughts on which they are founded and supervene. To allow the thoughts on which such interior passions are founded to go unevaluated is obviously tantamount to inviting confused thinking and thus to neglecting virtue. Interior passions such as joy, which can provide our greatest contentment, or sadness, which can prompt intelligent apprehension, are indeed useful to life. But only we can keep them useful by examining our thoughts to see if our contentment is based on a solid good and our sadness on genuine evils. Wisdom in managing this examination of our interior passions dictates our remembering that sadness, by alerting us to a possible evil, may incline us to a calm evaluation, while joy, by reaping the comforts of contentment, may divert us from a careful appraisal of the 'good' on which it is founded.

Chapter 14. PASSIONS, OR EMOTIONS, CAUSED BY THE BODY, AND PHYSIOLOGY

Elisabeth and Descartes thought it part of virtue to try to learn the physiology of the passions in order to be better able to control them. The details of Descartes' physiological theory are antiquated. But by reviewing them briefly the reader will better understand the jargon of the Correspondence. Doing so also points up some notable aspects of the passions—their external manifestations and self-sustaining quality. The physiology of the passions is continuous with that of sensation, memory, and imagination.

1. THE PHYSIOLOGY OF SENSATION, MEMORY, AND IMAGINATION

According to Descartes, the human body is composed of many organs, internal and external, that themselves are composed from fundamental physical particles. Some particles are called "humors"; they replenish the body and play a crucial role in nutrition and growth. Following tradition, some particles are called "spirits." Nonetheless, for Descartes, the only force one particle can exert upon another is the force of physical impact by means of collision (no action at a distance, no entelechies, are allowed). Thus the external sense organs can be affected only when they are impinged upon by particles that, in accordance with the laws of motion governing collisions, are suited to move certain of the many nerve fibers present in them. These fibers are enclosed in nerve tubes, and both tubes and fibers extend to the interior of the brain. When a fiber is pushed by external particles impinging upon a sense organ, the end of its incasing nerve tube at the interior of the brain is opened to some degree. At this point certain particles, called "animal spirits," do their work. These animal spirits originally got to the interior of the brain by a complicated process we cannot describe here. Suffice it to say they derive from the blood that makes its way to the brain after it has passed through the heart. These animal spirits follow certain laws of motion governing floating bodies, and when one or more nerve tubes are opened, the animal spirits rush toward them. Some of these animal spirits pass into the nerve tubes and go to muscles, thus tending to create motions that are reflex reactions to external stimuli. For example, when the optic fibers are violently pushed by intense light rays, the nerve tubes in the brain open so much that many animal spirits pass into them. These animal spirits then proceed to muscles of the eye and cause the eyelids to shut. Similarly, if particles constituting fire are applied to the nerves, the animal spirits may proceed to muscles causing us to retire the part of the body being burnt and even clutch it.

When a number of nerve tubes are opened, as is always in fact the case, the animal spirits rush to them in a pattern corresponding to the distribution of the opened nerve tubes. This pattern in turn corresponds to differences in the particles impinging upon the sense organs. Some of these animal spirits that rush in a pattern to the opened nerve tubes create impressions among the fibers of the brain in the region of the nerve tubes. These impressions lay the foundation for memories and imaginations; they constitute what Descartes calls the "corporeal phantasy" or "corporeal imagination." Thus, objects contingently connected to each other, yet once experienced together, such as the feeling of pain and the sight of a black cat, can be associated together in the corporeal memory or imagination and thus might become the basis for what could seem an induction—an induction obviously capable of being very misleading if it prejudiced a rational being from using his reason to examine the true connections between objects thus associated.

At the same time as the animal spirits lay these corporeal memories and imaginations, they also dispose the fibers in the brain in such a way as to make it easier in the future for other animal spirits to move toward the same muscles that cause the movements that have been associated with the stimulus, such as closing the eyes, retiring the limbs, clutching the place of one's pain. Thus the animal spirits lay the sensory-motor basis for the activities displayed toward physical objects. That basis, and the ensuing behavior, will accordingly vary with impairments of the sensory-motor apparatus, such as blindness and deafness. The associations in individual cases are always particular—for example, when not everyone has had a bad experience of a black cat. Thus not everyone will have been disposed in his motor responses to the avoidance or pursuit of the same objects.

Descartes' metaphysical view maintains that sense experiences, such as color, smell, feeling, and so on, occur, not in the brain, but in the mind. They are not the same as the brain movements that occasion them. Thus, even the feelings of pleasure or pain, of delight or fear, that accompany our seeing or hearing or touching of things, or accompany our motor activities, such as walking serenely or cringing, occur in the mind. Nevertheless sense experiences always correspond to a cerebral activity. In his particular physiological theory they correspond to a motion of the animal spirits toward the nerve tubes opened by physical particles impinging upon the senses. Similarly, Descartes argues that our sensuous imaginations and memories, as well as our feeling of being disposed to perform motor activities that have been associated with such memories and imaginations, are mental experiences and do not occur in the brain. Nevertheless they always correspond to cerebral motions. In his particular physiological theory they correspond to motions of the animal spirits toward muscles and into those cerebral memories and imaginations that have been implanted among the fibers of the brain during previous processes of sensation.

2. THE PHYSIOLOGY OF THE PASSIONS, OR EMOTIONS, CAUSED BY THE BODY

For reasons that will soon become apparent, Descartes believed that the animal spirits in the brain can move into corporeal memories and imaginations even without the presence of an external stimulus and despite one's wish. Thus unsettling memories and imaginations characteristic of the passions occur. At the same time, the animal spirits also tend toward nerve tubes adjacent to these corporeal memories. Thus the animal spirits will proceed to muscles that can cause overt actions, such as sudden arrest of movement, or cringing, that are characteristic of the passions, such as astonishment or fear. The animal spirits also go to muscles controlling such internal organs of the body as the liver or spleen. That, in turn, determines from which of these organs the heart receives its supply of blood. Depending upon the organs that supply blood to it, the heart produces animal spirits of various sizes and speeds. Thus, animal spirits, by affecting the internal organs, can even produce animal spirits constituted similarly to themselves and accordingly sustain the same sort of passion despite one's wish. Furthermore, associated with the activity of the internal organs will also be other kinds of bodily symptoms of the passions such as pallor, blushing, hunger.

Descartes claims that people's nervous systems vary. Thus not all people are so susceptible to the same passions. The same overt actions or movements need not be characteristic of the same passions in everyone, nor need the bodily symptoms of the passions, such as pallor and blushing, be the same in everyone.

Chapter 15. BENEFITS OF ATTENDING TO PHYSIOLOGY

Attention to Descartes' physiological views, however antiquated, alerts us to the fact that the physiological basis of the passions tends to be self-sustaining and makes it clear that our strategies against harmful passions can only benefit from a knowledge of the physiological processes involved. Thus, for example, although their specific recommendations may often be best forgotten, we must admire the intention as Elisabeth and Descartes discuss the regimen of diet, drugs, "waters," and meditations that produce animal spirits and humors favorable to health and composure.

Similarly, knowledge of the frequently automatic and self-sustaining character of the passions helps us better understand the relation of mind to body and our nature as a person. It prevents us from thinking that a person can be divided within himself in ways that he is not, and it wards off unnecessary guilt without allowing us to excuse our "irrationalities" as driven or compelled.

Thus rather than postulating a part of the mind at war with the rational part, Descartes traces the appearance of such a division to the mind-body relation. For example, the sound of a certain language can have become associated with fear. Hence, when we are confronted with such speech, we will automatically be disposed to fearful imaginations and to motor responses characteristic of fear. Yet, unless we recognize that the occurrence of such imaginations is automatic, we might think ourselves responsible for them and guilty of some bigotry. However, if we realize that such imaginations are automatic, not only will we hold ourselves guiltless, but we will be less distracted from exercising our powers of volition to think what our response ought to be. Similarly, the passions can be complex, with the less dominant, and in the short run more intense, passions interlacing themselves with others. Thus the sight of a comrade's distress might move us to display signs of compassion. Were we then to be vividly reminded how narrowly we escaped the same tragedy, that might automatically cause in us some temporary signs of joy. Yet, that joy need not be construed as diminishing our dominant concern for him. Indeed, it may lead us to a more profound humanity, to appreciating the depth of his loss and the role that fortune plays in life. Similarly, our dominant attitude toward someone might be a callous neglect of him, yet if we see hospital paraphernalia, it might automatically evoke a temporary grief that in no way alters our basically insouciant attitude. In other words, while not always responsible for the thoughts that come to us automatically, we do become responsible for them if we persistently neglect to examine their merits and try, when warranted, to change them. For our associations can be idiosyncratic, having no firm logical or evidential connection, and can dispose us to reactions without our ever having reasonably judged that such reactions are apropos. Thus, we must try to determine what our reactions tend to be and what they ought to be.

But, most important, when we, as rational beings, seriously reflect upon what our associations and reactions tend to be, we will necessarily be led to consider what they ought to be. We cannot but scrutinize them with a heightened consciousness, with a new concern for their validity. Irrationality, we will see, can only be a misuse of reason—a bestowing upon experience of a content that it does not have. And thus the very process of observing ourselves must necessarily develop ourselves—must make us want to learn how to become adequate 'perceivers' of things.

Chapter 16. PERCEPTION

Descartes argued that sensation, memory, imagination, and the passions involve more than raw sense quality. They are products of raw sense quality and 'ideas' applied to that raw sense quality. Such perceptual experiences can, of course, be extremely confused, inadequate, and mistaken, particularly when we make no effort to consider our ideas reflectively and determine the sorts of objects to which it is appropriate to apply them. Thus our innumerable ideas of number, geometry, time, substance, attribute, mode, cause, effect, matter, extension, motion, mind, intellect, will, sensation, imagination, other minds, and other bodies must be reflectively explored if our cognitions of the raw data of sense are to be intelligent and if we are not to mistake what sense can and cannot exemplify, or can and cannot exemplify directly.

Without our 'ideas' our perceptions—not just our reasonable perceptions but our worst passions and dreams—could not acquire the contents they do. And until reason explores its ideas critically, seeking to determine, for example, whether sense can directly exemplify one's own mind or that of others, or whether it can directly exemplify even extension or matter, we are bound to remain in a cave—in a cave that only unclarified human perceptions could invent.

Chapter 17. CLARIFICATION OF PERCEPTION, GENERAL CONCEPTS, AND PHILOSOPHY

Relieved of the bogy of a determinism that makes mental effort seem pointless, indeed impossible, reason should try to acquire habits of volition, interior passions or virtues, that enable it to clarify its perceptions. Doing so requires, not the improvement of one's optical equipment, but the repeated methodical exploration of the necessary and contingent connections among our ideas. The effect of such an exploration will be the acquisition of richer general concepts that allow reason's subsequent perception of 'particulars' to be more correct and adequate. If the mathematician, for example, reflects upon a diagram, he is led to reflections that go well beyond that diagram. And such reflections will, in turn, produce pregnant general concepts that make even more correct and adequate his subsequent perception of that same diagram and new ones. What mathematics trains us to do in a limited sphere, philosophy, which should exercise all our ideas in their interconnection, makes us do even more adequately or comprehensively.

By exercising all our ideas, and by taking full account of

our intelligence, philosophy helps reason perceive each particular by reference to its principles, which is the only way that completely satisfies reason's potential. A true theory of perception is accordingly circumscribed by no one discipline. Our philosophical intelligence tells us that we would forfeit the benefits of mathematics and render our perception myopic where we to think all reality describable in mathematical terms. Similarly, assuming physiological studies have only so much to offer, and that they do not enable us to determine how reason must relate its ideas to one another, we could never learn how to perceive adequately and comprehensively by studying only the nervous system. Nor could we ever educate our perceptions by guiding them by the unmeditated principles that seem to rule in 'normal' life. The search for a true theory of perception remains what it always has been, the search for those who can help us—can teach us—to discover and exercise the comprehensive use of our reason.

Chapter 18. GENERAL CONCEPTS, GENERAL PRINCIPLES, IMAGES, AND MEDITATION

Our sensations and imaginations become more intelligent experiences as we more cautiously excogitate general concepts to apply to subsequently encountered particulars. The mind has an ability to think of objects without images of such objects, as when having used a particular diagram for a while, it then thinks, without any images of diagrams, about general principles that at once govern that diagran and others. Similarly, the mind has an ability to imagine sensuously, or at least to discriminate in sensation, those particulars properly describable by reference to such general principles. The more our reason repeatedly meditates such general principles of interpretation, and probes the grounds for their validity, the more clearly does it recognize what constitutes confused principles and the grounds of their invalidity. The more our reason repeatedly meditates such general principles, the more automatically do they come to mind when appropriate sensuous particulars present themselves—reasoning increasingly tends to correctly associate sense qualities and appropriate ideas. Accordingly, since meditated principles will be remembered with their justifications, they will of necessity exclude whatever weight had been assigned to confused principles logically incompatible with them. The fostering of correct perceptions by logical necessity diminishes the tendency to confused ones.

There is a difference, however, between really meditating one's principles and coming upon them haphazardly. Only if they are remembered with their justifications or with the assurance they have been justified can we expect to reduce the hold upon us of those confused principles that vary from person to person, and that could derive from hearsay, reading, authority, perhaps even from some chance associations between ideas and raw sense quality set up while one was still in the womb.

Chapter 19. MEDITATION AND LANGUAGE

Genuine meditation is reflection upon ideas. It means not allowing language, or whatever is normally said in response to sensible objects, to substitute for probing our ideas. Thus, reason must practice bringing language and sensuous examples into association with fitting ideas or significations. Otherwise, on crucial occasions, for which philosophy should have prepared us, we will slip into and be carried away by the language and responses of the plebian.

The sensuous character of language and imaginations is, for Descartes, a clue to the obstacle that the passions might always pose. Yet the ability of the mind to think its objects through general concepts and without the use of images provides a clue to mastery of such passions. For, however much the mind practices associating certain of its ideas with words or imagery, the cerebral impressions of those words and images might nevertheless be connected with other impressions and motor responses in such a way that, despite our wish, and despite our realizing them unwarranted, we will be disposed to physical movements and passionate imaginations. Thus where the imagining of some topic will clearly be fraught with troublesome consequences for us, so that we will be sent into a passion, we have the advantage of heading it off by thinking about the topic, not with the help of images or too specific descriptions, but under general concepts.

In those cases where physiological causes of themselves or an unavoidable external stimulus triggers the unwarranted imaginations and motor dispositions, we can still master the passion. To do so, we clearly must have been 'virtuous' enough to have meditated worthwhile rules we can then remember. But it is likewise part of virtue never to neglect the power of things sensuous to excite our passions. Thus, we should also have fostered in ourselves dispositions to worthwhile passions that can be called into play to subdue the harmful ones. We should have cultivated the imaginations, the poetry, and the readings that can be used to produce salutary passions and quell troublesome ones. Virtue, then, forms man from the top down, but it forms the whole of man.

Chapter 20. PASSIONS, OR EMOTIONS, RECONSIDERED

Sensation, memory, and imagination are syntheses of raw sense quality, or feeling, and ideas. Thus they are, on the one hand, susceptible to confusion and falsity, and, on the other hand, capable of truth, only because of the ideas constituting their content. A passion, whatever the physiological activities that cause and sustain it, is not a mere reflex, but involves memories and imaginations giving it a content, object, intentionality, or direction. Only because of such content is the passion susceptible to confusion, irresolution, irrationality, and falsity. And only if reference is made to its content can the passion be identified. However, Descartes seems to think that not only reference to verbal behavior or introspective data, but also to physiology, is required to work toward an adequate taxonomy of the various passions and to explain otherwise puzzling irrationalities or inclinations that certain passions display.

Actual passions, we recall, are formed from combinations of the primitive passions of wonder, love, hate, desire, joy, and sadness. Although the primitive passions are not experienced in complete isolation, nevertheless not all of them are always found together. Thus, by noticing concomitant variations in external movements such as running and cringing and in external symptoms such as pallor and blushing, one can isolate those movements and symptoms indicative of the primitive passions in various persons or groups of persons. This kind of observation, whether made with reference to the self or others, obviously calls for care and practice.

Similarly, it is not a matter of simple introspection, but an art, to notice and define the various complex passions. The texture of a complex passion is often elusive. Thoughts tinged with attitudes of joy, sadness, love, hate, desire, optimism, or despair can follow one another without our being able to attend to these changing attitudes, to evaluate their foundations, and to notice the feelings and nervous dispositions that accompany them as we experience them. Thus behavior—verbal behavior together with the external movements and symptoms indicative of the primitive passions—may have to be combined to obtain an index to the various attitudes experienced in the course of a complex passion.

Descartes, I pointed out, refers to physiology to explain

the puzzling irrationalities or inclinations that certain passions display. One's irrational fear of black cats, he suggests, could be due to the fact that while one was still in one's mother's womb, she was frightened by such a cat, transferring the same disposition to one's brain. Similarly, one's natural inclination to favor some persons over others, for example, one's fondness for girls with a squint, could be due to specific forgotten experiences that set up a disposition in one's brain. Undoubtedly, were such dispositions to go unnoticed and never checked, they could get one into trouble. Stretch our imagination, and we will readily conceive a life turned into comedy or nightmare on such account. Yet while Descartes refers to physiology to explain reactions that lack a 'reason,' he never suggests that a single theme, such as sex, dominates all our choices, so that our rational life is but a camouflage for a subconscious logic in terms of which it is to be reinterpreted. Rather, the point of emphasizing the mechanistic character of the body is to remind us that we might have fallen into untoward dispositions for no good or worthy reason; he thus prods us to rational consideration of genuine values and to efforts toward reforming or reconstituting the self.

Chapter 21. VIRTUE RECONSIDERED

The rational and critical consideration of values is, of course, the exercise of virtue, or correct reasoning. Descartes does not deny that the correct moral perceptions may belong to the 'common' man. If unburdened by insanity, superstition, or corrupt mores, the common man will recognize certain moral axioms, for example, that all men are of equal inherent dignity, that the whole is more valuable than himself, that whatever the person's status he may be susceptible to committing breaches of justice, and that whoever has transgressed justice should realize he deserves punishment.

But the common man's virtue is incomplete, requiring that higher virtue that knows how to apply and defend itself. And the discovery of that higher virtue, which uses reason not to invent obstacles or sophistries, but to help man see his nature, requires that we push toward a correct metaphysics of man. Now that the reader is acquainted or reacquainted with Descartes' metaphysics, I leave it to him to examine the values Descartes rooted in it. But before closing, it will be helpful to consider briefly the general process of moral evaluation, because misdescription of that process can blind us to seeing the kinds of things that possess ultimate value for a rational human being.

In moral reflections, where the aim is to reason correctly about values, and to find out whether joys, sadnesses, and desires are justified, our volitions will likely be classified as likes, dislikes, hates, or loves. It is clear that all such species of volition cannot be raw feelings, twinges of pleasure or pain. A raw sense quality or feeling is dumb. It cannot be an attitude toward, or an evaluation of, anything, including itself. But likes, dislikes, fears, hates, are evaluations of what merits pursuit or avoidance, that is, of values and evils. Thus such volitions consist in the use of our intellect, or in the employment of ideas. Certainly, if our evaluation of what is desirable or fearful is false, then our estimates of value, our likes and dislikes, are going to be mistaken. Similarly, if our evaluation of what is desirable or fearful is inconclusive, then we will have no firm rule for judging the various suggestions that cross our minds when we undergo passions caused by the body, and more important when, in the crucial decisions of life, we may be torn by opposing interior passions—opposing joys or sadnesses.

Likes, hates, and fears are sometimes confused with feelings because, particularly during passions caused by the body, feelings are present when various objects seem to us desirable or fearsome. Nonetheless, even while experiencing such a passion, the only way the object can present itself to us as desirable or hateful is by ideas that suggest to us that the object is, as it were, making a claim as to its merits.

And although we may not have time to evaluate our various joys and fears or remember them as they fleetingly pass during complex passions caused by the body, still, this oblivion to our attitudes is always a matter of more or less. The very fact that while in the excitement of such a passion we can occasionally further express our attitude toward a content, as when we recognize that our fear of the new president deals with the likelihood he will remove our sinecure, shows that fears and joys are not the dumb feelings that may accompany them, but thoughts, even if inchoate.

Our more reflective, reasonable, and voluntary likes and dislikes consist, then, in considered evaluations of things. Sensible feelings are of course among the things upon which we must reflect in order to see in what their value consists and to determine whether other things have a value only as a means to the sensible feelings they produce. By considering this matter it will be clear that we cannot derive any general criterion of value from the sensible feelings of pleasure and pain. The types of mental contentment, of joy and love, and the types of mental distress, of sadness and fear, cannot generally or exclusively be a contentment regarding sensible pleasure or a distress regarding sensible pain, as though these were the ultimate goods and evils that enter human life. Sensible pleasures, and the avoidance of sensible pains, are *for* the worthwhile life, but life is not for them.

If, for example, we consider the mental contentment, the mental joy or pleasure, we take in our abstract reflections, we find that neither the object of our contentment, the good we value, nor the contentment we take in it, is sensible pleasure. Indeed, we would lose the valued good together with the contentment we take in it were sensible pleasure to distract our attention from it. Such mental contentment, or pleasure, is more compatible with a slight sensible pain that with such repose of the senses as inclines one to anything but the rational discussion with oneself that meditation is meant to be. Moreover, it is clear that even where sensible feelings of pleasure and pain may be noticeably present, such as in our experiences of human relationships, the object of our contentment or distress, the good or the evil, must be other than sensible pleasure or pain.

We willingly suffer physically distressing pains on behalf of child, friend, or state without being distressed by our paternity, friendship, or citizenship. We can derive many incidental pleasures from persons and institutions without being satisfied by their character. What moves us to suffer physical pain on behalf of something valued or to fail of contentment despite physical pleasures, is not some elusive, indeed meaningless, calculation designed to maximize sensible pleasures and minimize sensible pains. Thought creates those relations to ourself and others which alone make us rational human beings. The values that can fulfill us and promise contentment are accordingly inseparable from the correct relations, or the correct ordering of our thoughts. Similarly, distress is inescapable if our thoughts are misordered and our relations thereby ill-constituted. Paternity, friendship, citizenship, and so on consist in some ordering of our thoughts. Thus the business of virtue will remain what Plato knew it to be, the exploration of the correct ordering. Neither individual nor society can steal, nor could anything grant them, contentment. As Descartes implies, the beginning of foolishness is to fancy a contentment that does not know the labors of reason or virtue:

But just as when from some point of view there is a reward for shooting at the white, those to whom one shows this reward are made desirous of shooting at it, yet they cannot on that account gain this reward unless they see the white; and just as those who see the white are not thereby induced to shoot at it unless they see there is a reward to gain; so too virtue, which is the white, does not make itself very desirable when one sees it all alone; and contentment, which is the reward of virtue, cannot be acquired unless one follows virtue.[45]

THE CORRESPONDENCE

CCXXVI.   Descartes to [Pollot?].

Leiden, mid January 1641.

Monsieur,

1 I have just learned the sad news of your affliction, and
while I do not promise myself to say anything in this letter
that has great force in allaying your grief, I am nevertheless
unable to refrain from the attempt, so as to show you at least
that I share in it. I am not one who thinks tears and sorrow
belong only to women, and that to appear a man of gallant
soul one should force oneself always to display a tranquil
visage. I recently experienced the loss of two persons very
close to me; * and I discovered that they who wished me
forbear from sorrow only exacerbated it, whereas I was
comforted by the kindness of those I saw moved by my
grief. And so I assure myself that you will more easily endure me if I do not oppose your tears than if I tried to turn
you away from a feeling I believe just. However, some re-
straint is nevertheless required; and as one would be a barbarian not to be afflicted in the least when there are grounds
for it, so too one would be excessively weak to abandon
oneself entirely to grief; and one certainly would not do
well by oneself not to try with all one's power to deliver
oneself from so uncomfortable a passion. The profession of
carrying arms in which you are raised accustoms men to see
their best friends die unexpectedly; and nothing in the

---

* Descartes' father, Joachim Descartes, and Descartes'
eldest sister, Jeanne Descartes. See *Correspondance,
Oeuvres,* vol. IV, p. 373.

world is so troublesome that familiarity does not render it bearable. There is, it seems to me, very great similarity between losing one's hand and losing one's brother; you have previously suffered the former, without my ever noticing you were afflicted by it; why should you be more so as regards the latter? For, if it is for your own interest, it is certain you can better repair this latter situation, inasmuch as acquiring a faithful friend can be as valuable as the affection of a good brother. And if it is for the interest of him whom you are lamenting—as your generosity undoubtedly does not allow you to be touched by anything else—you know that neither reason nor religion gives cause for fearing evil after this life to those who have lived as people of honor, but that, on the contrary, both promise joys and rewards. Finally, Monsieur, all our afflictions, whatever they be, depend save very slightly on the reasons we give for them, but solely on the emotion and interior commotion nature excites in us; for when this emotion is subsided, although all the reasons we previously had remain the same, we no longer feel ourselves afflicted. But, now, I do not wish to advise you to employ all the forces of your resolution and constancy to stop all at once the interior agitation you feel: that remedy would perhaps be more annoying than the malady; but I also do not counsel you to wait upon time itself to cure you—and certainly even less to sustain and prolong your ill by your thoughts. I beseech you try just little by little to soften it by looking upon what happens to you only from the point of view that enables it to appear the most bearable, and by diverting yourself the most you can by other occupations. I well know I am telling you nothing new here; but one ought not scorn good remedies simply because they are common, and since I myself have used this one to good effect, I thought I was obliged to write you about it; for I am, . . . etc.

CCLXXXIII.   Descartes to Pollot.

Endegeest, 6 October 1642.

Monsieur,

2   I had already hitherto heard so many marvellous things about the excellent mind of Madame, the Princess of Bohemia, that I am less surprised to learn she reads metaphysical writings than thankful that, having deigned read mine, she gives evidence she does not disapprove of them; and I attach much more weight to her judgment than to that of those messieurs the Doctors, who take for a rule of truth the opinions of Aristotle rather than the evidence of reason. I shall not fail to repair to The Hague, as soon as I know you will be there, so that with your introduction I can have the honor of paying her reverence and receiving her commands. And because I hope that will be soon, I will wait until then to discuss matters more at length with you, and to thank you for the obligations I owe you . . . etc.

CCCI.   Elisabeth to Descartes.

The Hague, 6/16 May 1643.

Monsieur,

3   I have learned, with very great joy and regret, the intention you had to see me a few days ago, and I have been equally moved, both by your charity in consenting to communicate with an ignorant and indocile person, and by the misfortune that stole me away from so profitable a conversation. M. Pollot greatly augmented this latter passion by repeating to me the solution you gave him of the obscurities in the physics of M. Regius, concerning which I would have been better instructed from your own mouth, as also about a

question I proposed to the said professor when he was in this city, and in regard to which he directed me back to you to receive the required satisfaction. The shame of showing you so unruly a style has prevented me to date from asking this favor of you by letter.

4 But today M. Pollot gave me such assurance of your good will toward everyone, and especially toward me, that, banishing every other consideration from mind, save that of availing myself of it, I beseech you tell me how the soul of man (since it is but a thinking substance) can determine the spirits of the body to produce voluntary actions. For it seems every determination of movement happens from an impulsion of the thing moved, according to the manner in which it is pushed by that which moves it, or else, depends on the qualification and figure of the superficies of this latter. Contact is required for the first two conditions, and extension for the third. You entirely exclude extension from your notion of the soul, and contact seems to me incompatible with an immaterial thing. That is why I ask of you a definition of the soul more particular than in your Metaphysic—that is to say, for a definition of the substance separate from its action, thought. For although we suppose them inseparable (which nonetheless is difficult to prove regarding infants in their mother's womb and deep faints), still, like the attributes of God, we can, by considering them separately, acquire a more perfect idea of them.

5 Knowing you to be the best doctor for my soul, I therefore freely reveal to you the weaknesses of its speculations, and I trust that in observing the oath of Hippocrates you will furnish it remedies without publicizing them; that I ask of you, as likewise, that you bear these importunities of . . . etc.

CCCII.   Descartes to Elisabeth.

Egmond du Hoef, 21 May 1643.

Madame,

6 The favor with which your Highness has honored me,
in granting me receive her commands in writing, surpasses
anything I had ever dared hope for; and it compensates for
my flaws better than would that which I passionately
desired—to receive those commands from your lips had I
been able to be admitted to the honor of paying you reverence, and of offering you my very-humble services, when
I was last at The Hague. For I would have had too many
marvels to admire at the same time; and seeing a discourse
more than human flow from a frame so similar to those pain-
ters bestow upon angels, I would have been ravished, just
as, it seems to me, are bound to be they who, in coming
from earth, enter for the first time upon heaven. In such
wise was I rendered less capable of responding to your
Highness—who undoubtedly already noticed this flaw in
me—when I previously had the honor of speaking to her;
and it is your clemency that has wished to compensate for
that flaw by placing the traces of your thoughts upon paper,
where, rereading them several times, and accustoming myself to consider them, I am indeed less dazzled, yet have
only so much the more admiration for them, recognizing
that they do not seem ingenious merely at first sight, but
proportionately more judicious and solid the further one
examines them.

7 And I can in all honesty say that the question your
Highness proposes seems to me that which can be asked
with the greatest justification in sequel to the writings I
have published. For, there being two things in the human
soul on which depends all the knowledge we can have of its
nature—the first, that it thinks, and the second, that being
united to the body, it can act and suffer with it—I have said

nearly nothing of this latter, and have studied only to understand well the first, since my principal design was to prove the distinction that exists between the soul and the body, for which the first alone could suffice, while the other would have been an impediment. But since your Highness is so discerning that one cannot hide anything from her, I shall try here to explain the manner in which I conceive the union of the soul with the body, and how it has the force to move the body.

8 Firstly, I consider that in us are certain primitive notions that are like originals on whose model we form all our other knowledge. And there are but very few such notions; for, after the most general ones—of being, number, duration, etc.—which refer to everything we can conceive, we have, as regards body in particular, only the notion of extension, from which follow those of figure and movement; and, as regards the soul alone, we have only that of thought, in which are comprised the perceptions of the understanding and the inclinations of the will; finally, for the soul and the body together, we have only that of their union, on which depends that of the force of the soul for moving the body, and of the body for acting upon the soul by causing its feelings and passions.

9 I consider also that all human knowledge consists only in carefully distinguishing these notions, and in attributing each of them only to the things to which they pertain. For when we wish to explain some difficulty by means of a notion that does not pertain to it, we cannot fail to make a mistake. And that occurs whenever we wish to explain one of these notions by another—for since they are primitive, each of them cannot be understood except through itself. And inasmuch as the use of the senses has rendered the notions of extension, figures, and movements very much more familiar to us than the others, the principal cause of our errors consists in that we ordinarily wish to employ them to explain things to which they do not pertain, as when one wishes to employ the imagination to conceive

the nature of the soul, or else, when one wishes to conceive the manner in which the soul moves the body after the fashion in which a body is moved by another body.

10 That is why, having tried to clarify in the *Meditations* your Highness has deigned to read, the notions that pertain to the soul alone and distinguish them from those that pertain to the body alone, the first thing I should in sequel explain is the manner of conceiving whatever pertains to the union of the soul with the body, leaving aside things that pertain to the body alone or to the soul alone. In this regard it seems to me that what I wrote at the end of my Response to the sixth objections can be of use; for we cannot seek these simple notions other than in our soul—in our soul which, although it has all of them in it by its nature, does not always sufficiently distinguish them one from another, or else fails to attribute them to the objects to which they should be attributed.

11 Thus I believe that we hitherto confused the notion of the force by which the soul acts on the body with that by which one body acts upon another; and that we have attributed both, not to the soul, for as yet we did not recognize it, but to different qualities of bodies, such as weight, heat, and so forth which we imagined as being real—or, as having an existence distinct from that of body, and consequently as being substances, although we called them qualities. And in order to conceive them, we have sometimes used the notions that are in us for knowing body, and sometimes those that are for knowing the soul, according as what we attributed to them has been material or immaterial. For example, in supposing weight a real quality, of which we possess no other knowledge save that it has the force of moving the body in which it exists toward the center of the earth, we have no difficulty conceiving how it moves this body, nor how it is joined to it; and we do not think that happens by means of an actual touching of one surface against another, for we experience in our own selves that we have a particular notion for conceiving it; yet I believe

that in applying this notion to weight—which, as I hope to show in physics, is nothing really distinct from body—we are abusing what has been given us for conceiving the manner in which the soul moves the body.

12 I would show myself insufficiently aware of the incomparable wit of your Highness if I employed more words in explaining myself, and I would be too presumptuous if I dared think my response ought satisfy her entirely; but I shall try to avoid both by adding nothing further here save that, if I am capable of writing or saying anything that can be agreeable to her, I will always consider it a very great favor to take up my pen or to go to The Hague on such account; and that there is nothing in the world so dear to me as to obey her commands. But I can find no room here for observing the oath of Hippocrates as she enjoins me; for she has communicated nothing to me that does not merit being seen and admired by all. I can only say, regarding this matter, that infinitely esteeming your letter, I shall treat it as misers do their treasures—which they stash away all the more they esteem them, and, by begrudging everyone else the sight of them, take their sovereign contentment in looking upon them. And thus I shall be very willing to enjoy all to myself the good of looking upon it; and my greatest ambition is to be able to say, and truly to be, . . . etc.

CCCVIII.   Elisabeth to Descartes.

The Hague, 10/20 June 1643.

Monsieur Descartes,

13 Your good will not only shows forth, as I had been given to understand it would, in pointing out and correcting the flaws in my reasoning, but also in that, to render my recognizing them less annoying, you try—to the prejudice of your judgment—to console me by means of false praises that would have been necessary to encourage me to take the remedy had not my nourishment, in a place where the ordinary fashion of conversation has accustomed me to hear praises from persons incapable of speaking the truth, led me to suppose I could never err in believing the opposite of their discourse, and thereby to render reflection upon my imperfections so familiar as to cause me no more emotion than I require in connection with the desire to rid myself of them.

14 That makes me confess, without shame, that I have discovered in myself all the causes of error you note in your letter, and that I have been as yet unable to banish them entirely, since the life I am constrained to lead does not allow me enough free time to acquire a habit of meditation in accordance with your rules. Sometimes the interests of my household, which I must not neglect, sometimes conversations and civilities I cannot eschew, so thoroughly deject this weak mind with annoyances or boredom that it remains, for a long time afterward, useless for anything else: which will serve, I hope, to excuse my stupidity in being unable to comprehend, from what you had previously said concerning weight, the idea by which we should judge how the soul (nonextended and immaterial) can move the body; nor why this power, that you have then under the name of quality falsely attributed to it as carrying the body toward the center of the earth, ought persuade us that body can be pushed by something immaterial any more than the demonstration of a contrary truth (as you promise in your physics) confirms us in the opinion of its impossibility; principally, because this idea (not being able to claim to the same perfection and objective reality as that of God) can be feigned out of ignorance of what truly moves these bodies toward the center; and then, since no material cause presents itself to the senses, one would have attributed it—which I have only been able to conceive as a negation of matter—to its contrary, the immaterial, which cannot have any communication with it.

15 And I admit it would be easier for me to concede matter and extension to the soul, than the capacity of moving a body and of being moved, to an immaterial being. For, if the first occurred through 'information,' the spirits that perform the movement would have to be intelligent, which you accord to nothing corporeal. And although in your metaphysical meditations you show the possibility of the second, it is, however, very difficult to comprehend that a soul, as you have described it, after having had the faculty and habit of reasoning well, can lose all of it on account of some vapors, and that, although it can subsist without the body and has nothing in common with it, is yet so ruled by it.

16 But, since you have undertaken to instruct me, I entertain these opinions only as friends that I do not intend to keep, assuring myself you will explain the nature of an immaterial substance and the manner of its actions and passions in the body just as well as all the other things you have wished to teach. I ask you also to believe there is no one upon whom you can bestow this charity more aware of the obligation she owes you for it than . . . etc.

CCCX.   Descartes to Elisabeth.

Egmond du Hoef, 28 June 1643.

Madame,
17 I am very greatly obliged to your Highness in that, having experienced from my preceding remarks that I badly explain myself concerning the question it has pleased her to propose to me, she again deigns to have the patience to listen to me regarding the same subject, and to give me an opportunity to note the things I had omitted. The principal omissions seem to be that, having distinguished three kinds of ideas or primitive notions, each of which are recognized

in a particular manner and not by the comparison of one with another, namely, the notion we have of the soul, of the body, and of the union existing between the soul and the body, I should have explained the difference that exists among these three sorts of notions, and among the operations of the soul by which we have them, and should have stated the means of rendering each of them familiar and easy for ourselves; then, in sequel, having said why I used the comparison to weight, I should have made it plain that, although one wishes to conceive the soul as material (which is properly to conceive its union with the body), one cannot fail to recognize afterward that it is separable from it. That, I believe, is everything your Highness has enjoined me discuss here.

18 First, then, I note a great difference among these three kinds of notions, in that the soul conceives itself only by the pure understanding; body—that is to say, extension, figures, and movements—can likewise be recognized by the understanding alone, but very much better by the understanding aided by the imagination; and finally, the things that pertain to the union of the soul and the body are recognized only obscurely by the understanding alone or even by the understanding as aided by the imagination; yet they are known very clearly by the senses. From that it comes about that those who never philosophize, and who make use only of their senses, do not doubt that the soul moves the body and the body acts upon the soul; but they consider the one and the other as a single thing, that is to say, they conceive their union; for to conceive the union existing between two things is to conceive them as one thing alone. The metaphysical thoughts that exercise the pure understanding serve to render the notion of the soul more familiar to us; and the study of mathematics, which principally exercises the imagination in considering figures and movements, accustoms us to form very distinct notions of body; and finally, it is by availing oneself only of life and ordinary conversations, and by abstaining from meditating and studying things that exercise the imagination, that one learns to conceive the union of the soul and the body.

19 I almost fear that your Highness may think I am not speaking seriously here; but that would be contrary to the respect I owe her and shall never fail to render her. And I can truly say that the principal rule I have always observed in my studies, and of which I believe I have made very good use in acquiring some knowledge, has been that I have never employed save very few hours each day at thoughts that occupy the imagination, and very few hours per year at those that occupy the understanding alone, and that I have devoted all the rest of my time to the respite of my senses and the repose of my mind; I even reckon among the exercises of the imagination all serious conversations, and everything that requires attention. That is what made me retire to the country. For although, were I in the most densely occupied city in the world, I could have as many more hours to myself as I now employ at studying, nevertheless I could not so usefully employ them, since my soul would be wearied by the attention required by the bustle of life. And I here take liberty of writing to your Highness to testify to her how truly I admire that, among the affairs and cares never relenting for persons who are at once of great mind and great birth, she has yet been able to devote herself to the meditations required to recognize well the distinction that exists between the soul and the body.

20 But I have judged that it was those meditations, rather than thoughts that require less attention, that have made her find obscurity in the notion we have of their union; for it does not seem to me that the human mind is capable of conceiving very distinctly, and at the same time, both the distinction between the soul and the body, and also their union; because to do so it is necessary to conceive them as one thing alone, and at the same time to conceive them as two, which is the contrary. And for this reason (supposing your Highness still had the reasons that prove

the distinction of the soul and the body very present to her mind, and not wishing to ask her to rid herself of them in order to represent the notion that everyone always experiences in himself without philosophizing—namely, that it is one person alone who, at the same time, has a body and thought of such nature that this thought can move the body and feel the accidents that happen to it), I previously made use of the comparison with weight and other qualities we commonly imagine united to some body, just as thought is united to ours; and I am not concerned that this comparison limped in that such qualities are not real, as one is wont to image them, because I believed your Highness was already entirely persuaded that the soul is a substance distinct from the body.

21 But, since your Highness notes it is easier to attribute matter and extension to the soul than to attribute to it, when it has no matter, a capacity to move a body and be moved by one, I ask her to please freely attribute this matter and this extension to the soul; for that is nothing but to conceive it united to the body. And having conceived that well, and having experienced it in herself, it will be easy for her to appreciate that the matter she shall have attributed to this thought is not thought itself, but rather that the extension of this matter is of another nature than the extension of this thought, in that the first is determined to a certain place, from which it excludes every other extension of body, which the second does not. And thus your Highness will not fail to return easily to the knowledge of the distinction of the soul and the body, notwithstanding that she has conceived their union.

22 Finally, just as I believe it very necessary, once in one's life, to have well understood the principles of metaphysics, since it is they that provide us with knowledge of God and our soul, I also believe it would be very harmful to occupy one's understanding in frequently meditating upon them because it could not be so healthy to abandon the functions of the imagination and senses; but the best procedure is to content oneself with retaining in one's memory and belief those conclusions one has once extracted from them, and then to devote the rest of the time remaining for studying to thoughts wherein the understanding acts along with the imagination and the senses.

23 My extreme devotion to the service of your Highness makes me hope my frankness will not be disagreeable to her, and it would have led me to engage here in a longer discourse, wherein I would have tried to clarify on this occasion all the difficulties attaching to the question proposed; but troublesome news from Utrecht, where the magistrate summons me to verify what I have written about one of their ministers—that he is indeed a man who has most scandalously calumniated me, and that what I have written about him in my just defense is only too well known to everyone—compels me to finish here, in order to go consult about the means of extricating myself, as soon as possible, from these chicaneries. * I am, . . . etc.

CCCXI.   Elisabeth to Descartes.

The Hague, 1 July 1643.

Monsieur Descartes,
24 I see that my regard for your instructions, and the desire to avail myself of them, does not inconvenience you as much as does the ingratitude of they who deprive themselves, and would wish deprive all mankind, of them; nor would I have dispatched this new effect of my ignorance before knowing you acquitted of that of their bigotedness,

---

* Descartes was summoned to defend what he had written in his *Epistle to Voetius*.

except that M. Van Bergen obliged me write sooner by his civility in resolving to remain in this city until I should give him a response to your letter of 28 June in which you clearly point out the three sorts of notions we possess, their objects, and the manner of using them properly.

25 I too find that the senses show me that the soul moves the body; but they fail to teach me (any more than the understanding and the imagination) the manner in which she does it. And, in regard to that, I think there are unknown properties in the soul that might suffice to reverse what your metaphysical meditations, with such good reasons, persuaded me concerning her inextension. And this doubt seems founded upon the rule you lay down there in speaking of the true and the false—namely, that all our errors occur from forming judgments about what we do not sufficiently perceive. Although extension is not necessary to thought, yet not being contradictory to it, it will be able to belong to some other function of the soul less essential to her. At least that avoids the contradiction of the scholastics—namely, that the entire soul is in the entire body and entirely in each of its parts. I do not excuse myself for confusing the notion of the soul with that of the body for the same reason as do ordinary people; but that does not dispel for me the first doubt, and I will despair of finding certitude in any matter unless you provide me with it—you who alone have prevented me from being the skeptic I was inclined to be by my first reasoning.

26 Although I owe you this admission, by way of rendering you thanks, I should nevertheless think it very imprudent, except that I know, as much from the experience I have already had of them as by reputation, that your good will and generosity equal the rest of your merits. You cannot give witness of them in any more obliging manner than by the elucidations and advice you share with me, and which I prize above the greatest treasures that could be possessed by . . . etc.

CCCLXXV.   Descartes to Elisabeth.

Egmond, 18 May 1645.

Madame,

27 I have been extremely surprised to learn from M. Pollot that your Highness has been ill for a long time; and I am annoyed with my seclusion, since it is the reason I had not known sooner. But although I am so withdrawn from the world as to learn nothing that passes there, nevertheless my earnestness to serve your Highness would not have allowed me to remain so long a time not knowing the condition of your health, when I should have gone to The Hague expressly to inquire about it, had not M. Pollot, who wrote me about two months ago, promised to write me again by the next mail; and because he never fails to inform me of the condition of your Highness, when I did not receive his letters, I supposed there was no change. But I have learned from his most recent letters that for three or four weeks duration your Highness has had a slow fever, accompanied by a dry cough, and that having been delivered from this illness for five or six days, it returned and, at the time he sent me his letter (which has been nearly fifteen days on route), your Highness began again to feel better. In these symptoms I notice the signs of an illness so serious—but that it nonetheless seems to me your Highness can certainly remedy—that I am unable to refrain from writing her my views. For although I am not a medical doctor, the honor your Highness bestowed upon me last summer, in wishing to know my opinion regarding another condition that indisposed her at that time, makes me hope my liberty will not be disagreeable to her.

28 The most ordinary cause of a slow fever is sadness; and the persistence of fortune in persecuting your household continually gives you subjects for anger so public and so scandalous, that there is no need to use many conjectures, nor to be accomplished in these matters, to judge that in this consists the principal cause of your indisposition. And it is to be feared you would be unable to be delivered from all these things, unless, by the force of your virtue, you render your soul content, despite the disgraces of fortune. I well know it would be imprudent to wish to persuade to joy anyone upon whom fortune everyday visits new subjects of displeasure; and I am not one of those cruel philosophers who wish their wise man to be insensible. I also know that your Highness is not so much affected by what has reference to her in particular as by what relates to the interests of her household and of persons to whom she is devoted; and this I esteem as the most amiable virtue of all. But it seems the difference between the greatest souls and those who are base and common consists principally in the fact that common souls abandon themselves to their passions and are happy or unhappy only according as the things that happen to them are agreeable or unpleasant; by contrast, the greatest souls possess arguments so strong and cogent that, although they also have passions, and passions indeed often more violent than those of ordinary people, their reason nevertheless always remains mistress, and even makes their afflictions serve them and contribute to the perfect happiness they enjoy in this life. For, on the one hand, considering themselves as immortal and capable of receiving very great contentments, and then on the other hand, realizing they are joined to mortal and fragile bodies that are subject to very many infirmities and will necessarily perish in a few years, they do everything they can to render fortune favorable in this life; but nevertheless they esteem this life so little in relation to eternity that they consider its eventualities only as we consider those things that come to pass in comedies. And just as the sad and lamentable stories we see represented in a theater often provide us with as many recreations as do those that are gay, even though they call forth tears from our eyes, so too, these greater souls of whom I speak derive satisfaction in themselves from everything that happens to them, even the most troublesome and hard to bear. And thus, feeling the pain in their bodies, they bend themselves to endure it patiently, and this proof that they have the force to do so is agreeable to them; likewise, seeing their friends in some great affliction, they sympathize with their trouble and do everything possible to deliver them from it, and, if necessary, they do not fear even to expose themselves to death in order to do so. Meanwhile, however, the testimony of their conscience that in acting in these ways they are performing their obligation, and doing a praiseworthy and virtuous deed, provides them a happiness that exceeds all the sadness with which their compassion afflicts them. And finally, just as the greatest prosperities of fortune never captivate them and render them more insolent, so also the greatest adversities cannot shatter them or render them so sad that the body, to which they are joined, becomes sick.

29 And I should fear that this style might be ridiculous were I using it to write to someone else; but because I consider your Highness as having the most noble and resilient soul that I know, I believe she should also be the happiest of souls and that she will truly be so, provided it pleases her to cast her eyes on all that is beneath her and compare the value of the goods she possesses, and that could never be taken from her, with those fortune has stripped from her and with the disgraces with which it persecutes her in the person of her relatives—for then she shall see the great occasion she has for being content with the goods in her very own person. The very great earnestness I feel toward her is the reason I have permitted myself to be so free in my language, and I very humbly beg you to excuse this as coming from a person who is, . . . etc.

CCCLXXVII.   Elisabeth to Descartes.

The Hague, 24 May 1645.

Monsieur Descartes,
    30   I see that the charms of the solitary life do not de-
prive you of the virtues required for society. I would be
annoyed if these generous kindnesses you display toward
your friends, and which you show toward me in the concern
you have taken in regard to my health, had led you to undertake a journey here, since M. Pollot told me you considered
rest necessary for the preservation of your health. And I
assure you that the doctors who came here everyday, and
examined all the symptoms of my sickness, did not find the
cause nor order remedies so salutary as those you have prescribed from afar. And should they have been wise enough
to suspect the role my mind played in this bodily disorder, I
would not have had the frankness to admit it to them. But to
you, Monsieur, I admit it without scruple, since I am assured that so candid a recitation of my faults will not rob me
of the place I hold in your friendship, but will confirm it to
me all the more, since you will see how necessary it is to
me.
    31   Know then that I have a body filled with a great many
of the weaknesses of my sex; it very easily feels the afflictions of the soul and does not have the force to bring itself
into harmony with the soul, since it is of such a temperament as to be subject to obstructions and remains in a condition that very much contributes to them—for in persons
who cannot take a great deal of exercise, it is not necessary
for sadness to oppress the heart for a long time before the
spleen becomes obstructed and infects the rest of the body
by its vapors. I imagine that this causes the slow fever and
the dry cough that are still with me, even though the heat of
the season and the walks that I take rally my strength a
little. And that is what inclines me to consent to the advice

of the medical doctors, that I drink here, one month hence, from the waters of the Spa (which are delivered this far without spoiling); for I have found by experience that these waters dispel the obstructions. But I shall not take them before knowing your opinion, since you have the kindness to wish me to cure the body together with the soul.

32 I will continue, and likewise confess to you that although I do not place my happiness in anything that depends upon fortune or the will of men, and although I will not esteem myself absolutely unhappy when I shall never see my household restored or my kin relieved of misery, I will still be unable to consider the harmful accidents that befall them under any other notion save that of evil, nor to regard the useless efforts I make for their advantage without some sort of discomfort that no sooner is calmed by reasoning than a new disaster produces another inquietude. And I think that if my life were entirely known to you, you would find more strange than the causes of this present malady, that a sensitive mind such as mine, when so thwarted, remains conserved for so long a time in so frail a body, having no advice save from her own reasoning and no consolation save her conscience.

33 I have employed all the past winter at such annoying matters as have prevented me from making use of the liberty you granted me to propose to you the difficulties I would find in my studies; these matters caused me still further troubles that would require even more stupidity than I have not to be phased by them. Only a little time before becoming indisposed, I found the leisure to read the philosophy of M. the Knight Digby, which he wrote in English; I hoped to take from it arguments to refute yours, since the summary of the chapters showed me there were two places where he pretended to have done it; but I was completely astonished when I reached those points to see he had understood nothing less than what he approved of in your view concerning reflection, and that, because of his misunderstanding, he denies what you say of refraction, as

he fails to make any distinction between the movement of a ball and its determination, and does not give consideration to why a soft body that gives way retards the one, and why a hard body only resists the other. Part of what he said about the movement of the heart is more excusable, if he has not read what you wrote to the medical doctor of Louvain. Doctor Jonsson told me he will translate these two chapters for you; and I think you will not be very curious about the rest of the book, because it is of the caliber and follows the method of the English priest who calls himself by the name Albanus *; but yet the book does have very pretty meditations. It would be difficult to expect more of someone who has passed the greatest part of his life pursuing the designs of love and ambition. I shall never be more determined, nor more constant, than in being, for all my life, . . . etc. Monsieur Descartes,

34 In rereading what I have let you know about myself, I recognize I have forgotten one of your maxims, which is never to put anything in writing that can be badly interpreted by uncharitable readers. But I so trust the care M. Pollot will take of my letter, that I know it will reach you without a problem, and that, at your discretion, you will consign it to the fire in the event that it might fall into bad hands.

CCCLXXX.   Descartes to Elisabeth.

Egmond, May or June 1645.

Madame,
35 In reading the letter your Highness did me the honor of writing, I could not but feel extremely upset to see that a virtue so rare and accomplished is not accompanied by

---

* Thomas White.

health, nor by the prosperities it merits; and I easily conceive the multitude of displeasures that present themselves continually to her, and are more difficult to overcome, inasmuch as they are often of such a nature that true reason ordains one not oppose them directly and try to dispel them. They are the domestic enemies with whom, since one is compelled to converse with them, one must constantly maintain one's guard to avoid being harmed by them; and I find but a single remedy for this—namely, to divert one's imagination and senses from them as much as possible, and to employ only the understanding to consider them when prudence obliges one to do so.

36   One can, it seems to me, easily recognize regarding this matter the difference between the understanding and the imagination or sense; for the difference is of such a kind that I believe a person who otherwise should have all sorts of subjects for contentment, but instead continually represented to himself tragedies in which all the acts were lugubrious, and occupied himself only with objects of sadness and pity he knew were imaginary and fabulous, so that they brought tears to his eyes and roused his imagination without regard to his understanding—I believe, I say, that by doing so, it alone would suffice to accustom his heart to contract and send out sighs; and in consequence of this, the circulation of the blood being retarded and slowed, and the largest parts of the blood attaching themselves to one another, they would easily obstruct his spleen, by entangling themselves in it and stopping in its pores, and the most subtle parts, retaining their agitation, would alter the lungs and cause a cough which, if prolonged, would be very much to fear. But, on the contrary, a person who would have an infinity of genuine subjects of displeasure, but yet would study with great care to turn his imagination from them, so that he never thought about them, except when the necessity of the matters should oblige him to do so, and who employed all his remaining time only to consider the ob-

jects which could bring him contentment and joy—indeed, other than the fact that this would be greatly useful to him in judging more sanely the things of importance to him, because he would regard them without passion, I also have no doubt it could restore him to health, even though the spleen and the lungs were already very badly disposed by the bad temperament of the blood which causes sadness. And that would result particularly if he also used medical remedies to dissolve the part of the blood which causes obstructions. And I deem the waters of the Spa very suitable for this, above all if in taking them your Highness observes what the medical doctors customarily recommend, namely that one must deliver one's mind entirely from all sorts of sad thoughts, and also even from all serious meditations regarding the sciences, and occupy oneself only at imitating those who, in looking at the verdure of a wood, the colors of a flower, the flight of a bird, and such things as require no attention, convince themselves that they are not thinking of anything. And to do so is not to waste time, but to employ it well; for in the meantime one can satisfy oneself by the hope that by this means one will recover a perfect health, which is the foundation of all the other goods one can have in this life.

37 I well know I have written nothing here your Highness does not know better than I, and I realize it is not so much the theory as the practice that is difficult in this matter; but the very great favor she has done me in stating she is not unwilling to listen to my opinions has made me take the liberty of writing them such as they are, and of adding here that in regard to myself I have experienced that a sickness nearly similar, and even more dangerous, has been cured by the remedy of which I spoke. For, since I was born of a mother who died a few days after my birth of a sickness of the lung caused by certain displeasures, I have inherited from her a dry cough and a pallid complexion which I kept until more than twenty years of age, and this

condition made all the medical doctors who saw me prior to that time condemn me to a young death. But I believe the inclination I have always had to regard whatever happened from the point of view that could render it more agreeable, and to arrange it such that my principal contentment depended only on me alone, is the cause why this indisposition, which was natural to me, has little by little entirely passed.

38 I am very much obliged to your Highness that it has pleased her to send me her opinion of the book of M. Digby, which I will be unable to read until someone has translated it into Latin. M. Jonsson, who was here yesterday, said that some people wish to make such a translation. He also told me I could address my letter to your Highness by ordinary messengers, which I had not dared do without him—and I had even deferred writing this letter because I was waiting for one of my friends to go to The Hague to give it to her. I definitely regret the absence of M. Pollot, because I could learn from him the condition of your disposition; but the letters sent to me by means of the messenger of Alkmaar do not fail to be delivered, and as there is nothing in the world I desire with so much passion as to be able to render service to your Highness, there is also nothing that can render me more happy than to have the honor of receiving her commands. I am, . . . etc.

CCCLXXXIV.   Elisabeth to Descartes.

The Hague, 22 June 1645.

Monsieur Descartes,

39 Although they would not 'instruct' me, your letters always serve me as an antidote against melancholy; they turn my mind from the disagreeable objects that befall it everyday and make it contemplate the happiness I possess in the friendship of a person of your merit, to whose counsel I can commit the conduct of my life. Were I as yet able to conform to your last precepts, there is no doubt I would promptly cure myself of the maladies of the body and the weaknesses of the mind. But I confess I find difficulty in separating from my senses and imagination the topics continually represented there by the conversation and the letters I could not avoid without sinning against my obligations. I well appreciate that in effacing from the idea of a matter everything that renders me angry (and I do believe that what makes me angry is represented by the imagination), I would judge the matter as sanely and find answers as quickly as I now do with all the affect I bring to these topics. But I have never known how to practice this except after the passion had played its role. There is something that overtakes one in the passions, and even though it is foreseen, I am mistress of it only after a certain time, and in the meanwhile my body becomes so greatly disordered that I require several months to restore it—months that hardly come to pass but there is some new subject of trouble. Besides being constrained to govern my mind with care so as to provide it with agreeable objects, the least sloth and I fall back upon those topics with which my mind afflicts itself. Moreover, I understand that if I do not employ my mind while I take the waters of the Spa, it will no longer become melancholish. Were I able to profit, as you do, from everything that presents itself to the senses, I would divert myself without thinking of it. But it is at that very time that I feel the inconvenience of being a little reasonable. For were I not at all reasonable, I would find pleasures in common with those among whom it is necessary for me to live, and thus take this medicine with profit. And were I as reasonable as you, I would cure myself as you have done. Furthermore, the curse of my sex prevents me the contentment which would come from voyaging to Egmond to learn the truths you have extracted from your new garden. Nevertheless, I console myself with the liberty you give me to ask occasionally about it, and I am, . . . etc.

Monsieur Descartes,
40 I have learned with very much joy that the Academy of Groningen has done you justice. *

CCCLXXXVI.   Descartes to Elisabeth.

Egmond, June 1645.

Madame,
41 I very humbly beg your Highness to pardon me if I am unable to pity her indisposition when I have the honor of receiving her letters. For I always notice therein such precise thoughts and firm reasonings that I find it impossible to persuade myself that a mind capable of conceiving them is lodged in a weak and sick body. However that may be, the knowledge your Highness shows herself to have about her illness and the remedies that can overcome it, assures me she will also not lack the ingenuity required to employ them.
42 I well know that it is nearly impossible to resist the first misfortunes new hardships excite in us, and even that it is ordinarily the best minds whose passions are the most violent and act more strongly upon their bodies; but it seems to me that the next day, when sleep has calmed the emotion that occurs in the blood under such circumstances, one can begin to restore one's mind and render it tranquil; and one does that by attending to consider all the advantages one can extract from the things one had the previous

---

* Descartes was upheld in his affair with Schoockius.

[128]

day taken as a great misfortune, and by turning one's attention from the evils one had imagined in them. For there are no eventualities so lugubrious nor so absolutely bad by the judgment of men that a person of wit cannot look upon them from some point of view such that they will appear favorable to him. And your Highness can extract this general consolation from the disgraces of fortune, namely, that perhaps they have very much contributed to making her cultivate her mind to the point which she has; that is a good she ought to esteem more than an empire. Great prosperities often overwhelm and intoxicate in such a way that, rather than being possessed by those whom they befall, these people are possessed by them; and although that does not happen to minds of your stamp, these prosperities always furnish minds such as yours less occasions to exercise themselves than do adversities. And I believe that, as there is no good in the world, save good sense, that one can absolutely name good, so also there is no evil from which one cannot extract some advantage, provided one has good sense.

43 I have previously tried to persuade your Highness to nonchalance, thinking occupations that are too serious may weaken the body by fatiguing the mind. But, for all that, I should never wish to dissuade her from necessary cares just to turn her thoughts from topics that can sadden her; nor do I doubt that the diversions of study, which would be very troublesome for others, would sometimes serve to relax her. I would esteem myself extremely happy if I could contribute to rendering them easier; and my desire to go learn at The Hague the virtues of the water of the Spa is much greater than to know those of the plants in my garden—and it is certainly greater than any care I have to know about what happens at Groningen or Utrecht to my advantage or disadvantage. That will oblige me to follow about four or five days after this letter, and I shall be all the days of my life, . . . etc.

CCCXCII.   Descartes to Elisabeth.

Egmond, 21 July 1645.

Madame,
   44 The air has been so inconstant since I had the honor of seeing your Highness, and there have been daytimes so cold for the season, that I have often had the concern and fear that the waters of the Spa might not be so healthful nor useful as they would have been in a time more serene; and because you did me the honor of indicating that my letters could offer you some diversion while the medical doctors recommend you not to occupy your mind at anything requiring its labors, I would do wrong to misuse the favor, which you have thus pleased to bestow upon me in permitting me to write to you, if I failed to take the first occasion to do so.
   45 I imagine that the greatest part of the letters you receive from others cause you emotion, and that even before reading them, you are apprehensive of finding therein some news to displease you, because the harshness of fortune has for a long time accustomed you to receiving such from her often; but as for those that come from here, you are at least assured that if they give you no subject for joy, neither will they cause you any sadness, and you can open them anytime without fear of them troubling the digestion of the waters you are taking. For not learning in this desert of anything that happens in the rest of the world, and having no thoughts more oft-repeated than those which, representing to me the virtues of your Highness, make me wish to see her as happy and content as she deserves, I have no other subject to discuss with you save to speak of the means concerning which philosophy instructs us for acquiring that sovereign happiness, which common souls await in vain from fortune, but which we shall be able to have only from ourselves.

[130]

46 One of these means, which seems to me most useful, is to examine what the ancients have written about it, and to try to go beyond them by adding something to their precepts; for in this way one can make them into something perfectly one's own and dispose oneself to put them into practice. That is why, to supplement the deficiency of my mind, which can produce nothing of its own accord; and so that I may deem myself deserving to be read by your Highness; and so that my letters are not entirely empty and useless: I propose to fill them in the future with considerations I shall take from the reading of a certain book, namely from the book Seneca has written *concerning the blessed life,* unless you may more prefer to choose another book, or unless this plan is disagreeable to you. But if I see you approve of it, which is my hope, and also, if it pleases you, if you are so obliging as to inform me of your observations on the same book, these observations, beyond serving very much to instruct me, shall give me occasion to render my own observations more exact, and I will develop them so much the more carefully the more I shall judge that this discussion shall be agreeable to you. For there is nothing in the world I desire with more enthusiasm than to show, in everyway within my power, that I am, . . . etc.

CCCXCVII.   Descartes to Elisabeth.

Egmond, 4 August 1645.

Madame,
47 When I chose Seneca's book, *concerning the blessed life,* to propose it to your Highness as an object of discussion that should be agreeable to her, I had in mind only the author's reputation and the dignity of the subject matter, and had not taken notice of the manner in which he treats it.

Having since considered his manner of treating the subject, I do not find it exact enough to merit being followed. But in order that your Highness can more easily judge of this, I shall try here to explain in what fashion it seems to me that this matter ought to have been treated by a philosopher such as he, who, not having been illuminated by faith, had only natural reason as a guide.

48 He speaks very well in the beginning when he says that *everyone wishes to live blessedly, but as to forseeing what brings about the blessed life, they grope in the dark.* But we need to know what it is to live blessedly; I would say in French to live happily, except that there is a difference between luck and blessedness in that luck depends only on things outside us, from which it results that those who have received some good they themselves have not procured are considered more happy than wise, whereas blessedness, it seems to me, consists in a perfect contentment of the mind, and in an interior satisfaction that those favored by fortune ordinarily lack; and this interior satisfaction the wise acquire without fortune. And thus *to live blessedly,* to live beatitude, is nothing but to have a mind perfectly content and satisfied.

49 Next, considering *what brings about the blessed life,* that is to say, considering the things that can give us this sovereign contentment, I notice they are of two sorts: namely, those that depend upon us, like virtue and wisdom, and those that do not depend upon us, like honors, riches, and health. For it is certain that a man who is well born, who is not sick, who lacks nothing, and who with all these things is also as wise and as virtuous as another man who is poor, in bad health, and deformed, can enjoy a more perfect contentment than the latter. Nevertheless, as a small vessel can also be as full as a larger one, even though it contains less liquid, so, taking the contentment of each person for the fullness and accomplishment of his desires regulated according to reason, I do not doubt that the most poor and disgraced by fortune or nature can be just as completely content and satisfied as are others, even though not enjoying as many goods. And it is only this sort of contentment that is here in question; for since the other kind is not in our power, to seek it would be superfluous.

50 It seems to me that everyone can render himself content with himself, and without counting on anything from others, provided only he observes three things, to which are related the three rules of morality I placed in the *Discourse on Method*.

51 First, that he try always to make the best possible use of his mind in order to know what he should do or not do in all the occurrences of life.

52 Second, that he have a firm and constant resolution to perform everything reason will advise him to do, and not allow his passions or appetites to lead him astray; and it is the steadfastness of this resolution that I believe should be taken as virtue, although I know nobody who has ever explained it so; rather, others have divided it into many kinds, to which they have given different names, because of the different objects to which it extends.

53 Third, that he realize that, when he is thus conducting himself as much as he can according to reason, all those good things he does not possess are, without exception, also entirely outside his power, and thus that by this means he accustom himself not to desire them. For nothing but desire, regret, or repentance can prevent us from being content. But if we always do everything our reason tells us, even though the outcomes might afterward make us see we have been mistaken, we will never have any subject for repentance, because we are not at fault. And what makes us not desire to have more arms or tongues than we have, but to desire more health or riches, is only that we imagine these latter things could be acquired by our conduct—or even that, unlike the former, they are owed to our nature. Yet we shall be able to free ourselves of this opinion by

[133]

considering that, since we have always followed the advice of our reason, we have omitted nothing which was in our power, and that maladies and misfortunes are no less natural to man than are prosperities and health.

54 Nevertheless, all sorts of desires are not incompatible with beatitude, but only those accompanied by impatience and sadness. Nor is it necessary that our reason not err; it suffices that our conscience show us we have never lacked the resoluteness and virtue to perform everything we have judged to be better; and accordingly virtue alone is sufficient to render us content in this life. But yet, because when not illuminated by the understanding, virtue can be false—which is to say, the will and resolution to do well can carry us toward bad things when we believe them good— the contentment that derives from it is not solid. And because one ordinarily opposes such virtue to pleasures, appetites, and passions, it is very difficult to put it into practice. However, the right use of reason, by giving us a true knowledge of the good, prevents virtue from being false; and even reconciling it with permissible pleasures, renders its practice so easy, and by making us know the condition of our nature, so limits our desires, that we must admit the greatest happiness of a man depends upon this right use of the reason, and that consequently the study which brings one to acquire it is the most useful occupation one can have, as it is also without a doubt the most agreeable and sweet of occupations.

55 Accordingly, it seems to me Seneca should have taught us all the principal truths required to facilitate the use of virtue and to regulate our desires and passions so as to enjoy natural blessedness—which would have rendered his book the best and most useful a pagan philosopher could achieve. Nevertheless, that is but my opinion, which I here submit to the judgment of your Highness; and if she does me the favor of advising me wherein I lack, I should be very greatly obliged and shall give evidence, in correcting myself, that I am, . . . etc.

CCCXCVIII.   Elisabeth to Descartes.

The Hague, 16 August 1645.

Monsieur Descartes,

56 In examining the book you recommended, I found a number of pretty phrases and well adorned sentences that provide an agreeable subject of meditation, yet do not instruct in the subject of which it treats, because they are without method, and the author does not pursue even what he had proposed. For instead of showing the shortest path toward blessedness, he contents himself with showing that its riches and delight do not render it negligible. I was obliged to write you this so that you might not believe me of your opinion out of prejudice or indolent imitation. Nor am I requesting you to continue to correct Seneca because your manner of reasoning is the more extraordinary, but because it is the most natural I have encountered and seems to teach me nothing new, save that I can extract from my mind knowledge I have not as yet noticed.

57 And thus, as yet, I am unable to extricate myself from doubting that one can arrive at the beatitude of which you speak without the assistance of what does not depend absolutely upon the will; for there are maladies that completely deprive one of the power of reasoning, and consequently of enjoying a reasonable satisfaction; others diminish the force of reasoning and prevent one from following maxims that good sense would institute; and these render the most moderate man subject to allowing himself to be carried away by his passions, and make him less capable of extricating himself from the accidents of fortune, which requires a prompt resolution. When Epicurus struggled hard, in his fit of stones, to assure his friends he felt no pain, he, instead of crying out like an ordinary man, led the life of a philosopher, not that of a prince, captain, or courtier, and he knew nothing would come from without to make him forget his role and cause him to cease to be regulated ac-

[135]

cording to the rules of his philosophy. And it is on those occasions that repentance seems to me inevitable; and even this knowledge that to fail is natural to man, just as to be sick is natural to him, cannot guard us against this repentance. For one also cannot ignore the fact that one cannot exempt oneself from each particular fault.

58 But I am assured you will illuminate these difficulties for me, as well as a number of others I am not clear-sighted enough to see now, when you shall teach me the truths that ought to be known in order to facilitate the practice of virtue. Do not fail, I beseech you, to oblige me by informing me of your teachings, and be assured I hold them in as great esteem as they deserve.

59 It is eight days since the bad humor of a sick brother prevented me from making this request of you; for I had constantly to keep at him in order to oblige him, by means of the respect he shows me, to submit himself to the directions of the doctors, or rather, to explain to him my own directions, trying to direct him toward theirs—for he is convinced I am capable in these matters. I wish to assure you I will be for all my life, ... etc.

CCCXCIX.   Descartes to Elisabeth.

Egmond, 18 August 1645.

Madame,
60 Although I do not know whether my last letters have been delivered to your Highness, and although I cannot write anything I dare think you do not know better than I regarding the subject I have chosen in order to have the honor of discussing it with you, I will nonetheless not fail to continue to write about it based upon my belief that my letters will not be more troublesome than the books you have in your library; for inasmuch as they contain no news

that you have an interest in knowing promptly, nothing will bid you read them at times when you must attend to affairs, and the time spent in writing them I shall consider very well employed if you bestow upon them only that you shall wish to lose.

61 I previously said what it seemed to me Seneca should have treated in his book, and I shall now examine what he does treat. In general, I note only three things: first, he tries to explain what the sovereign good is, and he gives different definitions of it; second, he disputes the opinion of Epicurus; and third, he responds to those who make the objection to the philosophers that they themselves do not live according to the rules they prescribe. But to see more particularly in what manner he treats these things, I will dwell somewhat upon each chapter.

62 In the first he reproves those who follow custom and example more than reason. *Never is life judged about,* says he, *it is always believed.* However, he indeed approves one's taking the advice of those one believes most wise; but he wishes that one also use one's own proper judgment to examine their opinions. In that I am very much of his opinion, for although very many are incapable of finding the right path by themselves, nevertheless but few people would fail to sufficiently recognize that path when it has been clearly pointed out to them by another; and, however that may be, one has grounds to be satisfied in conscience, and to assure oneself that one's opinions touching morals are the best one can have, when, instead of allowing oneself to be led blindly by example, one has employed all the forces of one's mind to examine what one ought to do. But while Seneca bends his efforts here to adorn his elocution, he is not always sufficiently precise in the expression of his thought; thus, when he says, *we shall be made healthy if only we be separated from the crowd,* he seems to teach that to be wise it suffices to be eccentric, which nonetheless is not his intention.

63 In the second chapter he does nothing but repeat, in

other terms, what he said in the first chapter; and he adds only that what one commonly esteems good is not good.

64 Next, in the third chapter, after having again used very many superfluous words, he finally states his opinion touching the sovereign good; namely, *that it is in accordance with the nature of things* and that *wisdom is to be formed in its law and example,* and that *the blessed life accords with one's nature.* All these explanations seem to me very obscure; for by nature he undoubtedly does not mean our natural inclinations, seeing they ordinarily lead us to follow pleasure, against which he argues; but the rest of his discourse makes one judge that by the *nature of things* he understands the order established by God in all the things in the world and, considering this order as infallable and independent of our will, he says that *wisdom is to be in accord with the nature of things and formed in the law and example,* which is to say, it is the wisdom of acquiescing to the order of things and of doing that for which we believe ourselves born; or better, to speak as a Christian, that it is the wisdom to submit ourselves to the will of God and to follow it in all our actions; and that *the blessed life accords with one's nature* is to say blessedness consists in thus following the order of the world, and taking in good stead all things that happen to us. But that explains hardly anything, nor can one sufficiently see the connection with what he adds immediately afterward, namely that this blessedness can occur *only if the mind is healthy, etc.,* unless one also understands that *to live according to nature* is to live following true reason.

65 In the fourth and fifth chapters he gives some other definitions of the sovereign good all of which have some relation with the meaning in the first chapter, but he does not explain any of them sufficiently; and seeing their diversity, it appears Seneca did not clearly understand what he wished to say; for the better one conceives something, the more one is more determined to express it in only one

way. The place where it seems to me he has succeeded best is in chapter five, where he says *he is blessed who has and does not fear the benefits of reason* and *the blessed life is established in right and certain judgment.* But since he does not teach the reasons why we ought not fear or desire anything, all that is of very little help.

66 He begins in these same chapters to dispute against those who place beatitude in pleasure, and he continues to do so in the following chapters. That is why, before examining them, I will say here my sentiment regarding this question.

67 I note, firstly, there is a difference between blessedness, the sovereign good, and the ultimate end or goal toward which our actions ought to tend; for blessedness is not the sovereign good; rather it presupposes it and is the contentment or the satisfaction of mind that comes from the fact one possesses the sovereign good. But, by the end of our actions, one can understand the one as well as the other; because the sovereign good is without doubt the thing we ought to propose to ourselves as the goal of all our actions, and the contentment of mind that comes from it, being the attraction that makes us seek after it, is also properly called our end.

68 I note, beyond that, that the word pleasure * has been taken in another sense by Epicurus than by those who dispute against him. For all these adversaries have restrained the signification of this word to pleasures of the senses; and he, on the contrary, has extended it to all the contentments of the mind, as one can easily judge from what Seneca and others have written of him.

69 Well then, there had been three principal opinions held among the pagan philosophers regarding the sovereign good and the end of our actions: namely, that of Epicurus, who said it was pleasure; that of Zeno, who

---

* *volupté.*

would have it to be virtue; and that of Aristotle, who had composed it from all sorts of perfections, as much from perfections of the body as of the mind. These three opinions can, it seems to me, be received as true and as in mutual accord, provided one interprets them favorably.

70 Aristotle considered the sovereign good of all human nature in general, that is to say, the sovereign good that can be had by the most accomplished of all men. Thus he had reason to compose it from all the perfections of which human nature is capable; but that does not serve our purpose.

71 Zeno, on the contrary, considered that which each man in particular can possess; that is why he also had very good reason for saying it consists in virtue, because, from among the goods we can possess, only virtue entirely depends upon our free decision. But, by making all vices equal, Zeno has represented this virtue as so stern, and as such an enemy of pleasure, that it seems to me it must have been only melancholics, or minds entirely detached from bodies, who were able to be his disciples.

72 Finally, Epicurus, when considering that in which beatitude consists, and the motive or end to which our actions tend, has not been wrong to say it is pleasure in general, that is, the contentment of the mind; for although the simple knowledge of our duty could oblige us to do good actions, that would nevertheless not make us enjoy any blessedness unless it returned us some pleasure for performing them. Yet, because one often attributes the name of pleasure to false pleasures that are accompanied or followed by disquietude, boredom, and repentance, many have accordingly believed this opinion of Epicurus taught vice and that, in effect, it does not teach virtue. But just as when from some point of view there is a reward for shooting at the white, those to whom one shows this reward are made desirous of shooting at it, yet they cannot on that account gain this reward unless they see the white; and just as those who see the white are not thereby induced to shoot at it unless they see there is a reward to gain; so too virtue, which is the white, does not make itself very desirable when one sees it all alone; and contentment, which is the reward of virtue, cannot be acquired unless one follows virtue.

73 That is why I believe I can here conclude that blessedness consists only in the contentment of the mind, that is to say, in contentment in general; for although there are contentments that depend upon the body, and others that do not, nevertheless there are no contentments except those in the mind: but to have a contentment that is solid, it is necessary to follow virtue, that is to say, to have a firm will, and to perform constantly all the things we judge to be the best, employing the entire force of our understanding to judge them well. I reserve to another time to discuss what Seneca has written about this; for my letter is already too long, and there remains only enough room as I require to say that I am, . . . etc.

CD.   Elisabeth to Descartes.

The Hague, August 1645.

Monsieur Descartes,

74 I believe you shall have already seen in my last letter of the 16th that yours of the 4th has been received by me. And I have no need to add that it sheds more light for me on the subject with which it deals than did everything I have been able to read or meditate. You know very well what you are doing and of what I am capable; and you have too thoroughly examined what others have done to leave any question about your examination; yet, by an excess of generosity, you wish to make yourself unaware of the very great obligation I owe you for having provided me with so useful and agreeable an occupation as to read and consider your letters. Without the last letter I would not have so well understood what Seneca thinks of beatitude as I now do. I have attributed the obscurity found in the said book, as in the greater part of the ancients, to their manner of explaining themselves, which is completely different from our's in that the same things that are problematic among us pass for hypotheses among them; next, there is the scant connection and order that Seneca observes, as he attempts to acquire admirers by surprising their imagination, rather than to make disciples by informing the judgment; moreover, there is his use of pretty words, like the other devices of poetry and fables, designed to entice the youth to follow his opinion. The manner in which he refutes the opinion of Epicurus seems to support this view. Seneca says of this philosopher, *what we say is the law unto virtue, he (Epicurus) says is a law unto pleasure.* And a little before he says, in the name of Epicurus' disciples: *for I deny anyone can live joyfully unless he at the same time lives honorably.* From which it would clearly seem that the followers of Epicurus gave the name pleasure * to the joy and satisfaction of mind that Senca calls *the consequence that is the highest good.* And nevertheless, in all the rest of the book, Seneca speaks of this epicurean pleasure as if it were purely sensual.

75 Yet I owe a great deal to Seneca, for his obscurity has caused you to take the pains to explain the ancient opinions and reconcile them better than the ancients themselves would have known how to do; moreover, by this reconciling of their opinions, you have thereby dismissed a potent objection against the search after this sovereign good, which none of these great minds has been able to define; furthermore, seeing their reason did not illuminate these excellent persons as regards the knowledge of what is most necessary

---

* *volupté.*

to them and the most to cherish, your explanations remove a potent objection against human reason itself. And I hope you will continue, based on what Seneca has said or ought to have said, to instruct me about the means of fortifying the understanding to judge best in all the actions of life; for this seems to me to be the sole difficulty, since it is impossible not to follow the good path once it is known. Be forthright, I pray you, and tell me if I abuse your kindness by asking too much of your leisure for the satisfaction of . . . etc.

CDI.   Descartes to Elisabeth.

Egmond, 1 September 1645.

Madame,

76 Because I was of late uncertain whether your Highness was at The Hague or Rhenen, I addressed my letter through Leiden, and the letter you did me the honor of writing was received only after the messenger who took mine to Alkmaar had left. That prevented me from being able to explain sooner how flattered I am both that my judgment of the book you have taken the pains to read does not differ from yours, and that my manner of reasoning seems to you natural enough. I am assured that if you had had the leisure to think as much as I have about the things it treats, I could write nothing that you would not have noticed more easily than myself; but since the age, birth, and occupations of your Highness have not allowed this, perhaps what I write will be able to serve you by sparing you a little time—perhaps even my faults will furnish you occasions to notice the truth.

77 Thus, when I spoke of a blessedness that depends entirely on our free decision, a blessedness all men can acquire without any assistance from elsewhere, you note very well that there are maladies which, by depriving one of the power of reasoning, also deprive one of enjoying the satisfaction of a reasonable mind; and this makes me recognize that what I had said generally of all men ought to be understood only of those who have a free use of their reason with which to know the path one must hold to so as to come to this beatitude. For there is nobody who does not desire to become happy; yet very many do not know the means; and often an indisposition of the body prevents the will from being free. That is like what happens in sleep—for the most philosophical person in the world would not know how to prevent himself from having bad dreams when his temperament disposes him to them. Nevertheless, experience makes us see that if one has often had some thought while one has had a mind in possession of its liberty, that thought still returns afterward, whatever indisposition the body suffers; and so I can say my own dreams never represent anything annoying, and undoubtedly there is great advantage in being for a long time accustomed not to have sorrowful thoughts. However, we can answer absolutely for ourselves only when we are in possession of ourselves; and it is less to lose one's life than to lose one's reason; for even without the teachings of the faith, natural philosophy alone makes our soul look forward after death to an estate happier than its present one; and it makes the soul fear nothing as more troublesome than being attached to a body that entirely robs it of its liberty.

78   As for the other indispositions that do not completely trouble sense, but only alter the humors and make one find oneself extraordinarily inclined to sadness, anger, or some other passion, they undoubtedly bring pain, but they can be surmounted and even provide the soul grounds for a satisfaction so much the greater the more they have been difficult to vanquish. And I also believe the same of all the impediments from without, such as the renown of great birth, the cajoleries of the court, the adversities of fortune, and also the great prosperities, which ordinarily more pre-

vent one from being able to display the role of philosopher than do disgraces. For when one has everything one has wished for, one forgets to think about oneself; and afterward, when fortune changes, one finds oneself the more surprised the more one was the more reliant upon good fortune. Finally, one can say generally that there is nothing that can entirely rob us of the means of rendering ourselves happy, provided only it does not disturb our reason—and it is not always those things that seem the most annoying that harm reason the most.

79 But, to know exactly how much each thing can contribute to our contentment, it is necessary to consider what causes produce it, and knowledge of these causes is one of the principal kinds of knowledge that can serve to facilitate the practice of virtue; for all the actions of our soul that bring us some perfection are virtuous, and all our contentment consists only in the interior testimony that we have to have some perfection. And thus we could never practice any virtue (that is to say, do something our reason persuades us we ought to do) from which we did not receive satisfaction and pleasure. But there are two sorts of pleasures: the ones pertain to the mind alone; and the others pertain to man, that is to say, to the mind inasmuch as it is united to the body; and these last pleasures, presenting themselves confusedly to the imagination, often seem very much greater than they are, principally before one possesses them—and that is the source of all the evils and all the errors of life. For, according to the rule of reason, each pleasure should have to be measured by the greatness of the perfection it produces, and it is thus that we measure those pleasures whose causes are clearly known to us. But passion makes us believe certain things very much better and more desirable than they are; then, when we have carefully taken the pains to acquire such things, thereby losing the opportunity to possess other and truer goods, their use makes us recognize their defects—from which issues dis-

dain, regret, and repentance. That is why the true office of reason is to examine the just value of all the goods whose acquisition seems to depend in some fashion upon our conduct, so that we never fail to employ all our efforts to try to procure for ourselves those things that are most desirable; and in this matter, if fortune is opposed to our goals and prevents them from succeeding, we will at least have the satisfaction of not having lost anything due to our fault, and we shall not fail to enjoy all the natural blessedness whose acquisition was in our power.

80 And so, for example, anger can sometimes excite in us desires of vengeance so violent that it will make us imagine more pleasure in punishing the enemy than in conserving our honor or our life, and on such an account it will make us risk both imprudently. On the other hand, if reason examines the good, or perfection, on which is founded this pleasure one extracts from vengeance, it will find it to consist in nothing else (at least when this vengeance does not serve to prevent another from offending us again) except that it makes us imagine that we have some sort of superiority and advantage over the one upon whom we avenge ourselves. And often that is but our vain imagination, which does not deserve to be esteemed in comparison to honor or life, nor even in comparison to the satisfaction one would have in seeing oneself master one's anger by abstaining from revenge.

81 And a similar thing happens in all the other passions; for there is none that does not represent to us the good to which it tends with more glitter than it merits; and there is none that does not make us imagine those goods, before we possess them, as very much greater pleasures than we afterward find them when once we have them. That explains why one ordinarily blames pleasure; for ordinarily one uses this word only to signify pleasures that frequently deceive us by their appearance and make us neglect others that are very much more solid, but whose expectation does not af-

fect us as much, such as those which pertain to the mind alone. I say ordinarily; for not all pleasures of the mind are praiseworthy, because they can be founded upon some false opinions, such as the pleasure one takes from slander, which is founded only upon the fact that one thinks the less other people are esteemed, the more one oneself ought to be esteemed; moreover, the pleasures of the mind can also deceive us by their appearance when some sort of passion accompanies them, as in the pleasure brought on by ambition.

82 But the principal difference between the pleasures of the body and those of the mind consists in the fact that the body, being subject to perpetual change, and having even its conservation and its good dependent upon this change, all the pleasures that have reference to it scarcely endure; for they proceed only from the acquisition of something useful to the body at the moment one receives it; and as soon as it ceases to be useful, the pleasures of the body cease as well; however, the pleasures of the soul can be immortal like the soul, provided they have so solid a foundation that neither knowledge of the truth, nor any false conviction, destroys them.

83 Accordingly, the true use of our reason in regard to the conduct of life consists only in examining and considering without passion the value of all the perfections, both of the body as well as of the mind, that can be acquired through our conduct; and thus, since ordinarily we must deprive ourselves of certain pleasures to have others, we may always choose the best. And because the perfections of the body are less than those of the mind, one can say generally that without them there is a way to become happy. Nonetheless, I am not of the opinion that one ought entirely to scorn them, nor even that one ought to exempt oneself from having passions; it suffices that one make them subject to reason; and, when one has thus sanctioned them, they are sometimes much more useful the more they lean toward

excess. And I shall never have any more excessive passion than that which leads to the respect and veneration I owe to you and which makes me, . . . etc.

CDII.   Elisabeth to Descartes.

The Hague, 13 September 1645.

Monsieur Descartes,

84 Were my conscience to remain satisfied with the excuses you provide as palliatives to my ignorance, I should be very much obliged for it, and should be exempt from repentance for having so badly employed the time I have enjoyed for using my reason; for that time has been much longer for me than for others of my age, since my birth and fortune forced me to employ my judgment at an earlier period in order to manage a life that is sufficiently troublesome and free of those prosperities which might prevent me from thinking about myself—for, from the beginning, there existed that constraint which would oblige me to rely upon my prudence as a ruler.

85 Nevertheless, it is not those prosperities, nor the flatteries that accompany them, that I believe absolutely capable of depriving well born souls of fortitude of mind and of preventing them from accepting a change of fortune in a philosophical way: rather, I am persuaded that the multitude of accidents that overwhelm persons governing the public, without allowing them time to examine the most useful expedient, often leads them, however virtuous, to perform actions which afterward cause the repentance you say is one of the principal obstacles to blessedness. It is true that the habit of esteeming goods according as they can contribute to contentment, of measuring this contentment according to the perfections that give birth to pleasures, and

of judging without passion these perfections and these pleasures, will secure them from many mistakes. But to thus evaluate the goods, it is necessary to know them perfectly; and to know all those goods about which one is constrained to make a choice in an active life, it would be necessary to possess an infinite knowledge. You will say that one does not fail to be satisfied when conscience testifies one has taken all possible precautions. But that never happens when one does not find one's goal. For one always plagues one's mind with the things that remained to consider. In order to measure contentment according to the perfection it causes, it would be necessary to see clearly the value of each thing so as to tell whether those that serve only us, or those that also render us useful to others, are preferable. It seems these latter things are esteemed excessively by one who torments himself for another, and the former by one who lives only for himself. And nevertheless both such persons support their own inclinations with reasons sufficiently strong to continue in that manner throughout their lives. It is similar with the other perfections of body and mind, which a quiet sentiment makes one's reason endorse. Nor ought this sentiment be called a passion—for one is born with it. Tell me then, if you please, how far it is necessary to follow this sentiment (since it is a gift of nature), and how does one correct it?

86 I would also wish you to define the passions,' so that they be well known; for those who name them perturbations of the soul would persuade me that the force of the passions consists only in overwhelming and subjecting reason, had not experience shown me there are passions that carry us to reasonable actions. But I am assured you will shed more light on this for me when you shall explain how the force of the passions renders them all the more useful when they are subject to reason.

87 I will receive this favor at Riswyck, where we are going to reside in the house of the Prince of Orange until

this present one is put in order; but you have no need on
that account to change the address of your letters to, . . .
etc.

CDIII.   Descartes to Elisabeth

Egmond, 15 September 1645.

Madame,

88 Your Highness has so exactly noted all the causes
that prevented Seneca from clearly explaining his opinion
regarding the sovereign good, and you have taken the pain
to read his book with so much care, that I fear lest I should
become importunate were I to continue here to examine all
its chapters seriatim; moreover, I fear that doing so would
make me delay in responding to the difficulty it has pleased
you to propose to me regarding the means of fortifying the
understanding to discern what is best in all the actions of
life. That is why, without now stopping to follow Seneca, I
shall try to explain only my own opinion regarding this
matter.

89 It seems to me there can be but two things required
for anyone always to be disposed to judge well: the one, a
knowledge of the truth; the other, the habit of remembering
and acquiescing in this knowledge every time the occasion
so requires. But since God alone perfectly knows everything, we must content ourselves with knowing those
things most to our advantage.

90 Among these the first and principal is that there
exists a God upon whom all things depend, whose perfections are infinite, power immense, decrees infallible: for
that teaches us to accept in good spirit everything that
comes to us as being expressly sent from God; and because
the true object of love is perfection, when we elevate our
mind to consider him such as he is, we find ourselves so

naturally inclined to love him that we extract joy even from our afflictions by thinking it his will that they come to us.

91 The second thing necessary to know is the nature of our soul, insofar as it subsists without the body, and is very much nobler than it, and capable of enjoying an infinity of contentments not found in this life: for that prevents us from fearing death, and so detaches our affections from things of the world that we regard only with disdain everything in fortune's power.

92 For that purpose, it can likewise be of much use if one judge worthily of the works of God and have that vast idea of the extension of the universe which I have tried to express in the third book of my *Principles:* for if one imagines that beyond the heavens are merely imaginary spaces, and that all these heavens are made only for the service of the earth, and earth only for man, it inclines one to think this earth our principal dwelling, and this life our best life; and that brings it about that, instead of recognizing the perfections truly in us, we attribute to other creatures imperfections they do not have in order to elevate ourselves above them; and so we fall into an impertinent presumption, wishing God to take us into his counsel and wishing to take charge with him of the conduct of the world, all of which causes an infinity of vain disquietudes and annoyances.

93 After one has thus recognized the goodness of God, the immortality of our souls, and the greatness of the universe, there still remains a truth the knowledge of which seems to me very useful: and it is this, that while each of us is a person separate from others, whose interests consequently are in some way distinct from the interests of others, nevertheless one should consider that one could not subsist alone and is, in effect, one of the parts of the earth, and more particularly, of this state, of this society, of this family, to which one is joined by one's residence, by one's oath, and by one's birth. And it is necessary to prefer always the interests of the whole, of which one is a part, to the interest of one's own person in particular; yet this is to be done with measure and discretion, for one would be wrong to expose oneself to a great evil to procure only a small good for one's parents or country; and if a man is worth more in himself than all the rest of his city, he would not be correct to wish to perish to save it. However, if one related everything to oneself, one would not fear to harm others a very great deal when one believed one would derive some small convenience from doing so; and such a person would provide no true friendship, no fidelity, and generally would lack all virtue; but, on the other hand, by considering oneself as a part of the public, one takes pleasure in doing good to everyone, and one does not fear even to expose one's life for the service of another when the occasion presents itself; thus, if one could, one would wish to lose one's soul to save others. Accordingly, this consideration is the source and origin of all the most heroic actions men perform; and as for those who expose themselves to death out of vanity, because by doing so they hope to be praised, or out of stupidity, because they do not apprehend the danger, I believe they are more to be pitied than esteemed. But, when one exposes oneself to death because one thinks it one's duty, or one suffers some other evil to bring good to others, even though one perhaps does not reflectively consider one is doing so because one owes more to the public of which one is a part than to oneself in particular, one still does it in virtue of this consideration which is confusedly in one's thought. And one is naturally led to act from such a consid·eration when one knows and loves God as one ought: for then, abandoning oneself completely to his will, one rids oneself of one's particular interests and has no other passion save to do what one believes agreeable to him; in consequence of which one has satisfaction of mind and contentments incomparably more valuable than all the small fleeting joys that depend upon the senses.

94 Beyond these truths, which refer generally to all our actions, it is necessary to know several others that relate more particularly to each of our actions. Of these the principal seem to be those I noted in my last letter: namely, that all our passions represent the goods to whose pursuit they incite us as very much greater than they truly are; and also, that the pleasures of the body are never so durable as those of the soul, nor so great when one possesses them as they might appear when one looks forward to them. We must pay careful attention to this, so that when we feel ourselves moved by some passion, we may suspend our judgment until the passion is calmed, and so that we do not easily allow ourselves to be deceived by the false appearances of the goods of this world.

95 To that I can add nothing except that it is necessary to examine in particular all the customs of the places where we live so as to know to what extent they should be followed. And although we cannot have certain demonstrations of everything, we nevertheless ought to take a position and embrace the opinions that seem to us the most probable in regard to all the things in practice, so that whenever it is a question of acting we may never be irresolute—which is what causes regrets and repentances.

96 Moreover, I said above that to be disposed to judge well always requires not only knowledge, but also habit. For, inasmuch as we are unable to be continually attentive to the same thing, however clear and evident might have been the reasons that formerly persuaded us of some truth, we can still afterward be turned away from believing it by false appearances—unless long and frequent meditation has so imprinted it upon our mind as to turn it into a habit. And in this sense they speak correctly in the School when they say the virtues are habits; for in effect we are hardly ever lacking because we fail to possess in theory the knowledge of what we ought to do; it is only because we fail to have practical knowledge of it, that is, a firm habit of believing it. And because while I am here examining these truths I am also further developing such a habit in myself, I am particularly obliged to your Highness for permitting me to discuss this matter with her; and there is nothing in which I esteem my leisure better employed than in doing that by which I can show that I am, . . . etc.

97 When I finished this letter I received yours of the 13th; but I found in it so many things to consider that I did not dare undertake to respond to them immediately; and I am sure your Highness will more prefer that I take a bit of time to think on them.

CDVI.   Elisabeth to Descartes.

Riswyck, 30 September 1645.

Monsieur Descartes,

98 Although your observations upon Seneca's opinions about the sovereign good would make my reading of them more profitable than I should be capable of finding it on my own, I am nevertheless not reluctant to exchange those observations for your reflections upon truths so necessary as are those dealing with the means of fortifying the understanding to discern what is best in all the actions of life: I am not reluctant to make this exchange, provided you still append an explanation my stupidity requires—namely, that you explain the utility of knowing the truths you propose.

99 The knowledge of the existence of God and of his attributes can console us concerning evils that come to us in the ordinary course of nature and due to the order God has established, such as losing something in a storm, health by infectious air, and friends by death. However, this knowledge does not console us concerning evils imposed upon us by men whose wills appear to us entirely free, for only faith can persuade us that God takes care to govern wills and that he has determined the fortune of each person before the creation of the world.

100   The immortality of the soul and the knowledge that it is very much nobler than the body can make us seek death as well as loathe it, since one could not doubt that we shall live more happily exempt from the maladies and passions of the body. And I am astonished that those who say they are persuaded of this truth and live without the revealed law would prefer a troublesome life to an advantageous death.

101   The great extension of the universe that you have shown in the third book of your principles serves to detach our affections from what we see in this extension; but it also removes from our idea of God that special providence which is the foundation of theology.

102   The consideration that we are a part of the whole, from which consideration we ought to seek a benefit, is indeed the source of all generous actions; but I find very many difficulties as regards the conditions you prescribe for such actions. How measure the pains one takes in serving the public against the good that will ensue, without these evils seeming greater insasmuch as their idea is the more distinct? And what rule shall we have to compare things not equally known, such as our individual worth and the worth of those with whom we live? One who is naturally arrogant will always tip the balance in his own favor; and one who is modest will esteem himself less than his worth.

103   In order to profit from the particular truths of which you speak, it is necessary to know exactly all those passions and preoccupations that, for the most part, are insensible. And in observing the customs of the country where we are, we will sometimes find some that are very unreasonable but yet must be followed in order to avoid greater inconveniences.

104   Since being here I have had a very annoying proof of this; for in sojourning in the country I hoped to find time to employ in study, and yet, because of the distractions of those who do not know what to do with themselves, I find incomparably less leisure than I had at The Hague; and although it is very unjust to deprive myself of real goods for imaginary ones, I am constrained, in order not to acquire enemies, to accede to impertinent established laws of civility. Since I have written this, I have been 'interrupted more than seven times by inconvenient visitors. It is your excessive generosity that prevents my letters from being an impediment such as this to you, and that obliges you to wish to foster the practice of your divers knowledge by communicating them to such an indocile person as . . . etc.

CDVII. Descartes to Elisabeth.

Egmond, 6 October 1645.

Madame,
105 I have sometimes proposed to myself a doubt: namely, is it better to be gay and content, imagining the goods one possesses greater and more estimable than they are, and ignoring or not stopping to consider those one lacks; or is it better to possess more consideration and knowledge, so as to recognize the true value of both and thus become more sorrowful? Did I think joy the sovereign good, I should not doubt one ought to try to become joyous whatever the price could be, and I should approve the brutality of those who drown their displeasures in wine or assuage them with snuff. But I distinguish between the sovereign good, which consists in the exercise of virtue, or what is the same thing, in the possession of all the goods whose acquisition depends on our free deciding, and the satisfaction of the mind that follows from this acquisition. That is why, seeing it is a greater perfection to know the truth, even though it is to our disadvantage, than to be ignorant of it, I admit it is better to be less gay and have more knowledge. However, it is not always the case that when

one has more gaiety one has a mind more satisfied; on the contrary, great joys are ordinarily dull and serious, and only mediocre and passing joys are accompanied by laughter. Thus I do not approve of one's trying to deceive oneself by feeding on false imaginations; for all the pleasures that come from that can but touch the exterior of the soul, which nonetheless feels an interior bitterness in perceiving that these imaginations are false. And although it could happen that the soul was so continually diverted by other things that she never perceived herself, she would not on that account enjoy the blessedness here in question, because this blessedness ought to come from our conduct, but what she would then enjoy comes only from fortune.

106 However, when there can be different considerations equally true, where certain of them incline us to be content, and the others, on the contrary, prevent us from being so, it seems to me prudence dictates we arrest ourselves principally upon those that give us satisfaction; and moreover, because nearly all things in the world are such that one can regard them from one side that makes them seem good and from another that lets us recognize their defects, I believe that if one ought to use his skill to some purpose, it is principally to know how to look upon things from the point of view that makes them appear more to our advantage, provided that we do so without deceiving ourselves.

107 Thus, when your Highness notices the circumstances why she has been able to have more leisure to cultivate her reason than very many others of her age, if it pleases her also to consider how much she has profited more than these others, I am confident she will have grounds to be content. Nor do I see why she prefers to compare herself to them more in a matter from which she can derive subject for complaining about herself than in one that would give her satisfaction. For since the constitution of our nature is such that our mind has need of very much relaxation in order that it can usefully employ certain times in the search after truth, and since the mind would suffocate itself rather than become refined if it applied itself too much to study, we ought not measure the time we have been able to employ at instructing ourselves by the number of hours we have had to ourselves, but rather, it seems to me, by the example of what we ordinarily see is the case with others, as that is an indication of the ordinary capacity of the human mind.

108 It also seems to me that one has no subject for repentance when one has done what one judged best at the time one had to make a decision to act, even though in rethinking the matter afterward, when one has more leisure, one judges oneself to have failed. Rather, one should be repentant if one has done something against one's conscience, even though one recognized afterward that one has done better than one had thought: for we are responsible only for our thoughts; nor is it man's nature to know everything, or always to judge so well at the moment as when he has very much time to deliberate.

109 Moreover, although the vanity that makes one have a better opinion of oneself than one ought is a vice that pertains only to weak and base souls, that is not to say the strongest and most generous souls should deprecate themselves; rather, it is necessary to do justice to oneself, by recognizing one's perfections as well as one's faults; and if good manners prevent one from boasting of one's perfections, they do not thereby prevent one from realizing them.

110 Finally, although one does not have an infinite knowledge, so as to know perfectly all the goods about which one must make a choice in the different contingencies of life, one ought, it seems to me, content oneself in having a moderate amount of the things more necessary to life, such as those I listed in my last letter.

111 In that letter I already declared my opinion regarding the difficulty your Highness proposes: namely, as to whether those who relate everything to themselves are more correct than those who torment themselves for others.

For if we think only of ourselves, we could enjoy only goods specific to us; whereas, if we consider ourselves as parts of some other body, we also participate in the goods common to it without on that account being deprived of any of those proper to ourselves. And it is not the same with evils; for, according to philosophy, evil is nothing real, but only a privation; and when we ourselves become saddened because some evil befalls our friends, we do not on that account participate in the defect of which this evil consists; and whatever sadness or pain we experience on such occasions, it could not be so great as the interior satisfaction that always accompanies good actions, principally those that proceed from a pure affection for others not related to oneself, that is to say, from the Christian virtue one calls charity. And so one can, even in crying and taking much pains, have more pleasure than when one laughs and is at rest.

112 And it is easy to prove that the pleasure of the soul in which beatitude consists is not inseparable from gaiety and from the comfort of the body: that is proved both by the example of tragedies, which all the more please us the more they excite sadness in us, and also by bodily exercises, such as the chase, table-tennis, and other similar things, which do not cease to be agreeable even though very laborious; and one even finds that often it is the fatigue and the toil that augment the pleasure. And the cause of the contentment the soul receives in these exercises consists in that they make her notice the force, or the skill, or whatever other perfection of the body to which she is joined; but her contentment in crying when she sees some pitiable and lugubrious actions represented in the theater comes particularly from the fact that it seems to her she is doing a virtuous action in having compassion for those who are afflicted; and generally the soul is pleased to feel moved by the passions, whatever their nature, provided she remains mistress of them.

113 But I must examine these passions more particularly so that I can define them; that will be easier for me to do here than if I wrote to someone else; for since your Highness has taken the trouble to read the treatise I previously drafted regarding the nature of the animals, you already know how I conceive different impressions are formed in their brains. Some are formed by exterior objects which move the senses; others by the interior dispositions of the body, or by the vestiges of preceding impressions that have remained in the memory, or by the agitation of the spirits that come from the heart, or also, in man, by the action of the soul, which has a force to change the impressions in the brain as, reciprocally, these impressions have the force to excite in her the thoughts that do not depend upon her will. In consequence of this, one can generally name 'passions' all the thoughts thus excited in the soul without the concurrence of her will, and consequently solely by the impressions in the brain, and without any action that proceeds from her—for everything that is not an action is a passion. But ordinarily one restricts this name to thoughts caused by some particular agitation of the spirits. For those thoughts that come from external objects, or else from the interior dispositions of the body, such as colors, sounds, odors, hunger, thirst, pain, and the like, are called sentiments, some exterior, others interior. Those that depend only on what the preceding impressions have left in memory and upon the ordinary agitation of the spirits are reveries, whether they come in a dream or when one is awake, and they depend upon the fact that the soul, not then being determined to anything by herself, follows heedlessly the impressions found in the brain. But when the soul uses her will to determine herself to some thought that is not simply intelligible, but imaginable, this thought makes a new impression in the brain, and that is not a passion of the soul but an action properly called imagination. Finally, when the ordinary course of the spirits is such that it commonly excites sorrowful or gay thoughts, or similar thoughts, one does not attribute it to passion but to what is natural to, or to the humor of, the one in whom they are

[160]

excited, and that makes one say this man is naturally sad, this other of a gay humor, etc. And so it remains that only the thoughts that come from some particular agitation of the spirits, of which one feels the effects as in the soul herself, are properly named passions.

114 It is true we hardly ever have any thoughts that do not depend upon several of the causes I just distinguished; nonetheless they are denominated from that cause which is principal, or to which one gives principal consideration: that accounts for the fact that many confuse the feeling of pain with the passion of sorrow, and the feeling of titillation with the passion of joy, which they also name delight or pleasure, and the feeling of thirst or hunger with the desire to drink or eat, which are passions: for ordinarily the causes that make for pain also agitate the spirits in the manner required to excite sadness, and those that make one feel some titillation agitate the spirits in the manner required to excite joy, and so too with the others.

115 Also we sometimes confuse inclinations or habits that dispose one to some passion with the passion itself, but nevertheless they can easily be distinguished from the passion. For example, when one announces to a city that enemies are coming to besiege it, the first judgments the inhabitants make concerning the evil that can happen to them is an action of their soul, not a passion. And although this judgment is similarly found in many people, they are nevertheless not equally moved; rather, some are moved more and others less, according as they possess a greater or lesser habit or inclination toward fear. And before their soul receives the emotion in which alone the passion consists, it is necessary that she make this judgment; or else, without judging, that she at least conceive the danger and imprint the image of it upon the brain (which happens by a different action called "to imagine"); and it is also necessary that, by the same means, the soul determines the spirits, that travel from the brain by the nerves into the muscles, to enter those muscles that serve to close the openings of the heart, thus retarding the circulation of the blood; in consequence, all the body becomes pale, cold, and trembling, and the new spirits, which come from the heart to the brain, are agitated in such a manner that they can assist in forming there those images that excite in the soul the passion of fear—all of which events so closely follow each other that it seems but a single operation. And so too in all the other passions there occurs some particular agitation in the spirits that come from the heart.

116 That is what I thought of writing eight days ago to your Highness, and my goal was to add to it a particular explanation of all the passions; but having found difficulty in enumerating them, I was constrained to allow the messenger to depart without my letter; moreover, having received in the meantime the letter your Highness did me the honor of writing, I have a new subject for response obliging me to postpone this examination of the passions to another time and to say here that it seems to me that all the reasons that prove the existence of God, and that he is the first and immutable cause of all the effects that do not depend upon the free decision of men, likewise prove in the same way that he is also the cause of all those that do depend upon it. For one could not demonstrate that God exists save by considering him as a being sovereignly perfect; and God could not be sovereignly perfect if something could happen in the world that did not come entirely from him. It is true that only the faith teaches us about the grace by which God elevates us to a supernatural blessedness; but philosophy alone suffices to give us the knowledge that the least thought cannot enter the mind of man if God has not wished and willed from all eternity that it enter therein. And the distinction of the school between universal and particular causes is not in place here: for what makes it that the sun, for example, being the universal cause of all flowers, is not on that account the cause that tulips differ from roses, is that the production of these flowers also depends upon other subordinate causes not subordinate to the sun; God, however, is such a universal cause of everything that he is in the same manner total cause; and thus nothing can happen without his will.

117   It is also true that the knowledge of the immortality of the soul, and of the happiness of which she shall be capable outside this life, could give pretext for leaving it to those bored with it, if they were assured they would afterward enjoy all those felicities; but no reason assures them of that; and there is only the false philosophy of Hegesias whose book Ptolemy condemned, because, having read this book which tried to prove that this life is bad, many killed themselves;* true philosophy, on the contrary, teaches that, even among the most sorrowful accidents and the most pressing pain, one can always be content, provided one knows how to use one's reason.

118   As regards the extension of the universe, I do not see how, in considering it, one is inclined to think it at odds with the special providence contained in our idea of God: for the case is completely different with God than with finite powers. Since finite powers can be exhausted, we have reason to judge, in seeing them employed for very many great effects, that it is improbable they also extend to lesser ones; but the more we esteem the works of God to be great, the more we note the infinity of his power; and the more this infinity is better known to us, the more we are more greatly assured it extends to all the particular actions of men.

119   I also do not believe that by the particular providence of God, which your Highness said is the foundation of theology, you meant some change that occurs in his decrees on the occasion of actions that depend on our free deciding. For theology does not allow this change, and when theology obliges us to pray to God, that is not so that we might teach him what we have need of, nor so that we

---

*See Cicero, *Tusculanes* (Cambridge, Mass.: Harvard University Press, 1971), p. 84.

might try to persuade him to change something in the order established by his providence from all eternity: both would be blameworthy; rather, we pray only so that we might obtain what he has wished from all eternity to be obtained by our prayers. And I believe that all the theologians are in agreement on this matter, even the Arminians,* who seem the ones who most defer to the free will.

120 I admit it is difficult to measure exactly how far reason orders us to interest ourselves in the public; yet that is not something in which one must be very exact: it suffices to satisfy one's conscience, and in doing that, one can grant very much to one's inclination. For God has so established the order of things, and has joined men together in so connected a society, that although everyone related only to himself and had no charity for others, a man would nevertheless ordinarily not fail to employ himself on the behalf of others in everything that would be in his power, provided he used prudence, and principally if he lived in a century where the customs were not corrupted. And beyond that, as it is a higher and more glorious thing to do good to other men than to procure it for oneself, so too the greatest souls have more inclination to do so and place less value on the goods they themselves possess. Only weak and base souls esteem themselves more than they ought and are like small vessels that three drops of water can fill. I know your Highness is not of this number, and whereas one cannot incite these base souls to undergo toils for others without making them see some profit in it for themselves, it is necessary for the interests of her Highness to make clear to her that, if she neglects herself, she could not long be of use to those of whom she is fond; and I must beseech her take care of her health. That is the plea . . . etc.

---

* James Arminius (1560–1609) was a Dutch Protestant who opposed the tenets of strict Calvinism.

CDIX.   Elisabeth to Descartes.

The Hague, 28 October 1645.

Monsieur Descartes,
    121 After giving such good reasons for showing it more
worthwhile to recognize the truth to our disadvantage than
to deceive ourselves agreeably, and after demonstrating so
well that only when things admit of different considerations
equally true should we dwell upon that consideration
which will bring us more contentment, I am astonished that
you wish me to compare myself to those of my age more in
regard to something unknown to me than in regard to something I cannot ignore, even though doing so would be more
to my advantage. For nothing can make it manifest to me
whether I have profited more in cultivating my reason than
others have profited from the things to which they are devoted; and I have no doubt that, given the amount of rest my
body would require, there does not still remain enough
time for me to advance beyond where I am. And in measuring the capacity of the human mind by the example of ordinary men, it would be found of very small extent, because
the greater part use their thought only with reference to the
senses. Even among those who apply themselves to study,
few use anything but their memory, and few take truth as
the goal of their labor. Thus if there is a vice involved in my
not being pleased to consider whether I have gained more
than these people, I do not think it is an excessive humility,
which is also as harmful as presumption, but not so ordinary. We are more inclined to fail to recognize our faults
than our perfections. And in dodging repentance concerning the faults we have committed, as though it is an enemy
to our happiness, one could run the risk of losing the desire
to correct oneself, principally when some passion has produced those faults—for we have a natural love to be roused
by our passions and to follow their movements, and it is
only the inconvenience proceeding from following them

that teaches us they can be harmful. And it is this which, in my judgment, makes tragedies the more pleasing the more they excite in us sadness—for we know they will not be strong enough to carry us to extravagance nor durable enough to destroy our health.

122 However, that does not suffice to support the doctrine contained in one of your preceding letters: namely, that the passions are the more useful the more they tend to excess, as long as they are subjected to reason. For it seems to me that they cannot both be excessive and subjected to reason. But I believe you shall clarify this doubt by taking care to describe how the agitation of the spirits serves to form all the passions we experience, and by describing the manner in which they vitiate the reasoning. I would not dare ask this of you did I not know you do not leave off work that is incomplete, and were I not aware that in undertaking to instruct a stupid person such as I you have prepared yourself for such inconveniences as it brings.

123 That is what makes me continue to say to you that the reasons that prove the existence of God and that he is the immutable cause of all the effects that do not depend upon the free deciding of man, do not persuade me he is cause of all those that do depend on it. It necessarily follows from his sovereign perfection that he could be the cause of these effects, which is to say, he would be capable of not having given free decision to men; but since we feel we have it, it seems to me contradictory to common sense to believe that free deciding is dependent upon God in its operations as it is in its being.

124 If one is very much persuaded of the immortality of the soul, it would be impossible to doubt that the soul will not be happier after its separation from the body (which body is the origin of all the displeasures of life, just as the soul is the origin of life's greatest contentments) were it not for the opinion of M. Digby. That is the opinion taught him by his preceptor (whose writing you have seen); and it has led him to believe in the necessity of purgatory, by persuading him that the passions which have dominated over reason during the life of man still leave some traces in the soul after the death of the body and all the more torment the soul the more they find no means of assuaging themselves in so pure a substance. I do not see how that accords with the immateriality of the soul. Rather, I have no doubt that, although life is not evil in itself, it ought to be abandoned for a condition one will know to be better.

125 By that special providence which is the foundation of theology, I understand that by which God has, from all eternity, prescribed such strange means, like his Incarnation, on behalf of a part of his creation that, in comparison with the rest, is so inconsiderable as you represent this globe to be in your physics; and, by that special providence, I also understand that God has done so to be thereby glorified—which seems an end very unworthy of the creator of this universe. But, in regard to this matter, I have presented what is more the objection of our theologians than of myself; for I have always believed it something very impertinent that finite persons judge the final cause of the actions of an infinite being.

126 You do not believe one has need of an exact knowledge about the extent to which reason orders us to interest ourselves in behalf of the public; for you think that, although each person related everything to himself, he would still also work for others were he to use prudence. And this prudence is the end-all of which I ask from you but a part. For in possessing it one would not fail to do justice to others as to oneself, and want of such prudence is the cause why a sincere mind sometimes loses the means of serving his fatherland by abandoning himself too lightly for its interests, and similarly, why a timid person perishes along with it instead of hazarding his well being and fortune for its conservation.

127 I have always been in a condition that rendered my life very useless to persons I love; but I seek to conserve my condition with very much more care ever since having the

happiness of knowing you—for you have shown me the
means to live more happily than I did. I have want only of
the satisfaction of giving you sufficient testimony how much
obligation is felt by . . . etc.

CDXI.   Descartes to Elisabeth.

Egmond, 3 November 1645.

Madame,
128 So infrequently do I encounter such good reasonings—not only in the discussions of those whom I meet
in this desert, but likewise in the books I consult—that I
cannot read those of your Highness without feeling an extraordinary joy; and so strong do I find them that I more
prefer to admit I am captivated by them than to undertake to
resist them. For although the comparison your Highness
refuses to make to her own advantage can be sufficiently
verified by experience, it is nevertheless so praiseworthy a
virtue to judge others favorably, and it accords so well with
the generosity that prevents you from wishing to measure
the capacity of the human mind by the example of men, that
I cannot fail to esteem both traits very greatly.
129 I would also not dare to contradict what your Highness has said about repentance, seeing it is a Christian virtue that serves to make one correct oneself—not only of
faults voluntarily committed, but of those one has done out
of ignorance when some passion has prevented one from
knowing the truth. And I indeed admit that the sadness of
tragedies would not please as it does were we able to fear it
would become so excessive that we would be inconvenienced by it. However, when I said certain passions are
more useful the more they incline toward excess, I wished
only to speak of those that are all good—to which I testified
when I added they ought to be subject to reason. For

there are two sorts of excess: one which, by changing the nature of the thing and rendering what is good evil, prevents the passion from remaining subject to reason; the other augments but the measure of the passion and serves only to render what is good better. And thus fortitude has rashness as its excess only when it goes beyond the limits of reason; but while not passing beyond reason's limits, it can still have another excess that consists in being accompanied by no irresolution or fear.

130 I have thought during these days about the number and order of all these passions in order to be able to examine their nature more particularly, but I have not as yet sufficiently pondered my own opinions touching this subject to dare to write them to your Highness, and I shall not fail to inform her as soon as it shall be possible for me to do so.

131 As for what concerns the free deciding, I confess that in thinking only of ourselves we cannot fail to deem it independent; yet when we think of the infinite power of God we cannot fail to believe all things depend upon him, and consequently that our free deciding is not exempt from such dependence. For it implies a contradiction to say that God has created men of such a nature that the actions of their will do not depend upon his will, because that is the same as if one said God's power is both together finite and infinite: finite, since there is something that does not depend upon it; and infinite, since he has been able to create this independent thing. But as the knowledge of the existence of God ought not prevent us from being assured of our free deciding, since we experience it and feel it in ourselves, so also the knowledge of the free deciding should not make us doubt the existence of God. For the independence we experience and feel within us, and which suffices to render our actions praiseworthy or blamable, is not incompatible with a dependence of another nature according to which all things are subject to God.

132 As regards what relates to the state of the soul after this life, I certainly have less knowledge about it than does M. Digby; for leaving aside what faith teaches, I admit that by natural reason alone we can indeed make very many conjectures to our advantage and have pretty hopes in the matter, but not any assurance. And because the same natural reason also teaches us that we have always more goods than evils in this life, and that we should not forgo the certain for the uncertain, it seems to me it teaches us that we ought truly not to fear death, but also ought never seek it.

133 I have no need to respond to the objection that the theologians can make respecting the vast extension I have attributed to the universe, because your Highness has already responded on this matter for me. I add only that, if this extension could render the mysteries of our religion less believable, then the extension the astronomers have always attributed to the heavens would do the same, since they have considered them so great that in comparison the earth is, as it were, merely a point; and nevertheless the same objection is not made to them.

134 Furthermore, if prudence were the mistress of events, I have no doubt your Highness would accomplish everything she wished to undertake; however, that would require all men to be perfectly wise, so that, knowing what they ought to do, one could be assured what they would do. Or else it would be required that one know in particular the humor of everyone with whom one has some dealings; and even that would not suffice since, beyond their humor, they also have their free decision, whose movements are known only to God. And because one ordinarily judges concerning what others will do by reference to what one would wish to do were one in their place, it often happens that ordinary and mediocre minds, being similar to those with whom they deal, better penetrate their designs and are more easily successful in what they undertake than are more elevated souls, who in dealing only with those very much inferior in knowledge and prudence, judge very differently of things

than do they. And that ought to console your Highness when fortune opposes itself to your designs. I pray God to favor those designs and I am . . . etc.

CDXII.   Elisabeth to Descartes.

The Hague, 30 November 1645.

Monsieur Descartes,
   135 You shall have subject for astonishment that, having testified to me that my reasoning did not seem completely ridiculous to you, I remain for so long a time without extracting from it the advantage your responses provide me. And it is with shame I avow to you the cause, since this circumstance has turned around everything your lessons seemed to have established in my mind. I believed that a strong resolution to seek after blessedness only in the things that depended upon my will would render me less sensitive to those that came to me from elsewhere—but then the foolishness of one of my brothers made me know my weakness! For that has more disturbed the health of my body and the tranquility of my soul than all the unfortunate things that have as yet happened to me. And if you take the trouble to read the newspaper, you could not fail to see that he has fallen into the hands of a certain sort of people who have more hatred for our household than affection for their cult, and has allowed himself to be caught in their traps to the point of changing religion to become a Roman Catholic, displaying not even the least grimace to persuade the more gullible that he was doing so despite his conscience. It is necessary that I see a person, whom I loved with the greatest tenderness possible, subjected to the contempt of the world and (according to my belief) to the loss of his soul. If you did not have more charity than bigotry, it would be an impertinence to discuss this matter with you, and even that

would not be sufficient permission were I not in the position of telling you all my faults, as to the person most capable of correcting them.

136 In the same way, I admit to you that, although I do not comprehend any lesser contradiction between the independence of the free deciding and the idea we have of God, than between the dependence of the free deciding and its liberty, it is impossible for me to reconcile them, since it is as impossible for the will to be at the same time free and attached to the decisions of providence as for the divine power to be infinite and limited both together. I do not see their compatibility, of which you speak, nor do I see how this dependence of the will can be of another nature than its liberty, unless you take the pains to teach me about it.

137 As regards contentment, I admit that the present possession of it is very much more assured than awaiting it in the future, however good be the reason upon which this future hope is founded. But on that basis I have difficulty in persuading myself that we always have more goods than evils in this life, since more is required to constitute goods. For man has more situations from which to receive displeasure than pleasure: there are an infinite number of errors for one truth; very many ways to go astray for the one that leads along the right path; and a quantity of persons with the design and power to harm one in proportion to the few able and willing to serve one. Finally, everything that depends upon the will and the course of the rest of the world is capable of providing inconvenience; and according to your proper opinion, only that which depends absolutely on our will suffices to give a real and constant satisfaction.

138 As regards prudence, as far as human society is concerned, I do not await an infallible rule; but I should be very pleased to see those rules you would give to one who, in living only for himself, in whatever profession he has, would nevertheless not fail to work for others—that I should wish to see were I to dare ask of you more light after having so badly employed that which you have already given to . . . etc.

CDXIX.   Descartes to Elisabeth.

Egmond, January 1646.

Madame,

139 I cannot deny my surprise in learning that your Highness has been annoyed, to the extent that her health has been upset, by a matter which the greatest part of the world will find good, and that very many cogent reasons will be able to render excusable in the view of others. For everyone of my religion (and undoubtedly they are the largest part of Europe) are obliged to approve this matter even though they see there circumstances and apparent motives that were blameworthy; for we believe God uses different means to attract souls to faith, and that such people as have entered the cloister with a bad intention have afterward led a very holy life. As for those who are of another belief, if they speak evil of this, one can challenge their judgment: for as in all other matters where there are different factions, it is impossible to please one faction without displeasing the others. Moreover, if they consider that they would not be of the religion of which they are had not they or their fathers or their grandfathers left the Roman religion, they will have no reason to mock or label inconstant those who leave theirs.

140 As for what pertains to the prudence of the century, it is true that those who have fortune on their side are correct to stay with her and press to join their forces together to prevent her from escaping them; but those of a household whose fortune is fled do not, it seems to me, do badly to agree to follow separate ways, so that, if they cannot all find her, at least one of them may meet with her. And in the meanwhile, since it is believed each of them has many resources, having friends in different factions, all of them are thereby rendered more formidable than if they were all to be engaged in a single faction. That is what prevents me from being able to imagine that those who have been the author of this advice have thereby wished to harm your household. However, I do not pretend that my reasons could prevent the resentment of your Highness. I hope only that time shall have diminished it before this letter is presented to you, and I would fear to arouse it anew were I to discuss this subject further.

141 That is why I pass to the difficulty your Highness proposes regarding the free deciding, whose dependency and liberty I shall try to explain by a comparison. If a king who has condemned duels and very assuredly knows that two gentlemen of his kingdom, residing in different cities, are quarrelling, and have such animus against each other that nothing could prevent them from battling if they meet; if, I say, this king charges one of them to go one day to the city where the other resides and also gives this other the charge to go the same day to the place where the first resides, he very assuredly knows they will not fail to meet and do battle, and thus to contravene his ban, but for all that he has not constrained them to do so; and his knowledge, and even the will he has had to determine them in this way, does not prevent them from as voluntarily and freely battling when they come to meet as they would have done had he known nothing about it and it were because of some other circumstance that they met; and they can also be justly punished for having contravened his ban. Well, what a king can do regarding certain free actions of his subjects, God, who has an infinite prescience and an infinite power, infallibly does regarding all the actions of men. And before he had sent us into the world, God knew exactly what would be all the inclinations of our will; it is he himself who placed them in us; it is he also who has disposed all the other things which are without us in order to bring it about that such and such objects would present themselves to our senses at such and such times; and he knew that on these occasions our free decision would determine us to this or that thing; and he has willed it so, but for all that he has not willed to constrain us to such actions. And as one can distinguish in this king two different degrees of will, the one by which he wished these gentlemen would battle, since he arranged that they would meet, and the other by which he has not wished it, since he condemned the duels, so too the theologians distinguish in God an absolute and independent will, by which God wills that everything would happen as it happens, and another which is relative, and which relates to the merit or demerit of men, by which he wishes that they obey his laws.

142 It is also necessary for me to distinguish two sorts of goods in order to bring into an accord what I have previously written (namely that in this life we always have more goods than evils) and what your Highness objects to me regarding all the inconveniences of life. When one considers the idea of good to serve as a rule for our actions, one takes it for all the perfection that can be in the thing one calls good, and one compares it to the straight line that is unique among an infinity of curved lines to which one compares evils. And it is in this sense that the philosophers are accustomed to say that *good is from a faultless cause, evil from any defect whatever.* But when one considers the good and evils which can be in the same thing, in order to know the worth one ought to set on it, as I did when I spoke of the worth we ought to set on this life, one considers as good everything one finds there from which one can draw some convenience, and one calls evils anything from which one can receive inconvenience; as for the other defects which can be there, one does not count them. Thus, when one offers employment to someone, the latter considers, on the one hand, the honor and the profit he can attain as

goods, and, on the other hand, the pain, the peril, the loss of time, and other such things as evils, and in comparing these evils with these goods, according as he finds these goods more or less great than these evils, he accepts or rejects the employment. But what made me say, in this last sense, that there are always more goods than evils in life is the little importance I believe we ought to place on all those things that are without us, and that do not depend upon our free deciding, in comparison with those that do depend upon it and that we can always render good when we know how to use them well; and by their means we can prevent all the evils that come from elsewhere, however great they be, from entering any more intimately into our soul than the sadness the comedians excite in her when they represent certain very lugubrious actions before us; but I admit it is necessary to be strongly philosophical to arrive at this point. And nevertheless I also believe that even those who most allow themselves to give way to their passions always inwardly judge there are more goods than evils in this life, although they do not perceive it themselves; for while they occasionally call upon death to assist them when they are in great pains, it is only so that it may help them bear their burden, as happens in the fable, and they do not on that account wish to lose their life; or rather, if there are some who wish to lose it, and who kill themselves, it is due to an error of their understanding—not to a well reasoned judgment nor to an opinion imprinted upon them by nature, such as that which makes one prefer the good of this life to its evils.

143 The reason that makes me believe that those who do nothing save for their own utility ought also, if they wish to be prudent, work, as do others, for the good of others, and try to please everyone as much as they can, is that one ordinarily sees it occur that those who are deemed obliging and prompt to please also receive a quantity of good deeds from others, even from people who have never been obliged to them; and these things they would not receive did people believe them of another humor; and the pains they take to please other people are not so great as the conveniences that the friendship of those who know them proves to be. For others expect of us only those .deeds we can render conveniently, nor do we expect more of them; but it often happens that deeds that cost others little profit us very much, and can even save our life. It is true that occasionally one wastes his toil in doing good and that, on the other hand, occasionally one gains in doing evil; but that cannot change the rule of prudence that relates only to things that happen most often. As for me, the maxim I have most often observed in all the conduct of my life has been to follow only the grand path, and to believe that the principle shrewdness is not to wish at all to use shrewdness. The common laws of society, which all tend to do each other mutual good, or at least not evil, are, it seems to me, so well established that whoever follows them frankly, without any dissimulation or artifice, leads a life very much more assured than those who seek their utility by other ways. It is true these other ways occasionally succeed for those who follow them, because of the ignorance of other men and the favor of fortune; but it happens much more often that such people go wrong and, thinking they are establishing themselves, they ruin themselves. It is with this truthfulness and candor, which I profess to observe in all my actions, that I also make especial profession of being, . . . etc.

CDXXXI.   Elisabeth to Descartes.

The Hague, 25 April 1646.

Monsieur Descartes,
144 The treaty my brother Philip concluded with the Republic of Venice has, ever since your departure, thrust upon me an occupation very much less agreeable than what

you had left for me. I had to busy myself regarding a matter that surpasses my knowledge, and to which I was summoned only to check the impatience of the young man to whom it was appealing. That prevented me up until now from taking advantage of the permission you gave me to tell you the obscurities my stupidity has made me find in your treatise concerning the passions; these obscurities are small in number, since one would have to be blind not to comprehend that the order, definition, and the distinctions you have given to the passions, and finally the entire moral part of the treatise, surpasses everything that has ever been said on this subject.

145 But the physical part is not so clear to the ignorant; and I do not see how one can know the different movements of the blood that cause the five primitive passions, since these passions never exist alone. For example, love is always accompanied by desire and joy, or by desire and sadness, and to the extent that love strengthens, the others grow as well . . . . * on the contrary. How is it possible then to detect the difference of the beat of the pulse, of the digestion of vittles, and of other changes of the body that serve to uncover the nature of these movements? Also, what you indicated as in each of these passions is not the same in all temperaments: and my temperament makes sadness always bring an appetite upon me, even though the sadness is not mixed with any hate—for example, when it issues just from the death of a friend.

146 When you speak of the exterior signs of these passions, you say admiration joined to joy makes the lungs inflate in a discontinuous manner so as to cause laughter. I ask you to add something about the manner in which admiration (which, according to your description, seems to operate only on the brain) can so promptly open the orifices of the heart so as to produce this effect.

147 Those passions you note as the cause of sighs do not

---

* Gap in ms.

seem always to be their cause, since custom as well as a full stomach can also cause them.

148   But I find still less difficulty in understanding everything you say about the passions than in practicing the remedies you order against their excesses. For how is one to forsee all the accidents that can happen in life—accidents it is impossible to enumerate? And how can we prevent ourselves from ardently desiring things that necessarily tend to the conservation of man (like health and the means to live), which nevertheless do not depend upon man's decision? As for knowledge of the truth, the desire for it is so just that it exists naturally in all men; but it would be necessary to have an infinite knowledge to know the just value of the goods and evils that customarily rouse us, since there are very many more of them than a single person should be able to imagine, and because, to imagine them, one would have to know perfectly everything that exists in the world.

149   Since you have already said what are the principles as regards private life, I would be satisfied to know further your maxims regarding civil life; I ask this of you even though civil life makes us dependent upon persons who are so little reasonable that until now I have always found myself doing better by using experience rather than reason in such matters.

150   I have been so often interrupted in writing to you that I am forced to send you my rough draft and to make use of the messenger of Alkmaar, because I have forgotten the name of the friend to whom you wished that I address my letters; for that reason I do not dare send you back your treatise until I know his name; for I cannot allow myself to risk in the hands of a drunkard so valuable a piece that has given so much satisfaction to . . . etc.

CDXXXII.   Descartes to Elisabeth.

May 1646

Madame,

151 I recognized from experience that I have been right in placing glory among the number of the passions; for I cannot prevent myself from being moved when I see the favorable judgment your Highness has made of the small treatise I have written about them. And I am not at all surprised that she also notes defects in it, because I did not doubt it had a great number of them, since the subject matter is one I have never previously studied, and one about which I drew only the outlines, without adding the colors and ornaments that would be required to make it show forth to eyes less clairvoyant than those of your Highness.

152 I also did not put down all the principles of physics I used to decipher the movements of the blood accompanying each passion, because I could not deduce them accurately without explaining the conformity of all the parts of the human body; and that is something so difficult that I would still not dare to undertake it, although I am nearly satisfied myself as regards the truth of the principles I have supposed in this treatise. The principles are: that the office of the liver and spleen is always to contain blood in reserve less purified than that in the veins; and that the fire in the heart requires continual sustenance, either by means of the juice of vittles that comes directly from the stomach, or else, when that is lacking, by this blood that is in reserve, because the other blood in the veins dilates too easily; and that there is such a connection between our soul and body that the thoughts that have accompanied certain movements of the body from the beginning of our life still accompany them at present in such a way that if the same movements are excited again in the body by some exterior cause, they also excite in the soul the same thoughts, and, reciprocally, if we have the same thoughts, they produce the same movements; and, finally, that the machine of our body is so made that a single thought of joy, or of love, or another similar thought, is sufficient to send the animal spirits through the nerves into all the muscles required to cause the different movements of the blood that I said accompany the passions. It is true I have had difficulty in distinguishing those movements pertaining to each passion, because these passions never exist alone; but nevertheless, because the same passions are not always joined together, I have tried to note the changes that would happen in the body when they changed in relation to each other. Thus, for example, were love always joined to joy, I would not know to which of these two it would be necessary to attribute the heat and dilation they make one feel around the heart; but, because love is also sometimes joined to sadness, and because one then still feels this warmth but no longer this dilation, I judged that the heat pertains to love and the dilation to joy. And although desire is nearly always together with love, nevertheless they are not always together to the same degree: for, although one loves very much, one desires little when one conceives no hope; and because one does not then have the diligence and alertness one would have were the desire greater, one can judge that the desire causes this and not the love.

153 I indeed believe that sadness destroys the appetite of very many people; but since I have always found in myself that it augments it, I myself was the example as far as that question is concerned. And I consider that the difference which exists in this matter derives from the fact that the first subject of sadness that certain people have had at the beginning of their life has been that they did not receive enough nourishment, and for others, that the nourishment they received was harmful to them. And in these latter the movement of the spirits that destroys the appetite is ever since joined with the passion of sadness. We also see that

the movements accompanying the other passions are not entirely similar in all men, and that too can be attributed to a like cause.

154 As for admiration, it has its origin in the brain; and the mere temperament of the blood can cause it, as it can often cause joy or sadness; but nevertheless, admiration, by means of the impression it makes in the brain, can act upon the body as much as any other passion, or even more in some fashion, because the surprise it contains causes the most prompt movements of all. And as one can move the hand or foot at nearly the same instant one thinks of moving them, because the idea of this movement which forms in the brain sends the spirits into the muscles serving for this effect, so too the idea of a pleasant thing overcoming the mind will immediately send the spirits into the nerves that open the orifices of the heart; and admiration does nothing else in this regard except that, by its surprise, it augments the force of the movement that causes joy and brings it about that the orifices of the heart, being suddenly dilated, the blood that enters within it by the *vena cava* and leaves by the arterial vein suddenly inflates the lungs.

155 The same exterior signs that customarily accompany the passions can indeed also sometimes be produced by other causes. Thus redness of the face does not always come from shame; but it can also come from the heat of fire or else from exercise. And the grin called sardonic is nothing but a convulsion of the nerves of the face. And so too one can sigh sometimes from custom, or from sickness, but that does not prevent sighs from being exterior signs of sadness or desire when it is these passions that cause them. I have never heard nor remarked that sighs might also be occasionally caused by a full stomach. But when that happens, I believe it is a movement that nature uses to make the juice of the vittles pass more promptly to the heart and thus to discharge the stomach of it sooner: for the sighs, by agitating the lungs, make the blood contained in them descend more quickly by the venal artery into the left side of the heart; and that makes the new blood—composed from the juice of the vittles that comes from the stomach by the liver and heart into the lung—more easily received by the lung.

156 As for the remedies against the excess of the passions, I admit they are difficult to practice, and even that they cannot suffice to prevent the disorders that arrive in the body, but only to make the soul untroubled and to enable her to retain her free judgment. Nor do I judge that this requires an exact knowledge about the truth of each thing, nor even that one have forseen in particular all the accidents that can befall one, for undoubtedly that would be impossible; but it is enough to have imagined in general the most annoying accidents, and to be prepared to suffer them. I also believe one could scarcely sin by excess in desiring things necessary for life; it is only desires for bad or superfluous things that need to be regulated. For those desires that tend only to good are, it seems to me, so much the better the greater they are; and although I have wished to flatter my faults by placing a sort of languor among the excusable passions, I nevertheless value very much more the diligence of those who always bear themselves with ardor to do the things they believe in some way their obligation, even though they do not anticipate much fruit.

157 My life is one of such retirement, and I have always been so separated from the management of affairs, that I would be no less impertinent than that philosopher who wished to teach the obligation of a captain in the presence of Hannibal, were I to undertake to write the maxims one ought to observe in civil life. And I have no doubt that what your Highness proposes is the best of all, namely, that it is better to regulate herself in that matter by experience rather than reason, because one rarely deals with persons so perfectly reasonable as all men ought to be that one could judge what they will do by merely considering what they

should do; and often the best advice is not the happiest. That is why one is constrained to risk and to place oneself in the power of fortune; and fortune, I hope, is as obedient to your desires as am I, . . . etc.

CDXXXIV.   Descartes to Elisabeth.

Egmond, May 1646.

Madame,

158 The opportunity to give this letter to my very-intimate friend, M. de Beclin, whom I trust as much as myself, is my reason for taking the liberty to confess herein a very conspicuous fault I committed in the treatise on the passions. For, in order to flatter my negligence, I included in the enumeration of the excusable emotions of the soul a sort of languor that occasionally prevents us from putting into execution things already approved by our judgment. And what has most caused me scruples about this is that I remember your Highness has particularly referred to that place as evidence that I do not disapprove practice in a subject where I do not see it will be useful. I indeed admit that one has great reason to take time to deliberate before undertaking things of importance; but once an affair is begun and one is settled on the principle, I do not see that one reaps any profit in seeking delays and disputing about conditions. For, if the affair succeeds despite all that, all the small advantages one might have acquired by this means are of no avail in so far as the unpleasantness ordinarily caused by these delays is thereby prolonged; if the affair does not succeed that procrastination would only serve to make known to everyone that one had defective plans. Besides, it very often happens that when the design one undertakes is very good, if one delays its execution the affair escapes one, whereas that does not happen when the affair in question is bad. That is why I am persuaded that resolution and alertness are very necessary virtues for designs already begun. And one has no subject to fear that of which one is ignorant; for often things about which one has most apprehension before knowing them are found to be better than those one desired. So the best thing to do as regards such matters is to trust to divine providence and allow oneself to be led by it. I am assured your Highness very well understands my thoughts, although I explain them very badly, and I am assured she pardons the extreme concern that obliges me to write this; for I am, as much as I can be, . . . etc.

CDXXXIX.   Descartes to Chanut.

Egmond, 15 June 1646.

Monsieur,
  159 I have been very pleased to see, from the letters with which you honored me, that Sweden is not so far from here that one cannot receive news in a few weeks, and thus that I shall occasionally be able to have the good fortune to discuss matters with you in writing, and to participate in the fruits of the study for which I see you prepared. For since it pleases you to take the pains to review my *Principles* and examine them, I am assured you will notice in them many obscurities and faults that I ought very much to know, and of which I cannot hope to be made aware by anyone so well as by you. I fear only that you may very soon lose a taste for this reading inasmuch as what I have written leads but by a very long path to morals, which you have chosen as your principal study.

[185]

160   It is not that I am not entirely of your opinion when you judge that the most assured means for knowing how we ought to live is to know, beforehand, what we are, what the world in which we live, and who the Creator of this world, or the master of the house we inhabit. But besides the fact that I neither pretend nor promise, in any fashion, that everything I have written is true, there is a very great gap between the general notion of heaven and earth that I have tried to give in my *Principles,* and the specific knowledge that deals with the nature of man, of which I have not as yet treated. Nevertheless, so that it does not seem I wish to turn you away from your design, I will say to you, in confidence, that such notion of physics as I have tried to acquire has greatly served me in establishing certain foundations in morals; and that on this point I am more easily satisfied than on many others bearing upon medicine even though I have employed very much more time at them. For, in place of discovering the means for conserving life, I have found another, very much easier and more certain, which is not to fear death; without, however, being on that account chagrined, as ordinarily are they whose wisdom is completely taken from the teachings of others and rests upon foundations depending only on the prudence and authority of men.

161   I will further say to you that, while I allow the plants in my garden to grow, from which I await certain experiments in order to try to advance my physics, I stop myself also from time to time to think of particular questions in morals. And thus I have sketched this winter a small treatise on the passions of the soul, without, however, having the intention of publishing it, and I would now be in a humor to write still something further except that I am made negligent by my dismay at seeing how few people there are in the world who deign to read my writing. But negligent I shall never be in whatever has reference to your service: for I am with heart and affection, . . . etc.

[186]

CDXLV.   Descartes to Elisabeth.

Egmond, September 1646.

Madame,

162 I have read the book about which your Highness
commanded me to write her my opinion, and I find very
many precepts that seem very good; as, among others, those
in chapters 19 and 20: *That a Prince ought always avoid the
hate and contempt of his subjects and that the people's
love is worth more than fortresses.* But there are many
other things I could not approve. And I believe the author
most lacking in that he has not made a great enough distinction between princes who have acquired a state by just
means and those who have usurped it by illegitimate
means; and also in that he has given to all princes generally
precepts proper only to the last sort. For, as in building a
house whose foundations are so bad that they could not
sustain high and thick walls, one is then obliged to make
the walls weak and low, so too, those who have begun to
establish themselves by crimes are ordinarily constrained
to continue to commit them and could not maintain themselves if they wished to be virtuous.

163 It is as regards such Princes that he could say in
chapter three: *That they could not fail of being hated by
very many; and they often have more advantage in doing
very much evil than in doing less, because the lightest of-
fenses suffice to instill the will to revenge but the greatest
take away the power.* Then in chapter 15: *That if they
wished to be good men themselves, it would be impossible
for them not to ruin themselves among the great number of
evil men one finds everywhere.* And in 19: *That one can be
hated for good as well as for bad actions.*

164 On these foundations he supports very tyrannical
precepts, as when he wishes *that one ruin an entire country in order to remain its master; that one exercise great*

cruelties, provided one does so promptly and all at the same time; that one try to appear a good man but not be truly so; that one keep his word only as long as it will be useful; that one dissimulate; that one betray; and finally, that in order to reign, one rid oneself of all humanity and become the most ferocious of all the animals.

165 But it is a very bad subject for making books to undertake to lay down therein precepts such that, at the end of the tale, they provide no assurance to those to whom they are given; for as the author himself admits, the princes *cannot guard against the first person who would wish to neglect his own life in order to revenge himself upon them.* Whereas, to instruct a good prince, even if he be recently entered into the state, it seems to me one should propose to him maxims altogether contrary to these and suppose the means he used to establish himself have been just; as, in effect, I believe nearly all are when the princes who practice them deem them such: for justice among sovereigns has other limits than among private individuals, and it seems that in these confrontations God gives the right to whom he gives the force. But the most just actions become unjust when those who do them think them such.

166 One ought also distinguish between subjects, friends or allies, and enemies. For as regards the latter, one has permission to do nearly everything, provided one extracts some advantage for oneself or one's subjects; and I do not disapprove that on this occasion one join fox and lion and artifice to force. Moreover, I comprise under the name of enemies all those who are not friends or allies, because one has the right to make war upon them when one finds one's advantage lies there; and one has this right when, because they begin to become suspect and fearsome, there is reason to mistrust them. But I do exclude one sort of deception so directly contrary to society that I believe one is never permitted to use it, although our author approves of it in different places but thinks it too difficult to practice: that is to feign friendship to those one wishes to ruin in order to surprise them the better. Friendship is too sacred a thing to be abused in this way; and he who could feign to befriend someone in order to betray him deserves that those whom he would afterward truly wish to befriend not believe him at all and hate him.

167 As for what regards allies, a prince should exactly keep his word to them, even when that is detrimental to himself: for this detriment cannot be as great as the utility of his reputation for being one who fails not to do what he promises; and he can only acquire this reputation on such occasions where there exists some loss for himself; however, on those that would ruin him completely, the right of nations dispenses him from his promise. He ought also use very much circumspection before promising in order always to be able to keep his word. And, although it is good to have a friendship with the greater part of his neighbors, I nevertheless believe the best thing is not to have strict alliances except with those less powerful. For whatever trustworthiness one proposes to display toward others, one should not expect the same from them; rather, one should make it one's belief that one will be deceived by them every time they shall find it to their advantage; and the more, not the less, powerful will find themselves able to extract such an advantage.

168 As regards subjects, there are two sorts: namely, the great and the people. I comprise under the name "great" all those who can form parties against the prince; and the prince should be very assured of their fidelity, or, if he is not so assured, all statesmen are agreed he should weaken them, and, insofar as they are inclined to upset the state, should consider them only as enemies. But, as regards his other subjects, he ought above all avoid their hate and disdain; and that I believe he can always do, provided he exactly observes their kind of justice (that is to say, if he follows the laws to which they are accustomed) without being too rigorous about punishments, or too indulgent about dispensations, and provided he does not refer all these things to his ministers, but rather, leaving them in charge only of the most odious condemnations, shows that he himself has care for all the rest; and provided also he so retains his dignity that he abstains from none of the honors and deferences the people believe due to him, but yet never demands more, and never makes public show except of his most serious actions or those that can be approved by all, reserving his own pleasures to be taken privately without it ever being at anyone's expense; and provided, finally, he is unchangeable and inflexible, not regarding the first plans that shall have been formed by himself—for inasmuch as he cannot have an eye everywhere, he must seek advice and listen to the reasons of many before making a decision—but regarding the things about which he shall have testified he has made a resolution, even though they be harmful to himself; for, as uncomfortable as they can be, so much also would be the reputation for being weak and fickle.

169 Thus I disapprove the maxim of chapter 15: *That the world being very corrupted, it is impossible to avoid ruining oneself if one wishes to be a good man, and that to maintain himself a prince must learn to be wicked when the occasion requires*—unless perhaps by a good man he means one superstitious and simple, who dares not do battle on the sabbath, and whose conscience cannot rest until he changes the religion of his people. But thinking of a good man as one who does everything true reason dictates to him, it is certain that the best thing is to try always to be good.

170 I also do not believe what is said in chapter 19: *That one can be as much hated for good as for bad actions,* except inasmuch as envy is a species of hate: but that is not the sense of the author. Nor are princes customarily envied by common subjects; they are envied only by the great or by neighboring princes; and the same virtues that give neighboring princes an envy of some prince also give them a fear of him; that is why a prince should never abstain from doing good in order to avoid this sort of hate; and there is nothing that can harm princes but what derives from the injustice or arrogance the people judge to be in them. For one sees that even those who have been condemned to death do not customarily hate their judges when they think they have merited it; and one also suffers with patience the evils one has not merited when one believes the prince from whom one receives them is in some manner constrained to dispense them and is displeased by the fact; for it is considered just that the prince prefer the public utility to that of a private person. There is difficulty only when the prince is obliged to satisfy two factions who judge differently about what is just, as when the Roman emperors had to satisfy citizens and soldiers: in such a case it is reasonable to accord something to each, and one ought not undertake suddenly to make reasonable those unaccustomed to listen to reason; instead, it is necessary to try, little by little, be it by public writing, by the voices of the preachers, by other such means, to bring them to one's point of view. For, in short, the people suffer everything one can persuade them to be just, and take offence at everything they imagine unjust; and the arrogance of princes—that is to say, the usurpation of some authority, rights, or honors the people do not believe due to them—is odious to the people only because they consider it a species of injustice.

171   Furthermore, I am also not of the opinion of this author in what he says in his preface: *That as it is necessary to be in the plain to see better the figure of the mountains when one wishes to draw them, so too one must be in the condition of private person to know better the office of prince.* Now a drawing represents things only as seen from afar; but the principal motives of the actions of princes are often circumstances so particular that, unless one is a prince oneself, or else has for a very long time been participant in the secrets of princes, one could not imagine them.

172   That is why I should deserve to be mocked did I think myself able to teach anything about this matter to your

Highness; moreover, such is not my design; I wish only to make my letters provide her some sort of diversion different from those I imagine she derives from her journey, which I hope is perfectly comfortable: as undoubtedly it will be if your Highness resolves to practice those maxims which teach that the happiness of each person depends upon himself, and that it is necessary so to raise oneself above the empire of fortune that, without forfeiting occasions to hold on to the advantages fortune bestows, one nevertheless does not think oneself unhappy when they are refused; and that she consider that, because in all affairs there are a quantity of reasons *pro* and *contra,* one should stop principally to consider those reasons serving to make one approve the things one sees happen. What I deem most inevitable are sicknesses of the body, from which I pray God preserve you, and I am with all the devotion I can have, . . . etc.

CDL.   Elisabeth to Descartes.

Berlin, 10 October 1646.

Monsieur Descartes,

173 You are correct to believe that the diversion your letters afford me differs from that which I received from my journey, since they provide me a satisfaction that is greater and more durable. Although I found in journeying everything the intimacy and caresses of my relatives can give, I consider them as things that could change, whereas the truths your letters teach me leave impressions in my mind that will always contribute to the contentment of my life.

174 I have a thousand regrets for not having brought by land the book you have taken the trouble to examine in order to inform me of your opinion. For I allowed myself to be persuaded that the baggage I sent by sea to Hamburg would reach here sooner than us; but it has not yet arrived although we got there 7/17 September past. That is why I can represent the maxims of this author only insofar as a very bad memory assists me concerning a book that I have not looked at for six years. But I remember approving certain of its maxims then, not as being good in themselves, but because they cause less evil than those used by a quantity, of imprudent ambitious persons whom I knew; for such people tend only to stir things up and to leave the rest to fortune, whereas the maxims of this author all tend to the maintenance of things.

175 It also seems to me that to instruct in the governing of a state, he chooses to consider the one most difficult to govern, where the prince is a new usurper, at least in the opinion of the people; and in this case the opinion the prince himself shall have of the justice of his cause would be capable of serving for the repose of his conscience, but not for the tranquility of his affairs, when either the laws are opposed to his authority, or the great countermine his opinion, or the people condemn it. And when the state is thus disposed, large violences are less evil than small ones, because the small do damage as well as the large, and give a subject for a long war; but the large take away the courage for this, as well as the means by which the great will be able to undertake such a war. In the same way, when violences come promptly and all at once, they annoy less than they astonish, and they are also more supportable by the people than is the long series of miseries that civil wars bring.

176 It seems to me he further adds, or else teaches, by the example of the nephew of Pope Alexander, whom he holds up as a perfect politician, that the prince ought to employ for these great cruelties some minister whom he can afterward sacrifice to the hate of the people; and although it seems unjust for the prince to cause a man to perish who would have obeyed him, I find that persons so barbaric and unnatural as would wish to employ themselves as executioners of all the people for whatever consideration it be do not merit better treatment. As for myself, I should prefer the condition of the most poor peasant in Holland to either that of the minister who wished to obey such orders or the prince who is constrained to issue them.

177 When the same author speaks of allies, he likewise supposes them as wicked as can be, and that affairs are in such extreme condition that it is necessary to lose an entire republic or break his word to those who keep theirs only as long as it is useful to them.

178 However, if the author is wrong to erect general maxims on the basis of what one ought to practice on very few occasions, it is also true that he shares this sin equally with nearly all the holy fathers and ancient philosphers who do the same; and I believe this derives from their pleasure in uttering paradoxes that they can afterward explain to their pupils. When this man here says that one ruins oneself if one always wishes to be a good man, I believe he does not mean that to be a good man it is necessary to follow the laws of superstition, but to follow that common law requiring one to do to each person as one would wish done to oneself: something princes could hardly ever say to anyone of their subjects—namely, that he must lose each time the public utility so demands. And since, before you, nobody has said virtue consists only in following right reason, but have rather prescribed certain laws or more particular rules, one should not be astonished that they have failed to define virtue well.

179 I find the rule you note in his preface false, because he had not known someone, such as you, clairvoyant in all he proposes—someone who, though private and retired from the confusion of the world, would, as your writings about it show, nevertheless be capable of teaching princes how they must govern.

180 For myself, who has but the title, I study only to make use of the rule you place at the end of your letter; and that I do by trying to make my present circumstances as agreeable as I can. Here I do not encounter many difficulties, since I am in a household where I have been cherished since my childhood and where everyone vies to embrace me. And even though they sometimes divert me from more useful occupations, I bear this inconvenience easily, because of the pleasure involved in being loved by one's kin. And that, Monsieur, is the reason why I did not sooner have the leisure to inform you not only of the happy success of our journey, and how it has passed without any inconvenience and with the celerity of which I spoke above, but also of the miraculous fountain about which you spoke to me at The Hague.

181 I was only a little mile away from it, at Cheuningen, where we met with all the family who had just come from there. Monsieur the Elector wanted to take me to see it; but since the rest of our company decided on a different diversion, I did not dare contradict them and satisfied myself with seeing and tasting the water, of which there are different sources with different tastes; however, one principally uses only two, the first of which is clear, salty, and a strong purgative; the other is a bit more white, tastes like water mixed with milk, and is, according to everyone, refreshing. There is talk of the quantity of miraculous cures these waters effect; but I have been unable to learn of these from anyone worthy of trust. They are right in saying this place is filled with poor people who testify they have been born deaf, blind, lame, or hunchbacked, and have found their cure in this fountain. But since these are mercenary people and encounter a nation sufficiently credulous in regard to miracles, I do not believe reasonable people ought to be persuaded by that. In all the court of Monsieur the Elector my cousin only his grand equerry has found himself made well by the fountain. He had had a wound under the right eye of which he had lost the sight from one side due to a small skin that came over the eye; and the salt water of the fountain, being applied to the eye, dissipated that same skin so that he can, at this time, discern persons when he closes his left eye. Besides, since he is a man of strong constitution and bad diet, a good purge could not harm him as it did very many others.

182 I have examined the notation you sent me and found it very good, but too prolix for writing an entire message; and if one wrote only a few words, one would find them out by the quantity of letters. It would be better to make a key to the words by the alphabet, and then to mark some distinction between the numbers signifying letters and those signifying words.

183 I have here so little leisure for writing that I am constrained to send you this rough draft wherein you can note with each difference of pen the number of times I have been interrupted. But I more prefer to appear before you with all my faults than to give you any reason to believe that I have a vice so alien to my nature as to forget friends in their absence, principally a person, such as you Monsieur, for whom I could not cease to feel affection without also ceasing to be reasonable, and to whom I shall be all my life, . . . etc.

CDLII.   Descartes to Elisabeth.

November 1646.

Madame,

184 I have received a very great favor from your Highness in that she has wished to inform me by her letters of the success of her voyage and of her having happily arrived in a place where, being greatly esteemed and cherished by her kin, it seems to me she has as much good as one can reasonably want in this life. For knowing the condition of human things, it would be excessive to expect from fortune graces so abundant that one could find no subject for annoyance, even in one's imagination. When there are present no objects to offend the senses, nor any indisposition of the body to disturb it, a mind that follows true reason can easily be satisfied. And there is no need on that account that it forget or neglect things from which it is removed; it is enough to try to have no passion as regards those things that can displease: nor does this contradict charity, because often one can more easily find remedies for evils that one examines without passion than for those with which one is afflicted. But as the health of the body and the presence of agreeable objects very much aid the mind to rid itself of all the passions that participate in sadness and to give entrance to those that participate in joy, so too, in a reciprocal manner, when the mind is full of joy, that serves very much to make the body bear up the better and to make present objects seem more agreeable.

185 And I also even dare believe that interior joy has some secret force to render fortune more favorable. I would not wish to write this to persons of weak mind for fear of inducing them into some superstition; but, as regards your Highness, I fear only she might laugh at seeing me become too credulous. Nevertheless, I have an infinity of experiences, and with that the authority of Socrates, to confirm my opinion. For I have often noted that things I have done with a gay heart, and without any interior repugnance, ordinarily succeed happily for me, even to the point that in games of chance, where nothing but fortune alone reigns, I have always found it more favorable when I had in addition reasons for joy rather than subjects of sadness. And what one commonly calls the genius of Socrates was doubtlessly nothing but the fact that he was accustomed to follow his interior inclination, thinking the outcome of whatever he undertook would be happy when he had some secret feeling of gayety, and, on the contrary, unhappy, when he was sad. It is true, however, that one would be superstitious to believe so strongly in this as it is said Socrates did; for Plato tells us he remained in residence every time his genius counselled him not to go out. But, regarding the important actions of life, when we meet with circumstances so doubtful that prudence cannot teach us what we ought to do, it seems to me one has great reason to follow the advice of one's genius, and that it is useful to have a strong persuasion that the things we undertake without repugnance, and with the liberty that ordinarily accompanies joy, will not fail to succeed well for us.

186 Thus, I dare here to exhort your Highness, since she finds herself in a place where the present objects give her nothing but satisfaction, that she herself please coöperate with this in order to render herself content; and it seems to me she can easily do that by fixing her mind on present things and by never thinking of affairs save at times when the courier is about to leave. And I consider it fortunate that your Highness' books could not be brought to her so readily as she wished; for reading is not so fit to sustain gayety as to make sadness ensure, and principally reading such as the book of that doctor to princes, who, in repeating only the difficulties they have in maintaining themselves, and the cruelties or perfidies to which he counsels them, makes individual princes who read the book have less reason for envying than lamenting their condition.

187 Your Highness has perfectly well remarked his faults and mine; for it is true that his design to please Caesar Borgia made him establish general maxims to justify particular actions that can be difficult to excuse; and I have since read his discourse on Titus-Livy where I remarked nothing bad. And his principal precept, which is to extirpate entirely one's enemies, or else to render them one's friends, without ever following the middle way, is without doubt always the most sure; but when one has no reason for fear, it is not the most generous precept.

188 Your Highness has also very well noted the secret of the miraculous fountain—for there are very many poor people who publicize its virtues and who perhaps are hired by those who have hope of profit. For surely there is no remedy that can serve for all evils; yet very many people having used the waters, those who find themselves well speak well of them, whereas there is no talk of the others. However that may be, the purgative quality in one of these fountains, and the white color with the sweetness and refreshing quality in the other, give reason to judge they pass through mines of anitmony or mercury, which are two bad drugs, principally mercury. That is why I would not counsel anyone to drink them. The vitriol and the iron of the waters of the Spa are much less to fear; and because both diminish the spleen and make it eject melancholy, I think both worthwhile.

189 Your Highness will permit me, if it pleases her, to finish this letter where I began, and to wish for her principally satisfaction of mind, and joy, as being not only the fruit one awaits from other goods, but also just as often a means of augmenting the benefits one can receive from them. And although I am not capable of contributing to anything that has reference to your service, except only by my wishes, I still dare to give the assurance that I am more perfectly than anyone else in the world, . . . etc.

Addenda, excerpt from

CDLXI.   Elisabeth to Descartes.

Berlin, 29 November 1646.

190 I also hope never to be put in the circumstance of following precepts of the doctor to princes, since violence and suspicion are things contrary to my nature. However, I blame tyrants only for the first design of usurping a country and for the first attempt—for afterwards the way that serves to establish them, however harsh it be, always does less evil to the public than does a sovereignty contested by arms.

CDLXII.   Chanut to Descartes.

Stockholm, 1 December 1646.

191 M. de la Thuillerie did not deceive you in telling you wonders about our Queen of Sweden. In all truth, you would be astonished at the force of her mind. As for the conduct of her affairs, not only does she understand them, but she robustly carries their weight, and carries it nearly alone. Whereas in many other courts one speaks on affairs only with ministers, here we report only to the Queen and receive responses from her mouth. And in that she is so adroit that her age and small experience provide no advantage to those who speak with her, her judgment supplying in affairs everything she lacks by way of practice.

192 But I do not wish to speak of her now save to say she knows you in such wise as all the world ought to know you, and that, having a disposition marvellously detached from servitude toward popular opinions, she would understand as easily as anyone all your principles if the burden of governing a large state left her enough time to devote to these meditations. In the moments she can salvage from caring after public affairs, and frequently when the audiences she has granted me in regard to the affairs of the realm are over, she diverts herself in conversations that would pass as very serious among the learned; and I assure you it is necessary to speak in front of her with great circumspection.

193 The last time I had the honor of seeing her, matters brought her to fall upon a question concerning which she obliged me to speak my sentiment. The question was to know, when one makes ill-use of love or hate, which of these two disorders or ill-uses was worse. The term love was meant in the sense of the philosophers, not as it so frequently rings to the ears of girls, and the question was general. In that encounter I dared to take the side contrary to her thinking, and this debate made her say many things of great wisdom, subtly reasoned. Since I am not allowed to tell you our opinions, if only you will assume the risk of condemning a queen by giving your own judgment, I will then tell you what remains, and how she sustained her view. I await the copy of your French *Meditations* to present them to her; and if, in the question I propose to you, your sentiment favors her thinking, I will take the opportunity to admit to her I was mistaken and that you have confirmed her opinion. . . . etc.

CDLXVIII.   Descartes to Chanut.

Egmond, 1 February 1647.

Monsieur,

194 The obliging letter I received from you does not allow me to rest until I have responded; and although you therein propose questions that those more knowledgeable than I would find difficult to examine in a short time, nevertheless, since I know well that were I to employ even much time at them, I could not entirely resolve them, I prefer to place promptly on paper whatever the devotion driving me shall dictate rather than delay and write nothing better thereafter.

195 You wish to know my opinion regarding three things: 1. *What love is.* 2. *If the natural light alone teaches us to love God.* 3. *Which is worse if disordered and misused, love or hate?*

196 To respond to the first point, I distinguish between love that is purely intellectual or reasonable, and love that is a passion. The first, it seems to me, consists only in the fact that when our soul perceives some good, present or absent, which she judges suitable to herself, she joins herself willingly to it, that is to say, she considers herself, together with this good, as a whole, of which it is one part and she the other. In consequence of which, if it is present, that is to say, if she possesses it—either because she is possessed by it or finally because she is joined to it not only by her will but also really and in fact, in the manner it suits her to be joined to it—the movement of her will accompanying the knowledge that what she thus possesses is a good for her, is her joy; and if it is absent, the movement of her will accompanying the knowledge that she has been deprived of it constitutes her sorrow; but that movement which accompanies her knowledge that she possesses what it would be good to acquire is her desire. And all these movements of the will in which love consists—joy, sorrow, and desire—inasmuch as they are reasonable thoughts and not passions, could find themselves in our soul even though she did not possess a body. Thus, for example, if she perceived that there are very many very beautiful things to know in nature, her will would carry her infallibly to love the knowledge of these things, that is to say, to consider such knowledge as pertaining to her. And if with that she remarked she possessed such knowledge, she would receive joy from it; should she conclude she did not possess it, she would be sorrowful; if she thought it would be good for her to acquire it, she would be desirous of it. And in all these movements of her will there is nothing obscure to her, nor of which she had not a very perfect knowledge, provided she reflected upon her thoughts.

197 But while our soul is joined to the body, this rational love is ordinarily accompanied by the other, which one can call sensual or sensitive, and which, as I have summarily said of all the passions, appetites, and sentiments on page 461 of the French translation of my *Principles*, is nothing but a confused thought excited in the soul by some movement of the nerves that disposes her to this other, clearer, thought in which rational love consists. For, just as in thirst, the feeling of dryness of the throat is a confused thought that disposes one to the desire to drink, but is not that very desire; so also, in love one feels I know not what warmth around the heart, and a great abundance of blood in the lungs, that makes one even open one's arms as if to embrace something, and inclines the soul to join willingly to herself an object that presents itself. But the thought by which the soul feels this warmth is different from that which joins her to this object, and it even happens sometimes that this feeling of love is found in us without our will being inclined to love anything, because we meet with no object we deem worthy. It can, on the contrary, also happen that we know some very worthy good and willingly join ourselves to it, without on that account having any passion, our body not being disposed to such.

198 But ordinarily these two loves are found together; for there is such a connection between the one and the other that, when the soul judges an object as worthy of herself, that suddenly disposes the heart to movements exciting the passion of love, and when the heart finds itself thus disposed by other causes, that makes the soul imagine lovable qualities in objects in which she would at another time see only defects. And it is not astonishing that certain movements of the heart are so naturally joined to certain thoughts with which they have no resemblance; for, from the fact that our soul is of such nature that she could be united to a body, she also possesses this property, namely, that each of her thoughts can associate itself with certain movements or other dispositions of this body in such a way that when the same dispositions are found in it at another time, they induce the soul to the same thought; and reciprocally, when the same thought returns, it prepares the body to receive the same disposition. Thus, when one learns a language, one joins the letters or pronunciation of certain words, which are material things, to their significations, which are thoughts; accordingly, when one afterward hears the same words again, one conceives the same things; and when one conceives the same things, one recalls the same words.

199 But the first bodily dispositions that thus accompanied our thoughts when we entered the world ought undoubtedly have joined themselves more directly to them than those that accompany them afterward. And in order to examine the origin of the warmth one feels around the heart, and of other bodily dispositions accompanying love, I consider that, from the first moment our soul has been joined to the body, it is probable she felt joy, and suddenly afterward, love, and then perhaps also hate and sorrow, and that the same bodily dispositions that then caused these passions in our souls have naturally accompanied the thoughts of such passions afterward. I judge her first passion was joy—because it is unbelievable the soul was placed in the body except at a time when the body was well disposed, and that, when thus well disposed, this naturally gives us joy. I say also love came afterward, because, as the matter of our body flows incessantly, just like the water of a river, and as there is need for other matter to replace it, it is scarcely likely the body could have been well disposed had not there also been close to it some other matter very suitable to serve it as nourishment—new matter to which the soul willingly joined herself and for which she had love; and likewise if afterward it happened that this nourishment was wanting, the soul sorrowed after it. And if the other matter that came in its place was not suited to nourish the body, the soul had for it a hate.

200 Those are the four passions I believe were in us earliest, and the only ones we had prior to our birth; and I also believe that at that time they were merely feelings or very confused thoughts; because the soul was so attached to matter that she was as yet unable to devote her attention to anything save to receiving diverse impressions from it; and although, some years afterward, she began to have other joys and other loves than those that depend only on the good constitution and suitable nourishment of the body, nevertheless, whatever has been intellectual in her joys or loves has always been accompanied by the first feelings she had of them, as also even by the movements or natural functions that were then in the body: thus, inasmuch as love was caused before birth only by a suitable nourishment that, entering abundantly into the liver, heart, and lungs, excited in them more heat than ordinary, it comes about that this heat now always accompanies love, even though it comes from other very different causes. And if I did not fear to go on too long, I could show minutely that all the other dispositions of the body that have accompanied these four passions from the beginning of our life accompany them still. But I will say only that it is these confused sentiments of our childhood, which, remaining joined with the rational thoughts by which we love whatever we deem worthy, that explain why the nature of love is difficult for us to know. To which I add that several passions, such as joy, sorrow, desire, fear, hope, etc., mixing themselves diversely with love, prevent one from recognizing in what it properly consists. And this should principally be noted in the case of desire; for it is so ordinarily taken for love, that such is the reason why two sorts of love are then distinguished: one called the love of benevolence, in which this desire does not appear, and the other called concupiscence, which is only a very violent desire founded upon a love that is often weak.

201 But it would be necessary to write a large volume to treat all the things that pertain to this passion; and although its nature is to make one communicate the most one can, so that it incites me to try here to tell you more than I know about it, I nevertheless wish to restrain myself for fear the length of this letter may bore you. Thus I pass to your second question, namely, *whether the natural light alone teaches us to love God and whether one can love him by the force of this light.* I see there are two strong reasons for doubting it: first, the attributes of God most ordinarily considered are so far elevated above us that we can in no way conceive they can be suitable for us—which is the reason we do not willingly join ourselves to them; second, there is nothing in God we are able to imagine, and thus, while one would have for him some intellectual love, it seems one cannot have any sensitive love for him, because that would

have to pass through the imagination to come from the understanding into the senses. That is why I am not astonished if certain philosophers persuade themselves that only the Christian religion, in teaching us the mystery of the Incarnation, by which God is humbled to the point of rendering himself similar to us, makes us capable of loving him; and moreover, that those who have not known this mystery, but yet have seemed to have a passion for some divinity, did not, for all that, have a passion for the true God, but only for certain idols which they have called by his name—just as Ixion, according to the poets, embraced a cloud in place of the Queen of the Gods. Nevertheless, I do not doubt that we can truly love God by the sole force of our nature. I do not assert that this love is meritorious without grace—I leave it to the theologians to disentangle that matter. But I venture to say that in regard to this life, it is the most ravishing and most useful passion we can have—and even that it can be the strongest, although that requires a very attentive meditation because we are continually diverted by the presence of other objects.

202 But, now, here is the path I deem one ought to follow to arrive at the love of God: one must consider God a mind, or a thing that thinks; so that the nature of our mind, having some resemblance to his, we come to persuade ourselves it is an emanation of the sovereign intelligence & *divinae quasi particula aurae.** Indeed, because our knowledge seems able to grow by degrees to infinity, and God's knowledge, being infinite, already is at the point where ours aims, if we neglect to consider anything else, we can fall into the extravagance of wishing to be gods, and thus, by a very great error, to love only divinity in place of loving God. But if, in addition, we heed the infinity of his power, through which he has created so many things, of which we are the least part; the extension of his providence,

---

*and, as it were, a particle of the divine gold (Horace, *Satires*, 11, 2, 79)

that makes him see in one thought alone everything that has been, is, shall be, and could be; the infallability of his decrees, which, although they do not disturb our free will, nevertheless cannot in any fashion be changed; and finally, if, on the one hand, we heed our insignificance, and if, on the other hand, we heed the grandeur of all created things, by noting the manner in which they depend on God and by considering them in a fashion that has a relationship to his omnipotence, without confining them in a globe, as do they who think the world finite: meditation upon all this so abundantly fills the man who hears it with such extreme joy that, realizing he would have to be abusive and ungrateful toward God to wish to occupy God's place, he thinks himself as already having sufficiently lived in that God has given him the grace to reach such knowledge; and willingly and entirely joining himself to God, he loves God so perfectly that he desires nothing more in the world than that God's will be done. That is the reason he no longer fears either death, or pains, or disgraces, because he knows that nothing can happen to him save what God shall have decreed; and he so loves this divine decree, esteems it so just and so necessary, knows he ought so entirely to depend upon it, that even when he awaits death or some other evil, if *per impossible* he could change that decree, he would not wish to do so. But if he does not refuse evils or afflictions, because they come to him from divine providence, he refuses still less all the goods or licit pleasures one can enjoy in this life, because they too issue from that providence; and accepting them with joy, without having any fear of evils, his love renders him perfectly happy.

203 Certainly, to represent the truths that excite this love in her, the soul must detach herself very much from dealings with the senses; from which it seems to follow she cannot communicate this love to the imaginative faculty so as to make a passion of it. But nonetheless I have no doubt she does communicate it. For although there is nothing in God, who is the object of our love, susceptible of being imagined, we can imagine our very love, which consists in the fact we wish to unite ourselves to a certain object, that is to say, as regards God, to consider ourselves as a very small part of the entire immensity of things he has created; because, according as the objects are diverse, one can unite oneself with them or join them to oneself in different ways; and the single idea of that union suffices to excite warmth around the heart and to cause a very strong passion.

204   It is also true that the custom of our language and good manners forbid us from saying, to those whose condition is very elevated beyond our own, that we love them—but only that we respect, honor, and esteem them, and possess ardor and devotion after their service. The reason for that, it seems to me, is because the friendship of man for man renders equal in some sense those among whom it is reciprocated; hence, in trying to make oneself beloved of some noble, if one told him one loved him, he could think he was being treated as an equal and slighted. But, since philosophers are not wont to give different names to things that conform to one and the same definition, and since I know no other definition of love save that it is a passion that makes us join willingly to some object, without distinguishing whether this object is equal, greater, or less than ourselves, it seems to me that, to speak their language, I ought to say one can love God.

205   And if I asked you, candidly, do you love this great Queen upon whom you now wait, it would be idle for you to protest you have for her only respect, veneration, and astonishment—for I should not hesitate to judge you have a very ardent affection as well. For the style flows so felicitously when you speak of her, that although I believe everything you say about her, because I know you are very truthful and I have also heard others speak of her, nevertheless I do not believe you could have described her as you have unless you felt a very great devotion, nor that you could have attended so great a light without receiving of its

warmth. And, far from it being that the love we have for objects above us is less than what we have for other objects, I believe that in its nature it is more perfect, and that it makes one embrace more ardently the interests of what one loves. For the nature of love is to make one consider oneself, together with the object loved, as a whole of which one is only a part, and to make one so transfer the cares one usually has for oneself to the conservation of this whole, that one retains for oneself in particular only such part of that care as is sufficiently great or small, in proportion to what one believes constitutes a great or small part of the whole to which one has given one's affection: thus, if one is willingly joined with an object that one esteems less than oneself, for example, if we love a flower, a bird, a building, or a similar thing, the highest perfection that this love can attain, if it is not distorted, cannot lead us to place our life in any danger for the conservation of such things, because they are not the noblest parts of the whole they compose with us any more than are fingernails and hair of our body; and it would be an extravagance to place the entire body in jeopardy for the conservation of the hair. But when two men love each other charity dictates each of them esteem his friend more than himself; that is why their friendship is not perfect, unless they are ready to say in favor of each other: *Meme adsum qui feci, in me convertite ferrum, &c.** In the same way, when an individual willingly joins himself to his prince or country, he ought, if his love is perfect, to deem himself only as a very small part of the whole he composes with them, and thus he should no more fear going to a very assured death for their service than he fears extracting a little blood from his arm in order that the rest of his body may fare the better. And everyday one sees examples of this love, even among people of low condition who gladly give their life for the good of their country, or to defend a noble

---

* *I am here who did the deed, turn your swords on me, etc.* (Virgil, *Aeneid*, IX, 427.)

whom they love. In consequence of which it is evident that our love for God ought to be without comparison the greatest and most perfect of all.

206 I have no fear that these metaphysical thoughts provide your mind with too much difficulty; for I know it is very capable of everything; but I admit they fatigue mine, and that the presence of sensible objects does not allow me to dwell upon them for a long time. That is why I pass to the third question, namely: *which of the two disorders is the worse, love or hate?* But I find myself more prevented from responding to it than to the two others, because you have less explained your intention in regard to it, and because this difficulty can be understood in different senses that seem to me should be examined separately. One can say that one passion is worse than another, because it renders us less virtuous; or because it more conflicts with our contentment; or finally, because it carries us to greater excesses and disposes us to do more evil to other men.

207 As for the first point, I find it doubtful. For in considering the definitions of these two passions, I judge that love for an object that does not merit it can render us worse than hate for another we ought to love—because there is more danger in being joined to a thing that is bad, and in being, as it were, transformed into it, than in being willingly separated from one that is good. Yet when I attend to the inclinations or habits born of these passions, I change my opinion: for, seeing that love, however disordered it be, has always good for its object, it does not seem to me it can so corrupt our mores as does the hate that proposes to itself only evil. And one sees by experience that most good people gradually become malicious when they are obliged to hate someone, for, even though their hate is just, they so often represent to themselves the evils they receive from their enemy, and likewise those they wish for him, that, little by little, it accustoms them to malice. On the contrary, those who give themselves to love, even though their love be disordered and frivolous, frequently do not fail to become more honest and more virtuous than if they occupied their mind at other thoughts.

208 As for the second point, I find no difficulty there: for hate is always accompanied by sorrow and chagrin; and whatever pleasure certain people take in doing evil to others, I believe it like that of demons who, according to our religion, do not cease to be damned even though they continually imagine they avenge themselves against God by tormenting men in hell. On the contrary, love, however disordered it be, provides pleasure, and although the poets often complain about it in their verses, I nevertheless believe that men would naturally abstain from loving unless they found it involved more sweetness than bitterness; and also, that all the afflictions whose cause one attributes to love come only from the other passions that accompany it—namely, from rash desires and ill-grounded hopes.

209 But if one asks which of these two passions carries us to the greater excess and renders us capable of doing more evil to the rest of men, it seems to me I ought to say it is love—for by nature love has very much more force and vigor than has hate, and frequently one's affection for an object of little importance causes incomparably more evils than could one's hate for something else of more value. I prove that hate has less vigor than love by reference to the origin of each. For if it is true that our first feelings of love came from the fact our heart received an abundance of nourishment suitable to it, and on the contrary, our first feelings of hate were caused by a harmful aliment that came to the heart; and if it is also true that even now the same movements still accompany the same passions, as has already been said; it is evident that, when we love, all the purest blood in our veins flows in abundance toward the heart, which sends a quantity of animal spirits to the brain, and thus provides us with more force, more vigor, and more courage; whereas, if we hate, the bitterness of the gall and sourness of the spleen, in mixing themselves with our blood, are the cause why neither so many nor such kind of spirits come to the brain, and why, consequently, one remains weaker, colder, and more timid. And experience confirms what I say; for the Hercules, the Rolands, and generally those who have the most courage, love more ardently than the others; and, on the contrary, those who are weak and cowardly are most inclined to hate. Anger can well render men bold, but it borrows its vigor from the love one has for oneself, which always serves it as a foundation, and not from the hate that only accompanies it. Despair also produces great feats of courage, and fear makes one inflict great cruelties; however, there is a difference between these passions and hate.

210 It still remains for me to prove that love for an object of little importance, when disordered, can cause more evil than does hate for something else of more value. And the reason I give for it is that the evil that comes from hate extends itself only to the object hated, whereas disordered love spares nothing, except its object, and this object is ordinarily of such small importance in comparison with everything else whose downfall and ruin such love is ready to procure that it will look upon them as fuel for the raging of its fury. Perhaps one will say hate is the most proximate cause of the evils one attributes to love, because, if we love something, we hate, by the same means, everything contrary to it. But love is always more culpable than hate as regards evils done in this manner because it is the foremost cause of them, inasmuch as the love for one object can give birth to a hatred of very many others. Then, beyond that, the greatest evils stemming from love are not those she commits in this fashion by means of hate; the principal, and most dangerous, are those she commits, or allows to be committed, for the sole pleasure of the object loved, or for her own self. I recall an outburst of Théophile that can be taken here as an example; he has a person distraught with love say:

Dieux, que le beau Paris eut une belle proye!
Que cet Amant fit bien,
Alors qu'il alluma l'embrazement de Troye,
Pour amortir le sien! *

Which shows that even the greatest and most lugubrious disasters can sometimes be, as I have said, fuel for a disordered love and serve to render it agreeable the more they enrich its price. I do not know if my thoughts harmonize in this with yours, but I certainly assure you of their accord on another score—that just as you have promised me very much good will, so likewise I remain, with a very ardent passion, . . . etc.

CDLXXIX.**   Chanut to Descartes.

Stockholm, 11 May 1647.

Monsieur,

211 You would have had a prompt response to the letter you did me the favor of writing on 1 February had it been as easy for me to well understand it as it was for you to write it. It is not that my soul felt any hesitation about agreeing with you: the belief I have in you disposes me to accept everything that comes from you without discussion; but so that what you provide me may profit me the more, I wish to

_____

* *Gods, comely Paris had he his comely prey!*
  That lover, did he not do well?
  The fires of Troy must he lay,
  His own to dispel!
  (Stanzas for Mademoiselle de M . . . by Théophile)

** The French text of this letter is based on a manuscript copy, see *Oeuvres, Supplément a la correspondance*, vol. X, pp. 617–24.

review it with discernment, and that requires time—not a very long amount of it, but time calm and relieved from the pressure of other thoughts, a good I can but infrequently enjoy. The first occasion I found myself free to apply myself without interruption to this agreeable reading, I was so enthralled that for a few days hence I could not collect myself for affairs; and while my mind was still filled with these notions I had absorbed with so much pleasure, it happened that M. du Rier, medical doctor to the Queen of Sweden, a knowledgable and honorable man, came to pay me a visit. I immediately revealed my heart to him and told him of my joy. I reread for him, without his tiring, your letter of eight pages, which he admired no less than I. He asked me to let him have it for a time to consider it at his leisure. I excused myself civilly of that request, not wishing to give up so precious a writing. But, a few days hence, I was urged by the Queen, to whom he had spoken about it, to let her see it. I was very pleased her Majesty had this curiosity, hoping that the reading of this one piece would make her realize that everything I had told her about your person was still beneath the truth. All flattery aside, it is also true, Monsieur, that her judgment is so clear and detached from all prejudices that I think there is nothing in philosophy she could not understand with ease. I deferred matters from one audience to another to find a time free and relieved of affairs; and although for several days she asked for your letter, I made excuses in order to read it to her only at an opportune time. After she heard it, she remained very satisfied, and could not desist from bestowing praise upon you or from inquiring of me concerning all the details of your person and your life. I told her everything I knew, and after having thought for a moment, she said: *M. Descartes, as far as I can see by this writing and by the picture you have given me of him, is the happiest of men; and his condition seems to me worthy of envy. You would do me pleasure to assure him of the great esteem in which I hold him.* I will not relate here everything her Majesty said concerning all the points in your letter, which she did not allow me to read consecutively: indeed, she stopped me often to confirm by her reasoning what she heard very well; and I assure you, Monsieur, that I was not less astonished by her facility at penetrating into your thoughts than I was surprised by their profundity when first I read them.

212 In the first question, where you explain in general the nature of love, her Majesty paid close attention, but did not wish to stop to examine the doctrine *because,* said she, *not having felt this passion, she could not judge well a picture whose original she did not know.* I agreed that she did not know love as a passion; but I think that, had she wished, she could speak very pertinently concerning intellectual love, which concerns a pure good separated from sensible things—for in general I do not believe there is anyone in the world more moved by the love of virtue.

213 Finally, having heard all, she did not refuse her consent to any of your opinions, except where you suppose the world infinite. As regards this, her Majesty doubts whether one can admit this hypothesis without doing offense to the Christian religion; she told me succinctly her reasons, concerning which I am certain she will deem very agreeable the clarification you shall offer her—for her piety does not permit her to receive the least conjecture in physics that could wound the foundations of Christianity.

214 Firstly, she thinks that, if one once admits the world infinite in its matter and substance, then so much the more must one believe it infinite in the duration of all its parts, and thus the history of Creation, stated very clearly in the holy Scripture, would not retain its manifest authority; and as regards the other term of the duration, the end of the world, it is likewise difficult to conceive it in that large infinity of a production without limits, where God would not have extended the immensity of his power so as to bound it by the course of a few revolutions: whereas, in the Christian church, where we conceive the world as a small work of an immense power which is not entirely depleted, we see no obstacle to its having a beginning and an end.

215 Her Majesty adds, further, that it is the sentiment of the church that man is the end of Creation, that is to say, the most perfect of the works in the world, and the one for whom all the others have been made. The union of God with man in the Incarnation of the Word, and so many miracles made to keep the sun on its path and sustain its light, show well that human nature is the mistress of all the others that compose this great body that we see. And it is certain that, if we conceive the world in that vast extension you give it, it is impossible that man conserve himself therein in this honorable rank; on the contrary, he shall consider himself along with the entire earth he inhabits as in but a small corner, tiny and in no proportion to the enormous size of the rest. He will very likely judge that all these stars have inhabitants, or even that the earths surrounding them are all filled with creatures more intelligent and better than he; certainly he will at least lose the opinion that this infinite extent of the world is made for him or can serve him in any way.

216 I admit to you, Monsieur, there came to my mind something to respond by way of reconciling your hypothesis with the truth of the Christian religion; but the Queen's mind is not one to content itself with probable reasoning, and I thought I ought not weaken your case with a defective defense. I have reserved the matter entirely for you, and I cannot believe that having previously taken the pains to respond, in less important matters, to the objections of common men, you would refuse to offer clarification to a Queen who, although having as many soldiers at her command, gives you no pretext for fear as Emperor Hadrian gave to the philosopher Favorinus, but whose soul, whose generosity, and whose goodness merit that all men regard themselves her subjects.

217 However, Monsieur, I must advise you my nature is such to make me wish my return in all matters that pass through my hands; and persuading myself that I shall render you a service when I show the Queen your response to her difficulty, I ask you please to acknowledge my role with a certain liberality; and so that you have no pains in seeking out an appropriate present, I will say freely what I would urge.

218 I do not clearly see what constitutes that secret impulsion inclining us to befriend one person more than another before even knowing his merit; and so long as I seem not to recognize whatever confused opinion regarding the goodness of the one attracting me can cause this impulsion, my difficulty remains—namely, since I would not have distinctly recognized what characteristics and signs prejudiced me to this opinion, it is doubtful whether this secret attraction has its origin in the body or in the soul: if it is born of the body, I would wish it better revealed than by those general terms "sympathy" and "antipathy" with which the philosophers of the School mask their ignorance; and if this attraction of friendship issues from the disposition of our souls taken in their proper substance, although it seems beyond human capacity to render any explanation for it, nevertheless I am so accustomed to learning from you what I esteemed impossible to know, that I do not despair of your giving me some satisfaction. But, following my ordinary method, I intend to apply the knowledge you shall provide me to the conduct of my life for the sake of my improvement; and on that account I ask you, Monsieur, whether a good man, in choosing his friends, can follow those hidden movements of his heart and soul that have no apparent reason; and whether he does not commit an injustice in distributing his inclinations by any other rule save that of merit. This question has exercised my soul more than once, in that, separating friendship out from the two things one often confuses with it—namely, the esteem for virtue and that mutual exchange of employments among honorable men that in effect is but an exchange of benefits—this friendship remains, as it were, a simple

liaison and cement uniting all men in a single body and ought be of equal force among all the parts; otherwise, it could not escape division, which would breach natural equity, and by attaching us too strongly to certain people, would separate us insensibly from others. I do not think one can refuse the name "sage" to he who, taking as a foundation in his heart an equal love for all mankind, would add thereto only the distinction of different merits, as well as that obligation of acknowledgment in the exchange of good offices. And although his esteem for virtue and the reciprocation of good deeds would make it appear this sage loved some more than others—because these three affections very easily mix and seem to produce but one movement—it would nevertheless be true that he would have a very equal friendship for all.

219 I await, Monsieur, for you to relieve me of these doubts and make me see the true rule we should use in distributing our inclinations; but if your leisure does not permit you to provide me so much light; and should you wish me to remain silent and convince myself that I myself do not practice this equality, ask me only whether, beyond my veneration for your virtue, and beyond all obligation I have to you, I am not still inclined to love and honor you by some secret movement that I do not resist, and which makes me, more than of any other man, . . . etc.

CDLXXXVIII.   Descartes to Chanut.

The Hague, 6 June 1647.

Monsieur,
220 As I was passing through here on my way to France, I learned from M. Brasset that he had sent some of your letters for me to Egmond; and although my journey is pressing enough, I proposed to await them; but since they were

received at my home three hours after I had departed, they were sent on to me forthwith. I read them with eagerness. In them I have found great proofs of your friendship and tact. I was apprehensive in reading through the first pages, where you tell me M. du Rier had spoken to the Queen of one of my letters, and that she asked to see it. But later on I was reassured, as I came to the place where you say she listened with some satisfaction to what was read to her; and I doubt whether I have been touched more with admiration, because she so easily understood things the very learned deem very obscure, or with joy, because they have not displeased her. But my admiration is increased in seeing the force and weight of the objections her Majesty has remarked regarding the size I have attributed to the universe. And I should wish your letter had discovered me in my usual habitation, because being better able to gather together my wits there than in the room of some hostel, I would perhaps have been able to extricate myself a little better from so difficult, and so judiciously posed, a question. Nevertheless I do not think that provides me any excuse; and if only it be permitted to me to think it is to you alone that I write, so that veneration and respect do not render my imagination too confused, I will force myself to put down here everything I can say regarding this matter.

221 In the first place, I recall that the Cardinal of Cusa and several other doctors have supposed the world infinite, without their having been reproved by the church on that account; on the contrary, it is believed it does honor to God to conceive of his works as very great. And my opinion is less difficult to accept than theirs, because I do not say the world is infinite, but indefinite only. And the difference is noteworthy enough: for to say a thing is infinite, one ought to have some reason allowing one to recognize it such—which one cannot have save of God alone; but to say it is indefinite, it suffices not to have any reason by which one can prove it has limits. Thus it seems to me one cannot prove, nor even conceive, limits in the matter of which the world is composed. For, in examining the nature of this matter, I find it consists in nothing else save that it has extension in length, breadth, and depth, in such a way that everything having these three dimensions is a part of this matter; and there cannot be therein any space entirely empty, that is to say, containing no matter, because we could not conceive such a space except by conceiving in it these three dimensions, and, consequently, matter. But, now, in supposing the world finite, one imagines outside its limits certain spaces that have their three dimensions, and thus are not purely imaginary, as the philosophers call them, but rather contain in themselves matter, which, being unable to be any place else save in the world, makes us realize that the world extends beyond the limits we have tried to attribute to it. Thus, not having any reason sufficient to prove it, but yet being unable to conceive the world with limits, I call it indefinite. But I cannot on that account deny that perhaps there are some limits known to God, although they are incomprehensible to me: that is why I do not say absolutely that it is *infinite*.

222 When its extension is considered in this way, if one compares it with its duration, it seems to me it gives occasion for thinking only that there is no imaginable time before the creation of the world in which God could not have created it had he wished to do so; nor is there any ground, on that account, to conclude he in fact created it indefinitely long ago—because the actual or true existence that the world has had since five or six thousand years is not necessarily joined with the possible or imaginary existence it could have had beforehand in the way the actual existence of the spaces one conceives around a globe (that is to say, the earth supposed as *finite*) is joined with the actual existence of this same globe. Besides, if one could infer from the indefinite extension of the world the eternity of its duration in regard to past time, one would be even better able to infer the eternity of duration it should have in the future. For the faith teaches us that, although the earth and the heavens will perish, that is to say, will change appearances, nevertheless the world, that is to say, the matter of which they are composed, will never perish—as seems to follow from the fact that it promises an eternal life to our bodies after the resurrection, and consequently also to the world in which they will exist. And yet, from this infinite duration that the world ought to have in the future, one does not infer it has hitherto existed from all eternity, because every moment of its duration is independent one from the others.

223 As for the prerogatives religion attributes to man, but which seem difficult to believe if the extension of the universe is supposed indefinite, they merit some clarification. For, although we can say that all created things are made for us, inasmuch as we can extract some use from them, I nevertheless do not know that we are obliged to believe man the end of Creation. Rather, it is said that *all things are made because of him (God)*, that God alone is the final as well as efficient cause of the universe; and as for creatures, inasmuch as they reciprocally serve one another, each can attribute itself this advantage—namely that all those of service to it are made for it. It is true that the six days of Creation are so described in Genesis that it seems man is its principal object, yet one can respond that since this history of Genesis was written for man, it is principally the things pertaining to him that the Holy Spirit has chosen to detail there, and that he has not spoken therein of anything save as it relates to man. And because the preachers, whose task it is to incite us to a love of God, customarily describe for us the different advantages we receive from other creatures, and say that God has made them for us, but do not make us consider the other ends for which one can also say he has made them, since that does not serve their purpose, we are, as a consequence, very inclined to believe he has made them only for us. And they go even further: for they say each man in particular is indebted to Jesus Christ for all the blood he spent upon the Cross, just as if he had died for that man alone. In that they certainly speak the truth; but, just as that does not prevent him from having redeemed with the same blood a very great number of other men, so also I do not see that the mystery of the Incarnation, and all the other advantages God has rendered to man, prevent him from being able to have rendered an infinity of other very great advantages to an infinity of other creatures. And although I do not on that account infer that there are intelligent creatures in the stars or elsewhere, I also do not see there is any reason by which one can prove that there are none; but I always leave undecided questions of this sort rather than deny or affirm them. It seems to me no further difficulty remains here, except that when one has for a long time believed man has great advantages over other creatures, it seems he loses all of them once one changes that opinion. However, I distinguish between those of our goods that can become less from the fact others possess similar goods, and those that cannot be rendered less in that manner. Thus a man who has but a thousand pistols would be very rich if nobody else had as many; but the same man would be poor indeed if everyone else had a great deal more of them. And in a similar way, all praiseworthy qualities provide proportionally more glory to those who possess them the fewer the persons in whom they are encountered; that is why it is customary to envy the glory and riches of another. But virtue, science, health, and generally all the other goods, considered in themselves and without being related to glory, are not at all less in us from the fact they are also found in very many others; that is why we have no reason for being angered that they are in many. But, now, the goods that can be in all intelligent creatures in an indefinite world are of this number; they do not render less those we possess. On the contrary, when we love God, and through him willingly join ourselves to all the things he has created, then the greater, nobler, and more perfect we conceive those things, so much the more do we esteem ourselves as well, because the whole of which we are parts is more accomplished; and so much the more reason have we for praising God on account of the immensity of his works.

When holy Scripture speaks in different places of the innumerable multitude of angels, it entirely confirms this opinion: for we judge the least of the angels to be incomparably more perfect than men. And the astronomers who, in measuring the size of the stars, find them very much greater than the earth, likewise confirm this opinion: for if one infers from the indefinite extension of the world that there ought to be inhabitants elsewhere than upon earth, one can also infer the same thing from the extension the astronomers attribute to it, because there is none who do not judge the earth smaller in respect to all the heaven than a grain of sand in respect to a mountain.

224 I pass now to your question regarding the causes that often incite us to love one person rather than another before knowing their merit; and I note two such causes, the one being in the mind, and the other in the body. But as for that which is only in the mind, it presupposes so many things regarding the nature of our souls, that I would not dare undertake to deduce them in a letter. I will speak only of that which is in the body. It consists in the disposition of the parts of our brain, whether this disposition has been placed in it by the objects of the senses or by whatever other cause. For the objects that touch our senses move, by the intermediary of the nerves, certain parts of our brain, and make there, as it were, certain creases that undo themselves when the object ceases to act; however, the part where they were made remains afterward disposed to being creased again in the same manner by another object resembling the first in some aspect, even though not in everything. For example, when I was a child, I loved a girl of my age who had a slight squint. Because of that, the impression made upon my brain by the sight of her crossed eyes so closely joined itself to that made there to arouse in me the passion of love, that for a long time afterward, in seeing cross-eyed persons, I felt myself more inclined to love them than others, only because they had this defect; nevertheless, I did not know that was the reason. On the contrary,

[223]

since I have reflected upon it, and recognized it was a defect, I have no longer been affected by it. Thus, when we are drawn toward loving someone without knowing the cause for it, we can believe it stems from the fact there is something in them similar to what was in another object we loved previously, although we do not know what it is. And while it is more ordinarily a perfection than a defect that thus attracts us to love; nevertheless, because a defect can sometimes do so, as in the example I have adduced, a wise man ought not allow himself to go over entirely to this passion before having considered the merit of the person toward whom he feels himself moved. Yet, since we cannot equally love everyone in whom we note equal merits, I believe we are obliged only to esteem them equally; and since the principal good of life is to have friendship for certain persons, we are right in preferring those to whom our secret inclinations join us, provided we remark merit in them as well. Besides, when these secret inclinations have their cause in the mind, and not in the body, I believe they should always be followed; and what principally marks those that come from the mind is that they are reciprocated, which does not often happen with the others. However, the proofs I have of your affection assure me so strongly that the inclination I have for you is reciprocated, that I should have to be thoroughly ingrate, and lacking in all the manners I believe ought be observed in friendship, were I not, with the greatest zeal, . . . etc.

CDLXXXIX.   Descartes to Elisabeth.

The Hague, 6 June 1647.

Madame,

225 In passing through The Hague on my way to France, it seems I am obliged—since I cannot here have the honor of receiving your commands and of paying you reverence—to trace these lines so as to assure your Highness that my zeal and devotion will not change although I change soil. Two days ago I received from Sweden a letter from Monsieur the Resident of France, wherein he proposes to me a question on behalf of the Queen, to whom he has made me known by showing her my response to another letter he had sent to me previously. And the manner in which he describes this Queen, with the words he tells of her, makes me esteem her so highly, that it seems to me you would be worthy of each other's conversation; and so few of the rest of the world are meriting of it, that I think it would not be difficult for your Highness to form a very close friendship with her; and besides the contentment of mind it would bring, it would be desirable on divers accounts. I had previously written to my friend, the Resident at Sweden, by way of responding to a letter wherein he spoke of her, that I did not find unbelievable what he said of her, since the honor I had of knowing your Highness had taught me how much persons of high birth could surpass others, etc. But I do not recall whether it is in the letter he has shown her or else in another preceding letter; and because it is likely he will show her in the future the letters he receives from me, I will try always to place into them something to give her reason to desire the friendship of your Highness, unless you forbid me from doing so.

226 Someone has quieted the theologians who wished to harm me, but by flattering them, and by guarding against offending them as much as possible, which is now attributed to the time; yet I fear this time will last always, and that they will be allowed to take so much power that they will become insufferable.

227 The French publication of my *Principles* is finished; and because the *Epistle* will be printed last, I am here sending a copy of it to your Highness so that if there is something that does not agree with her, and that she judges should have been put differently, she may please do the favor of alerting him who will be, all his life, . . . etc.

CDXCI.   Descartes to Elisabeth.

Paris, July 1647.

Madame,

228 My journey could be accompanied by no distress—
for I have been so happy to be making it with the knowledge that your Highness is mindful of me. The very agreeable letter indicating her concern for me is the most precious thing that could happen to me in this country. It
would have rendered me completely happy had it not in-
formed me that the malady your Highness experienced before I departed from The Hague had left her still with a
certain residual indisposition of the stomach. The remedies
she has chosen, namely, diet and exercise, are, in my opinion, best of all—after, however, those of the soul, which
doubtlessly has great force over the body, as shown by the
large changes that anger, fear, and the other passions excite
in it. Yet it is not directly by her will that the soul leads the
spirits into the places where they can be useful or harmful;
it is only by wishing or thinking of something else. For the
construction of our body is such that certain movements
follow in it naturally from certain thoughts: just as one sees
redness of the face follow shame, tears compassion, and
laughter joy. And I know no more suitable thought for conserving health than the strong persuasion and firm belief
that so good is the architecture of our body that once one is
healthy, one cannot easily fall sick, unless one acts with
significant immoderation, or else the air or other exterior
causes harm one; and that having a malady, one can easily
restore oneself by the force of nature alone, especially
when one is still young. This persuasion is doubtlessly very
much more true and reasonable than that of certain people
who, based on the report of an astrologer or medical doctor,
make themselves believe they are to die within a certain
time, and on that account alone become sick, and often

enough even die, as I have seen happen to a number of persons. And as I could not fail to be extremely sorrowful if I thought your Highness' indisposition still remains, I prefer to hope it has entirely passed; and nevertheless the desire to be certain of that makes extreme my passion to return to Holland.

229 I propose to leave here in four or five days to go to Poitou and Brittany, the locations of the affairs that have brought me here; but as soon as I shall have been able to put them in some order, I look forward to nothing so much as to return to the places where I have been so happy as to have the honor of speaking occasionally with your Highness. For, although there are very many persons here whom I honor and esteem, nevertheless I have still seen nothing to keep me. And I am, more than any words can say, . . . etc.

CDXCV.   Descartes to Christina of Sweden.

Egmond, 20 November 1647.

Madame,
230 I have learned from M. Chanut that it pleases your Majesty that it be my honor to explain to her the opinion I hold regarding the sovereign good, considered in the sense that the ancient philosophers have spoken of it; and this command I deem so great a favor that my desire to obey it makes me turn from every other thought; thus, without excusing my insufficiency, I shall put down here, in a few words, everything I shall be able to determine in regard to this matter.

231 One can consider the goodness of each thing in itself, without relating it to others, in which sense it is evident that God is the sovereign good, because he is incom-

parably more perfect than creatures; but one can also relate it to us, and in this sense I see nothing we ought to esteem good, except what in some fashion pertains to us and is a perfection for us to possess. Thus the ancient philosophers—who, being unillumined by the light of faith, knew nothing of supernatural blessedness—would review only the goods we can possess in this life; and among such goods they sought the one that was sovereign, that is to say, the principal and greatest.

232 But, for me to be able to determine it, I consider that we ought to esteem good, from our point of view, only those things we possess, or else have the power of acquiring. That being assumed, it seems to me the sovereign good of all men together is an amalgamation or collection of all the goods, as much of the soul as of the body and fortune, that can be in individual men; but the sovereign good of each person in particular is a completely different thing, and consists only in a firm will to do well, and the contentment which that produces. The reason for saying this is that I remark no other good that seems to me so great nor is entirely in the power of each person. As for goods of the body and fortune, they do not depend absolutely upon us; and those of the soul all relate to two principal goods, namely, the one to know, and the other to will, what is good; yet such knowledge is often beyond our forces; that is why there remains only our will of which we can absolutely dispose. And I do not see that it is possible to use it better than by always preserving a firm and constant resolution to do exactly all the things one shall judge to be better, and to employ all the forces of one's mind to know them well. It is in that alone that all the virtues consist; it is that alone which, properly speaking, merits praise and glory; finally, it is from that alone that always results the greatest and most solid contentment of life. And thus I deem that in that consists the sovereign good.

233 And in this way I think I reconcile the two most

contrary and most celebrated opinions of the ancients, namely that of Zeno, who placed the sovereign good in virtue, or honor, and that of Epicurus, who placed it in the contentment to which he gave the name of pleasure.* For, as all the vices come only from that uncertainty and weakness which follow upon ignorance and give birth to regrets; so too virtue consists only in the resolution and vigor with which one pursues things one believes to be good, provided one's vigor does not issue from obstinacy but from the fact one knows oneself to have examined such things to the extent one is morally able. And although what one then does can be wrong, one is nevertheless assured one does one's duty; whereas, if one executes some action of a virtuous sort, but in the meanwhile thinks of oneself as doing evil, or else neglects to determine whether one does right or wrong, one is not acting as a virtuous man. As for honor and praise, one often attributes them to the other goods of fortune; however, since I am persuaded your Majesty places more importance upon her virtue than her crown, I shall have no fear in saying here that it seems to me there is nothing save this virtue that one has just reason for praising. All the other goods merit only to be esteemed, and not to be honored or praised, save insofar as one presupposes they are acquired or obtained from God through the good use of our free deciding. For honor and praise is a species of reward, and it is only that which depends on our will that one has reason to reward or punish.

234 It yet remains for me to prove here that from this good use of the free deciding issues the greatest and most solid contentment in life; which seems not difficult to show because, considering carefully that in which pleasure, or delight,** consists, and generally all the kinds of contentments one can have, I note, firstly, there are none that are

---

* volupté.
** la volupté ou le plasir.

not entirely in the soul—in the same way as it is also the soul that sees, although such occurs by means of the eyes. Next, I note, there is nothing that can give contentment to the soul, except her opinion that she possesses some good; and also, that this opinion is often in her only as a very confused representation, and indeed that her union with the body is the cause why she ordinarily represents to herself certain goods as incomparably greater than they are; but yet, that if she knew their just value distinctly, her contentment would always be proportioned to the magnitude of the good from which it would proceed. I note, furthermore, that the magnitude of a good, with regard to us, should not be measured only by the value of the thing in which it consists, but also, and principally, by the manner in which it relates to us; and that although the free deciding is of itself the most noble thing that can be in us—inasmuch as it renders us in some manner equal to God and seems to exempt us from being subjected to Him, so that, in consequence, its good use is the greatest of all our goods—it is also that which is most properly ours, and concerns us the most; whereupon it follows that our greatest contentments can proceed only from it. Also, one sees, for example, that the repose of mind and interior satisfaction felt in themselves by those who know they never fail of doing their best, as much in knowing as in acquiring the good, constitutes a pleasure, sweeter beyond comparison, and more durable and solid, than all those that come from elsewhere.

235 I am leaving out here very many other things because, in considering the numerous affairs encountered in running a large realm—affairs of which your Majesty herself takes charge—I dare not ask of her a longer audience. But I am sending to M. Chanut certain writings wherein I have placed at greater length my sentiments regarding the same question, so that, if it please your Majesty to see them, it gratifies me to present them to her, and it helps me testify with how much zeal, and devotion, I am, . . . etc.

CDXCVI.   Descartes to Chanut.

Egmond, 20 November 1647.

Monsieur,

236 It is true that I am accustomed to refusing to write my thoughts regarding morals, and for two reasons: the one, that there is no subject matter from which those who are malicious can more easily extract pretexts for their calumnies; the other, that I believe it pertains only to sovereigns, or to those authorized by them, to involve themselves in regulating the customs of others. But these two reasons cease to apply now that you have honored me, by writing on behalf of the incomparable Queen upon whom you wait, that it pleases her that I write her my opinion regarding the sovereign good; for this command is sufficient authorization, and I hope that what I write will be seen only by her and by you. Indeed, it is because my desire to obey her is so strong that, far from practicing reserve, I should wish to be able to put into one letter everything I have ever thought regarding this subject. In fact, I have wished to place so many things in the letter I dared writing to her, that I fear I did not explain any of them sufficiently. But, to make up for this defect, I am sending you a collection of some other letters wherein I have deduced the same things at length. I have joined thereto a small treatise on the passions, which is not the least part; for it is principally the passions that one must try to know in order to obtain the sovereign good that I have described. Had I dared also to include the responses I have had the honor of receiving from the Princess to whom these letters are addressed, this collection would have been more accomplished, and I could yet have added two or three of my own that are not intelligible without them; but I should have had to ask her permission for it, and she is now far removed from here.

237 However, I do not ask you to present this collection immediately to the Queen; for I should be fearful of not sufficiently guarding the respect and veneration I owe her Majesty if I sent her letters written for another rather than writing her directly about whatever I deem would be agreeable to her; yet, if you find it wise to speak to her about them, saying that it is to you I have sent them, and if, afterward, she desires to see them, I will be relieved of this scruple. And I am persuaded that she will perhaps be more pleased at seeing what I have thus written for another than if they had been addressed to her; for she will have more assurance that nothing has been changed or disguised in consideration of her person. But I pray you that these writings not fall, if possible, into other hands, and to assure yourself that I am, as much as I can be, . . . etc.

CDXCVII.   Descartes to Elisabeth.

Egmond, 20 November 1647.

Madame,
    238 Since I have already taken the liberty of mentioning to your Highness the correspondence I have begun with Sweden, I thought myself obliged to continue, and to tell her that a short time ago I received letters from my friend in that country informing me that the Queen, having been at Upsala, the location of that country's academy, had wished to hear a harangue of a professor of eloquence whom he deems the most capable and reasonable in that academy; and the Queen laid down as subject of the discourse the sovereign good of this life; but after having heard this harangue she had said these people but embellished matters, and that it would be necessary to know my opinion. To which he had responded that he knew I was very reserved about writing concerning such matters; but that, if it pleased her Majesty that he ask me about it on her behalf,

he did not think I would fail to try to satisfy her. Thereupon she had given him very express charge to ask me, and he had promised her he would write me concerning it by the next mail; so that he counsels me to respond, and to address my letter to the Queen, to whom he will present it, and he says he thinks it will be well received.

239 I thought I ought not neglect this opportunity, and considering that, when he wrote me this, he could not have yet received the letter in which I spoke of those I had the honor of writing to your Highness regarding the same matter, I thought that the design I had in that had failed and had to be pursued from another angle; that is why I wrote a letter to the Queen in which, after briefly stating my opinion, I add that I omit many things because, appreciating the number of affairs she faces in managing a large realm— affairs of which her Majesty herself takes charge—I did not dare ask of her a longer hearing; but I also add that I am sending to M. Chanut certain writings that contain at greater length my sentiments in regard to the same matter, so that, if it pleases her to see them, he can present her with them.

240 These writings are the letters I have had the honor of writing to your Highness regarding Seneca's book, *concerning the blessed life*—extending to half of the sixth letter, where, having defined the passions in general, I say I find difficulty in enumerating them. In consequence of which, I am also sending him the small treatise on the passions which I have had some pains to have transcribed from a rather confused rough draft that I had kept; and I am informing him that I wish him not to present these writings to the Queen forthwith, because I should fear not sufficiently guarding the respect I owe to her Majesty if I sent her letters prepared for another rather than writing to her whatever I should deem agreeable to her; however, I likewise add that, if he finds it advisable, he may speak to her of it, saying it is to him I have sent them, and if afterward she desires to see them, I would be relieved of

this scruple; and also, that I am certain she will perhaps find it more agreeable to see what has thus been written for another rather than for herself, because she will be able to assure herself the more that I have changed or disguised nothing because of her.

241 I have not judged it proper to say there anything further concerning your Highness, nor even to use her name, which he will nevertheless not fail to know in light of my previous letters. But considering that, despite his being a very virtuous man, who greatly esteems people of merit, so that he doubtlessly honors your Highness as much as he ought, he has still not spoken of her to me save rarely in his letters, although I have written something about her in all of mine, I have inferred that perhaps he took some scruple in speaking of her to the Queen because he did not know whether that would please or displease those who had sent them. But, if in the future I have the opportunity to write the Queen herself, I will have no need of an interpreter; and my goal this time in sending him these writings is to try to arrange it that she occupies herself further with these thoughts, and that, if, as I am made to hope, they please her, she may have occasion to confer about them with your Highness—of whom I shall be all my life, . . . etc.

DIII. Descartes to Elisabeth.

Egmond, 31 January 1648.

Madame,

242 I have received your Highness' letters of 23 December almost at the same time as the preceding ones, and I admit I am in distress regarding how I ought to respond to the earlier ones because your Highness there expresses her wish that I write the treatise on erudition of which I have formerly had the honor of speaking to her. There is nothing I wish with more ardor than to obey your commands; yet I

[234]

will say here the reasons why I had abandoned my design to write this treatise, and if they do not satisfy your Highness, I will not fail to resume it.

243 The first is that I could not place in it all the truths that ought to be there without overly arousing the gentlemen of the school against me—nor do I find myself in such condition that I can entirely disregard their hatred. The second is that I have already touched on some of the matters I had planned to put in it in a preface at the beginning of the French translation of my *Principles*, which I think that your Highness has by now received. The third is that I have now another writing in my hands that I hope will be more agreeable to your Highness: it is the description of the functions of the animal and of man. As for what I had roughly sketched of it, twelve or thirteen years ago, it has already been seen by your Highness—but only after being badly transcribed by several persons into whose hands it had fallen. Thus I have thought myself obliged to explain it more clearly, that is to say, to redo it. And I am even emboldened (but only since the past eight or ten days) to attempt to add an explanation of the manner in which the animal forms from the beginning of its origin. I say the animal in general; because, as for man in particular, I would not dare to undertake it for want of experiments adequate to the task.

244 Moreover, I consider what remains to me of this winter as perhaps the most tranquil time I will enjoy in my life; that is the reason I prefer to employ it at this study rather than at one that does not require so much attention. The reason I fear I will have less leisure in the future is that I am obliged to return to France next summer and to spend the following winter there; my domestic affairs and various reasons constrain me to do so. Also, someone has honored me in offering a pension on behalf of the King without my requesting it; that shant suffice to keep me—yet in a year many things can happen. Nothing, however, could prevent me from preferring the happiness of living wherever your Highness might be, if the occasion arose, even to

that of being in my own country, or whatever other place.

245 I do not expect any response for a while to the letter regarding the sovereign good—for it remained nearly a month at Amsterdam due to the fault of him to whom I had sent it for the purpose of having it addressed; but as soon as I will have news of it, I shall not fail to let your Highness know about it. The letter contained nothing new that merited being sent to you. I have since received certain letters from that country, informing me that mine are awaited, and according to what I am told of this Princess, she ought to be extremely inclined to virtue and capable of judging well. Moreover, I am told she is to be presented with the translation of my *Principles,* and I am assured she will read the first part with satisfaction, and that she would be very capable of the rest, if affairs did not deprive her of the leisure for it.

246 Along with this letter I am sending a booklet of little importance,* but I am not enclosing it in the same parcel because it is not worth the postage. The insults of M. Regius have constrained me to write it, and it was printed sooner than I knew; indeed, joined to it are verse and a preface of which I disapprove, although the verse is by M. Heydanus who dared not—as well he ought not—put his name to it. I am, . . . etc.

DXXXVI *bis.*   Descartes to [Pollot?].

[1648?].

Monsieur,

247 I am very thankful that the liberty I have taken in writing you my opinion has not been disagreeable to you, and I am obliged to you for wishing to follow it, in spite of

---

* Descartes' *Remarks on a Program.*

the fact you have reasons to the contrary that I confess are very strong. For I have no doubt that your mind can furnish you better divertissements than can the bustle of the world. And although custom and example esteem the profession of war as the noblest of all, for me, who considers it as a philosopher, I esteem it only as much as it merits; and indeed I have no little difficulty in ranking it among honorable professions, seeing that laziness and libertinage are the two principal motives that today attract the larger number of men to it—which is why I would be absolutely disconsolate were something to go amiss for you. Finally, I admit that a man inconvenienced by sickness should consider himself older than another, and that it is preferable to retire when winning rather than upon a loss. Nevertheless, because at the game now in question, I do not think there is any risk of losing, but only of winning or not winning, it seems to me there is time enough to retire from it when one no longer gains from it. And because I have often met old people who told me they were more unhealthy in their youth than many others who died before them, it seems to me that whatever weakness or indisposition of body we experience, we ought to use life and dispose its functions in the same manner as if we were assured of reaching an extreme old age. And, on the contrary, whatever force or health we possess, we ought also be prepared to accept death without regret whenever it shall come—because it can come at any moment, and there is no action we could perform not capable of causing it: if we eat a morsel of bread, perhaps it will be poisoned; if we go down a street, perhaps some tile will fall from a roof and crash down upon us, and so forth. That is why, since we live among so many inevitable risks, it seems to me wisdom does not forbid us to expose ourselves also to that of war, provided a noble and just cause obliges us do so, and provided we do so without rashness and do not refuse to carry arms, in so far as is possible, to the clash. Finally, I believe that however agreeable be the divertissements we choose of our own accord, they do not so well prevent us from thinking of our own discomforts as do those to which we are obligated by some duty; and also, that our body accustoms itself so strongly to our manner of life that, when one changes it, one's health is disturbed rather than improved—principally when the change is too sudden. That is why it seems to me the best thing is not to go from one extreme to the other except by degrees. As for myself, before I came to this country in search of solitude, I passed a winter in the French countryside where I made my apprenticeship; and were I engaged in some manner of life in which my indisposition did not permit me to remain for a long time, I would not conceal that indisposition, but would rather allow it to appear greater than it is, so as to be able to dispense myself honorably of all actions that could augment it, and thus, taking my comforts little by little, attain by degrees to a complete freedom. . . . etc.

DXXXIX.   Descartes to Elisabeth.

Egmond, 22 February 1649.

248 Among several upsetting pieces of news I have received from diverse places at the same time, that which touched me most vividly has been the sickness of your Highness. And although I am also told of her cure, there fails not to remain even now traces of sadness in my mind that shall not so soon be erased. The inclination of your Highness to compose verse during her illness made me remember Socrates, who, as Plato tells us, had a similar desire while he was in prison. And I believe this humor issues from a strong agitation of the animal spirits that would be able utterly to upset the imagination of those who do not possess a well settled brain, but can only make a little warmer those more stolid, and dispose them to poetry.

And I consider this transport a mark of a mind stronger and more elevated than the common.

249 Did I not know your's for such, I would fear you were extraordinarily afflicted in hearing the fatal conclusion of the tragedies of England; * but I promise myself that your Highness, being accustomed to the disgraces of fortune, and having seen herself just a little while past in great peril of her life, will not be so surprised nor so troubled to learn of the death of one of her kin, as if she had not previously received other afflictions. And although this death so violent seems to contain something more horrible than that which one awaits in one's bed, nevertheless, putting it in its best light, it is more glorious, more happy, and more calm—so that the thing about it that particularly afflicts the ordinary man ought to serve as a consolation to your Highness. For there is much glory in dying in a circumstance that causes one to be universally commiserated, praised, and mourned by everyone with any human sentiment. And it is certain that, without this ordeal, the clemency and other virtues of the dead king would never have been so noticed or so esteemed as they are now and will be in the future by all who will read his history. I am also certain that during the last moments of his life the satisfaction provided him by his conscience surpassed the vexation caused him by his indignation—which is the only sorrowful passion said to have been noticed in him. And as for his pain, I place no weight on it; for it is so short that, could the murderers employ fever, or whatever other maladies nature is wont to use to put men out of this world, one would have reason to deem them more cruel than when they kill with the blow of a hatchet. But I dare not linger long upon a subject so lugubrious; I add only that one is very much better off entirely delivered from a false hope than uselessly captivated by it.

----

* The execution of Elisabeth's maternal uncle, Charles I, 9 February 1649.

250 While writing these lines, I receive letters from a place whence I had none for seven or eight months; the person to whom I had sent the treatise on the passions a year ago has written one of them in her own hand in order to thank me for it. Since she remembers, after so long a time, a man so lowly as I, it is likely, even though she has delayed four months, that she will not forget to respond to the letters of your Highness. I am told she has charged one of her own with studying the volume of my *Principles* in order to facilitate her reading of it; I nevertheless do not believe she finds sufficient leisure for applying herself to it, although she seems to have the desire to do so. She thanks me in express terms for the treatise on the passions; but she makes no mention of the letters to which it was joined, and I learn nothing at all from that country that has reference to your Highness. With regard to that, I can divine nothing—except that the conditions of the peace of Germany not being so advantageous to your household as they could have been, those who have contributed to this are in doubt whether you do not wish them ill, and so for that reason restrain themselves from expressing friendship toward you.

251 I have always been troubled, ever since the conclusion of this peace, in not seeing that Monsieur the Elector, your brother, had accepted it, and I would have taken the liberty of writing sooner my sentiment about it to your Highness had I been able to imagine him taking my view into consideration. But because I do not know the particular reasons that might be moving him, it would be rash of me to make any judgment about it. I can only say, in general, that when it is a question of the restitution of a state occupied or disputed by others who have the forces in hand, it seems to me that those with only equity and the law of nations to plead for them ought never make it their aim to obtain all their claims, and that they have much more reason to be thankful to whomever offer them some part of those claims, however small it be, than to wish ill to those who retain the rest. And although one cannot disapprove their disputing their right the most they can, while those who havè the force are deliberating regarding it, I believe that once the conclusions are reached prudence obliges them to testify they are content with them, even though they are not; and to thank not only those who offer them something, but likewise those who do not take away everything from them, in order to acquire, by this means, the friendship of both, or at least avoid their hatred: for, afterward, that can serve very much in maintaining themselves.

252 Besides, there remains a long road in getting from promises to effect; and if those who hold the power work together by themselves, it is easy for them to find reasons to share among themselves what they had perhaps wished to give to a third party only out of jealousy of each other and in order to prevent whoever would enrich himself on these spoils from becoming too powerful. The smallest part of the Palitinate is worth more than all the empire of the Tartars or Muscovites, and after two or three years of peace, residence there will be as agreeable as in any other place on the earth. As for myself, who am not attached to residing in any one place, I would have no difficulty in leaving these Provinces, or even France, in order to go there if I could find a repose equally assured, even though no other reason save the beauty of the country took me. But there is no abode in the world, however crude and inconvenient, in which I would not deem myself happy to pass the rest of my days were your Highness there and I could render her some service; because I am entirely, and without any reservation, . . . etc.

PREFACE TO FRENCH VERSION OF THE
Principles of Philosophy

AUTHOR'S LETTER
to the Translator * of the book,
which can serve as its Preface

Monsieur,

253 The translation you have taken the trouble to make of my *Principles* is so clear and accomplished that it makes me hope more people will read them in French than Latin, and that they will be better understood. I fear only the title might put off some people who have not been nourished upon letters, or else have a bad opinion of philosophy, because what was taught them did not satisfy; and that makes me think it would be good to add thereto a preface explaining to them the subject matter of the book, my design in writing it, and the utility that can be derived from it. But although it should fall to me to write this preface, because I should know those matters better than anyone else, I can do no better than to state briefly the principal points it seems to me should be treated therein; and I leave to your discretion to make public however much you deem appropriate.

254 I would have wished, firstly, to explain in it what philosophy is, by starting from ordinary points: that the word philosophy signifies the study of wisdom, and that by wisdom one understands not only prudence in affairs, but a perfect knowledge of all the things man can know, both for

---

* M. l'abbé Claude Picot.

the conduct of his life, and for the conservation of his health and discovery in all the arts; and that for this knowledge to be such, it must be deduced from first causes, so that to study to acquire it, which is properly called to philosophize, one must begin by searching after these first causes, that is to say, principles; and that these principles should satisfy two conditions: the one, that they be so clear and evident that the human mind cannot doubt their truth when it applies itself attentively to consider them; the other, that the knowledge of all other things depend upon them, so that they can be known without these other things but not vice versa. And, after that, I would have wished to explain that it is necessary so to deduce from these principles the knowledge of the things that depend upon them that nothing be included in the entire chain of deductions that is not very manifest. Truly, only God alone is perfectly wise, that is to say, has an entire knowledge of the truth of all things. But one can say men have more or less wisdom in proportion as they have more or less knowledge of the most important truths. And I think there is nothing in this with which the learned are not in accord.

255 Next, I would have considered the usefulness of this philosophy, and shown that, since it extends to everything the human mind can know, one should deem that it alone distinguishes us from the most savage and barbarian, and that each nation is the more civilized and polished the better the men found therein philosophize; and that, accordingly, the greatest good a state can possess is to have true philosophers. And, beyond that, that for each man in particular, it is not only useful to live among those who apply themselves to this study, but it is incomparably better to apply himself to it; just as it undoubtedly is very much better to direct oneself by one's own eyes, and to enjoy the beauty of the colors and the light, than to have one's eyes closed and follow the direction of another; but even this last is better than to hold them closed and have only oneself to guide one. For to live without philosophy is truly to have one's eyes closed without ever trying to open them; nor is the pleasure of seeing all the things our sense of sight discovers comparable to the satisfaction derived from the knowledge of the things discovered by philosophy; and finally this study is more necessary to regulate our customs and guide us in this life than is the use of our eyes in guiding our steps. The dumb beasts, who have but their body to conserve, continually busy themselves in searching out nourishment for it; but men, whose principal part is the mind, ought to direct their principal care to searching after wisdom, which is its true nourishment; and I am also assured there are many who would not fail to do so had they hope of succeeding and knew how capable they were. And there is no soul so lowly, nor so strongly attached to the senses, who does not sometimes turn from them to wish after some other greater good, though ignorant of that in which it consists. Those whom fortune favors the most, who have abundance of health, honors, and riches, are not more exempt from this desire than these others; on the contrary, I am convinced that it is they who aspire with more ardor after another good more sovereign than all they possess. And this sovereign good, considered by natural reason, without the light of faith, is nothing but the knowledge of the truth by its first causes, that is to say, the wisdom of which philosophy is the study. And because all these things are absolutely true, it would not be difficult to persuade men of them were they well argued.

256 But, because one is hindered from believing these things by the experience which shows that those who make a profession of philosophy are often less wise and reasonable than they who have never applied themselves to this study, I would have wished here to explain summarily in what consists all the knowledge presently received and the degrees of wisdom to which it has attained. The first degree includes only notions so clear in themselves that one can acquire them without meditation. The second includes everything sense experience shows us. The third, what the

[245]

conversation of other men teaches us. And, as the fourth, one can add the reading, not of every book, but particularly of those that have been written by people capable of giving us good instructions—for such reading is a kind of conversation with their authors. And it seems to me that all the wisdom now familiar is derived only from these four means; for I am not including divine revelation here, because it does not teach by degrees, but elevates all at once to an infallible belief. Now, from all time there were great men who tried to find a fifth degree in order to attain to the wisdom incomparably higher and more certain than these other kinds: that is to say, to seek after the first causes and true principles from which one can deduce the reasons for everything one can know; and those who have labored at this have particularly been called philosophers. Nevertheless, I do not know that up to now anyone of them has succeeded. The first and principal whose writings we possess are Plato and Aristotle, between whom was no other difference save that the first, following the footsteps of his master Socrates, candidly confessed he had not as yet been able to find anything certain, and contented himself with writing things that seemed to him probable, imagining for this purpose certain principles by reference to which he then tried to give a reason for other things; whereas Aristotle had less frankness, and although he had been for twenty years Plato's disciple, and had no other principles but his, entirely changed the manner of retailing them and proposed them as true and certain although there was no appearance he ever deemed them such. Well, these two men were formidable wits and possessed much of the wisdom acquired by the four means mentioned above, which accordingly earned them great authority, in such a way that those who followed stopped more to acquiesce in their opinions than to seek anything better. And the principal dispute between their disciples was whether one should place all things in doubt or whether some things are certain. And on both sides of the issue they were led into extravagant errors: for those who favored doubt extended it even to the actions of life, in such a way that they neglected using prudence in conducting themselves; and those who held to certitude, supposing it ought to depend on the senses, trusted entirely in them, to the point that it is said Epicurus dared to uphold, against all the reasonings of the astronomers, that the sun is not larger than it seems. It is a defect one can notice in most disputes that, the truth being a mean between the two controverted opinions, each side goes more astray the greater the penchant to contradict the other. But the error of those who inclined too much to doubt was not long followed, and that of the others has to some small degree been corrected in that it has been recognized that the senses deceive us in many things. Nevertheless, I do not know that anyone has entirely removed that error by making it clear that certitude is not found in sense, but in the understanding alone, when it has evident perceptions; and that, as long as one has only the knowledge acquired by the first four degrees of wisdom, one should not doubt things that seem true so far as the conduct of life is concerned, but yet one also should not deem them so certain that one could not change one's opinion if the evidence provided by some reason obliged one to do so. Lacking knowledge of this truth—or else, if there were some who knew it, having failed to make use of it—the greater number of those who in these last centuries have wished to be philosophers have blindly followed Aristotle, in such a way that they have often corrupted the sense of his writings, attributing to him diverse opinions he would not recognize for his own were he to return to this world; and those who have not followed him (included among whom have been some of the best minds) have nevertheless been imbued with his opinions in their childhood (for they are the only ones taught in the schools), which has so preoccupied them that they have been unable to attain to the knowledge of true principles. And while I esteem all of them, and do not wish to make myself disagreeable by reproving them, I can give a proof of what I say that I do not think any of them denies, namely, that they all have supposed as a principle something they have not known perfectly. For example, I do not know anyone who has not supposed that weight is in terrestrial bodies; yet, although experience shows us very clearly that all the bodies called heavy descend toward the center of the earth, we do not on that account know the nature one calls weight, that is to say, the cause or the principle that makes them so descend—which we must learn from elsewhere. One can say the same of the vacuum, heat, cold, dryness, dampness, salt, sulfur, mercury, and all similar things supposed as principles by some of them. Moreover, none of the conclusions one deduces from a principle that is not evident can be evident, even though evidently deduced from it: from which it follows that all the reasonings based upon such principles could not have given them a certain knowledge of anything, nor consequently make them advance one step in the search after wisdom. And if they have discovered something true, it resulted only by one or more of the four means described above. Nevertheless, I do not at all wish to diminish the honor to which each of them can claim; I am obliged only to say, for the consolation of those who have never studied, that just as in journeying, when one turns one's back on the place one wishes to go, one goes the more astray the longer and more quickly one walks, in such a way that, even if one be afterward set upon the right path, one cannot as readily reach one's destination as if one had not marched at all; so likewise, when one has bad principles, the more one cultivates them and applies oneself more carefully to them to draw out various consequences, thinking that to be the same as philosophizing well, so much the more does one separate oneself from the knowledge of the truth, and from wisdom. From which it must be concluded that those who have least learned everything hitherto called philosophy are most capable of learning the real thing.

257 Having once made these things well understood, I

would have wished to state here the reasons proving that the true principles for attaining to this high degree of wisdom, or sovereign good of human life, are those contained in this book. And two reasons alone suffice to prove that: first, that these principles are very clear; and second, that one can deduce everything else from them—for those are the only two conditions they require. Now I easily prove these principles very clear: firstly, by the manner in which I have found them, namely, by rejecting everything in which I could find the slightest reason for doubt; for it is certain that those which could not be rejected when one has thus applied oneself to consider them, are the most evident and clear the human mind can know. Thus, in considering that he who wishes to doubt everything nevertheless cannot doubt that he exists while he doubts, and that what thus reasons, not being able to doubt itself and yet doubting all the rest, is accordingly not what we call our body, but what we call our soul or thought, I took the being or existence of this thought as the first principle from which I very clearly deduced the following: namely, that there is a God, who is the author of everything in the world, and who, being the source of all truth, has not created our understanding with such a nature that it can make a mistake in a judgment about something it perceives very clearly and very distinctly. These are all the principles I use regarding immaterial or metaphysical things, from which I very clearly deduce the principles of corporeal or physical things, namely, that there are bodies extended in length, breadth, and depth, which have diverse shapes and move in different fashions. These, in sum, are all the principles from which I deduce the truth of other things. The other reason proving the clarity of the principles is that they have been known from all time, and even received for true and indubitable by all men—except for the existence of God, which has been doubted by some because they have ascribed too much to the perceptions of sense, although God cannot be seen or touched. But while all the truths I place among my princi-

ples have been known from all time by everyone, nevertheless to the present nobody I know of has received them for
the principles of philosophy, that is to say, as being such
that one can deduce from them the knowledge of everything in the world: that is why it remains to me to prove
here that they are such; and it seems to me that for this
purpose nothing could be better than to let one see it by
experience, that is to say, by inviting readers to read the
book. For although I have not treated everything therein,
which would be impossible, I think that all the things I had
occasion to treat are explained in such a manner that whoever reads them attentively will have reason to persuade
himself that it is unnecessary to search after other principles than those I have given in order to attain the highest
knowledge of which the human mind is capable; principally if, having read my writings, he takes the trouble to
consider how many different questions are explained
therein and then, by looking through the works of others,
sees how few probable arguments have been able to be
given to explain the same questions by using principles
different from mine. And so that the readers might undertake this with more confidence, I would have been able to
assure them that those imbued with my opinions have
much less trouble understanding the writings of others and
recognizing their just value than do those not so imbued—
completely the contrary to what I just a little while ago said
of those who begin with the ancient philosophy, namely,
that the more they have studied it, the more they are ordinarily less suited to well understand true philosophy.

258 I would also have added a word of advice as to how
this book ought to be read, namely, that I should first of all
wish one to peruse it in its entirety like a novel, without
much forcing one's attention or stopping at the difficulties
one can meet there, in order to thus acquire an overview of
the matters I have treated; and that afterward, if one finds
they merit examination, and that one has the curiosity to
know their causes, one can read a second time to note the

sequence of my reasonings; but also that one should not become discouraged if one cannot sufficiently follow everything or understand all; rather one should simply mark with a pen those places where one will find difficulty, and continue to read without interruption right to the end; then, if one takes up the book for the third time, I dare to believe one will find therein the solution of the greater part of the difficulties one previously marked; and that, if some others still remain, one will find their solution by rereading.

259 I have noted in examining the nature of many minds that there is hardly anyone so dull or slow witted that they are incapable of laudible sentiments or even of acquiring all the highest sciences were they directed in the right way. And that can also be proved by reason: for since the principles are clear, and one can deduce nothing from them save by very evident reasonings, everyone has always sufficient wit to understand the things that depend upon them. But, beyond the obstacle provided by prejudices, of which nobody is entirely free—although those who have most studied the false sciences are most harmed by them—it nearly always happens that those of moderate wit neglect studying because they deem themselves incapable, and the others who are more eager hasten too quickly: from which it results that they often accept principles that are not evident and extract from them uncertain consequences. That is why I would wish to assure those who are too mistrustful of their forces that there is nothing in my writings they could not entirely understand, if they take the trouble to examine them; and nevertheless to warn the others that even the most excellent minds will require much time and attention to discern the things I have tried to include there.

260 After this, in order to make quite clear my goal in publishing them, I would here wish to explain the course it seems to me one should follow in instructing oneself. Firstly, a man who as yet has only that ordinary and imperfect knowledge one can acquire by the four means explained above, ought before all to try to make for himself a code of morals that can suffice for regulating the actions of his life, because that brooks no delay—and above all it is necessary to try to live well. After that, he ought also study logic: not that of the school, because properly speaking it is merely a dialectic that teaches how to make understood to another things one already knows, or even to thoughtlessly say many words about things one does not know, and thus it corrupts good sense more than augments it; instead, he should study a logic that teaches one to conduct one's reason well, so as to discover truths of which one is ignorant; and because that very much depends on habit, it is good to exercise himself a long time in practicing the rules regarding simple and easy questions, such as those of mathematics. Then, when he has acquired some talent for finding the truth in these questions, he ought immediately begin applying himself to true philosophy, whose first part is metaphysics, which contains the principles of knowledge, among which is the explanation of the principal attributes of God, the immateriality of our souls, and all the clear and simple notions that are in us. The second is physics, in which, after having found the true principles of material things, one examines in general how all the universe is composed, and then, in particular, the nature of this earth and of all the bodies customarily found around it, such as air, water, fire, the magnet, and the other minerals. After that it is necessary to examine specifically the nature of plants, animals, and above all, of man, in order that one be capable afterward of discovering the other sciences useful to one. And thus all philosophy is like a tree, whose roots are metaphysics, whose trunk is physics, and whose branches are all the other sciences, which reduce to three principal ones, namely, medicine, mechanics, and morals—I mean the highest and most perfect morals, which, presupposing an entire knowledge of the other sciences, is the last degree of wisdom.

261 But as it is not from the roots nor from the trunk of the trees that one gathers the fruits, but only from the extremities of their branches, so also the principal utility of philosophy depends on those of its parts one can learn only last. But, although I am ignorant of nearly all of them, the zeal I have always had to try to render service to the public is the reason I published, ten or twelve years ago, certain essays concerning things I seemed to have discovered. The first part of these essays was a *Discourse on the method for conducting one's reason well and for seeking truth in the sciences,* wherein I summarily placed the principal rules of logic and an imperfect morals that one can provisionally use while one as yet knows nothing better. The other parts were three treatises—*Dioptrics, Meteors,* and *Geometry.* In *Dioptrics,* I intended to show that one could advance far enough by philosophy to arrive by its means at the knowledge of the arts useful to life—for the invention of the telescope explained therein is one of the most difficult questions ever researched. In *Meteors,* I desired one to see the difference between the philosophy I cultivate and that taught in the schools, wherein it is customary to treat the same matter. Finally, in *Geometry,* I claimed to demonstrate that I had found certain things of which others have hitherto been ignorant, and thus to provide a reason for believing that one can discover still others, thereby inciting all men to search after the truth. Since that time, foreseeing the difficulty many would have in conceiving the foundations of metaphysics, I have tried to explain the principal points in a book of *Meditations,* which is not very large, but whose volume has been expanded, and whose matter very much clarified, by the objections that several learned persons have sent me in that regard, and by the responses I have made to them. Then, finally, when it seemed to me these preceding treatises had prepared the mind of the readers to receive the *Principles of Philosophy,* I also published them, and have divided the book into four parts, the first of which contains the principles of knowledge, which one can call first philosophy or else metaphysics: that is why, in order to understand it well, it is fitting to read beforehand the *Meditations* I have written on the same subject. The other three parts contain everything that is more general in physics, namely the explanation of the first laws or principles of nature, and the manner in which the heavens, fixed stars, planets, comets, and generally all the universe is composed; then, in particular, the nature of this earth, and of the air, water, fire, and magnet, which comprise the bodies one can most commonly find everywhere around it; and lastly all the qualities one notices in these bodies, such as light, heat, weight, and the like: by which means I think I have begun to explain all philosophy in orderly fashion, having omitted nothing that should come prior to the things treated last. But, to bring this goal to completion, I would still have to explain in the same fashion the nature of the other more specific bodies found on earth, namely, the minerals, plants, animals, and principally, man; then, finally, I would have to treat exactly of medicine, morals, and mechanics. That is what would be required for me to provide men with a fully completed body of philosophy; and I do not feel myself as yet so old, nor do I so much mistrust my forces or find myself so far removed from the knowledge of what remains, that I would not undertake to accomplish this design had I the means to perform all the experiments required to support and justify my reasonings. But seeing that great expenditure would be needed, which an individual like I could not make unless assisted by the public, and not seeing that I ought await this aid, I believe it henceforward my duty to content myself with studying for my own instruction, and I trust posterity will excuse me if in the future I fail to work for it.

262   However, to make plain that wherein I believe I have already served posterity, I will mention here the fruits I am persuaded one can derive from my principles. The first is the satisfaction of discovering many truths hitherto unknown; for although often the truth does not affect our imagination as much as do falsities and pretence, because it seems less wondrous and more simple, nevertheless the

contentment it provides is always more durable and solid. The second is that in studying these principles one will gradually accustom oneself to judge better all the things that present themselves, and so one will be more wise: therein their effect will be contrary to that of the common philosophy—for in those called pedants one easily notes that the common philosophy renders them less capable of reasoning than if they had never learned it. The third is that the truths they contain, being very clear and very certain, will dispel all subjects of dispute, and thus will dispose minds to sweetness and concord: completely the opposite of the controversies of the school, which, gradually rendering those who follow them more captious and obstinate, are perhaps the first cause of the heresies and dissensions that now try the world. The last and principal fruit of these principles is that by cultivating them one will be able to discover many truths I have not explained; and so, passing gradually from the ones to the others, will with time acquire a perfect knowledge of all philosophy and ascend to the highest degree of wisdom. For one finds in all the arts, that while crude and imperfect at the beginning, nevertheless, because they contain something true and whose effect experience demonstrates, they gradually perfect themselves; and so too, when one has true principles in philosophy, one cannot fail to discover other truths by following them; and one could not do better by way of proving Aristotle's principles false than to point out that no progress has been made by their means during the many centuries in which they have been followed.

263 I well know there are minds in such haste, and who use so little circumspection in what they do, that, despite having very solid foundations, they could build nothing certain; and because ordinarily they are readiest to publish, if one received their writings as mine, or as filled with my opinions, they could in a short period of time spoil all I accomplished and introduce uncertainty and doubt into my manner of philosophizing—from which I painstakingly have tried to banish them. I have recently had such an experience in the case of one believed most to follow me, of whom I had even written in one place that "I was so assured of his mind that I believed he held no opinion that I did not wish to admit as my own": for he published last year a book called the *Fundamentals of Physics:* and although he seems to have placed therein nothing regarding physics and medicine that he did not take from my writings—from those I have published as well as from another still incomplete that had fallen into his hands and that deals with the nature of the animals—nevertheless, because he has transcribed badly, and changed the order, and denied certain truths of metaphysics upon which all physics should be based, I am obliged to disavow his book entirely, and to here ask the readers that they never attribute to me any opinion they do not expressly find in my writings, and that they never receive any opinion as true, either in my writings or elsewhere, that they do not very clearly see to be deduced from true principles.

264   I also well know that it could take several centuries before one has thus deduced from these principles all the truths one can derive from them. For the greater part of those things yet to be discovered depend on certain particular experiments, which are not come upon by chance, but must be sought after with care and expense by very intelligent men. Moreover, rarely will it occur that those who have the ingenuity to make the experiments also have the means. And likewise, the larger number of the best minds, having conceived so bad an opinion of all philosophy because of the defects they have noted in that in practice until now, will be unable to apply themselves to seek after one that is better. But if the difference they will see between these principles and those of others, and the great series of truths one can deduce from them, makes them recognize how very important it is to continue in the search after these truths, and to what degree of wisdom, of perfection of life, and of felicity they can lead, I dare to believe that there will

be nobody who does not try to employ himself at so profitable a study, or at least who does not favor and wish to help with all his power those who fruitfully employ themselves therein. I hope our posterity will witness the success, etc.

NOTES

References to passages included in this volume are by paragraph numbers.

1. *The Passions of the Soul*, vol. I, pp. 329–427, *The Philosophical Works of Descartes*, 2 vols., tr. Haldane and Ross (Cambridge: Cambridge University Press, 1968).
2. René Descartes, *Oeuvres*, 11 vols., ed. Chalres Adam and Paul Tannery (Paris: Vrin, 1964–1974). *Correspondance*, vol. III (1971), vol. IV (1972), vol. V (1974), and *Supplément a la correspondance*, vol. X (1966). *Principes de la philosophie*, vol. IX–2 (1964), pp. 1–20.
3. Gregor Sebba, *Bibliographia Cartesiana: A Critical Guide to the Descartes Literature 1800–1960* (The Hague: Martinus Nijhoff, 1964).
4. *Les passions de l'âme*, ed. Geneviève Rodis-Lewis (Paris: Vrin, 1966), pp. 226–31.
5. *René Descartes: The Essential Writings*, tr. John J. Blom (New York: Harper & Row, 1977).
6. 255.
7. *Description du corps humain, Oeuvres*, vol. XI (1967), pp. 223–90; cf. 242–43.
8. *Traité de l'homme, Oeuvres*, vol. XI (1967), pp. 119–215; *Discours de la méthode, Oeuvres*, vol. VI (1965), pp. 45–60; 36, 151–55.
9. *Passions de l'âme, Oeuvres*, vol. XI (1967): Article XXXIX, pp. 358–59; Article CLXI, pp. 453–54.
10. Descartes specifically mentions only certain of his letters as containing his views on morals, 236, 238–40.
11. The correspondence concerning mind-body dualism is included in this volume, cf. 3–26.

12. *Passions de l'âme, Oeuvres,* vol. XI (1967), p. 326; cf. 145, 152–53, 260.

13. *Discours de la méthode, Oeuvres,* vol. VI (1965), p. 28.

14. Cicero, *Academica* I, x; *Tusculanes* IV, xiii.

15. Cf. *Tusculanes* IV, v.

16. Sainte-Beuve, C.-A., *Causeries du lundi,* 3rd edition, vol. 7 (Paris: Garnier Frères, 188?), pp. 261–263.

17. Seneca, *De vita beata* ix.

18. 105.

19. *Discours de la méthode, Oeuvres,* vol. VI (1965), p. 28.

20. Ibid., p. 14.

21. Ibid., p. 8.

22. Augustine, *Contra academicos, Oeuvres de Saint Augustin,* vol. 4 (Paris: Desclée de Brouwer et Cie, 1948), pp. 110–12; English translation by Patricia Garvey, R.S.M., *Against the Academicians* (Milwaukee: Marquette University Press, 1973), p. 49.

23. *Discours de la méthode, Oeuvres,* vol. VI (1965), pp. 16, 23.

24. Ibid., p. 10.

25. Ibid., pp. 9–10.

26. 256.

27. *Discours de la méthode, Oeuvres,* vol. VI (1965), pp. 13–14.

28. Ibid., p. 17.

29. *Meditationes de prima philosophia, Oeuvres,* vol. VII (1964), p. 3.

30. *Regulae ad directionem ingenii, Oeuvres,* vol. X (1966), p. 411; *Meditationes de prima philosophia, Oeuvres,* vol. VII (1964), pp. 30–31.

31. *Discours de la méthode, Oeuvres,* vol. VI (1965), pp. 56–60.

32. "Secundae responsiones," *Oeuvres,* vol. VII (1964), pp. 155–56.

33. *Discours de la méthode, Oeuvres,* vol. VI (1965), p. 32.

34. "Secundae responsiones," *Oeuvres,* vol. VII (1964), p. 161; cf. definitions of simple subject and composite from

simple subjects, *Notae in programma, Oeuvres,* vol. VIII-2 (1965), pp. 350–51.

35. "Quartae responsiones," *Oeuvres,* vol. VII (1964), p. 222; *Notae in programma, Oeuvres,* vol. VIII-2 (1965), p. 348.

36. *Principia philosophiae, Oeuvres,* vol. VIII-1 (1964), part 1, article LIII, p. 25.

37. *Meditationes de prima philosophia, Oeuvres,* vol. VII (1964), pp. 7–8, 12–14, 27.

38. Ibid., pp. 37–38.

39. "Secundae responsiones," *Oeuvres,* vol. VII (1964), pp. 164–65.

40. *Regulae ad directionem ingenii, Oeuvres,* vol. X (1966), p. 383; cf. *Meditationes de prima philosophia, Oeuvres,* vol. VII (1964), pp. 40–41.

41. *Meditationes de prima philosophia, Oeuvres,* vol. VII (1964), p. 53.

42. Ibid., p. 73.

43. *Passions de l'âme, Oeuvres,* vol. XI (1967); Article I, p. 328.

44. Ibid., Article XIX, p. 343.

45. 72.

46. *Passions de l'âme, Oeuvres,* vol. XI (1967), pp. 301–497.

CONCEPTUAL INDEX

The purpose of this conceptual index is to help the reader discern the structure of Descartes' moral philosophy and psychology. The basic structure is indicated by the major headings (outlined below). References to passages included in this volume are made by paragraph number. Bracketed numbers indicate passages drawn from Descartes' correspondents. References to passages in the *Passions of the Soul* [46] are indicated by *P*, together with article number.

I. BLESSEDNESS DISTINGUISHED FROM FORTUNE

Everyone desires happiness but many do not know proper means, 77. Many incapable of finding right path themselves, but can recognize it when clearly pointed out, 62. 'Blessedness' preferable to 'happiness'—latter may suggest dependence on fortune, or luck, 48. Fortune a chimera, P CXLV-VI; cf. fortune, divine providence, and fate, P CXLV-VI; cf. fortune, divine providence, and free will, P CXLVI, 119, [123], 131, [136], 141. Common souls abandon themselves to fortune and passion, 28. They are accounted more happy than wise because their well being does not issue from themselves, 48. To live blessedly is to have a mind perfectly content and satisfied, 48, 73. Those favored by fortune ordinarily lack interior contentment of mind, 48; cf. dangers of prosperities, 28, 42, 78, 172. The wise acquire interior contentment, satisfaction, or blessedness without help of fortune, 48, cf. [57], 77, 142, P CXLVIII. There are two sorts of contentments: those deriving from mind alone, and those deriving from mind united to body, 79. Goods that depend upon body and fortune such as health, riches, and honors can enhance contentment, so that different persons are capable of contentments of varying degrees of perfection, 49, 70, 231–32. To achieve any solid contentment whatever, one must make the best possible use of goods in one's person—namely, wisdom and virtue, 49, 232; cf. stages of wisdom and philosophy, 255–57.

II. BLESSEDNESS; THE SOVEREIGN GOOD; AND THE ULTIMATE END OF OUR ACTIONS

Blessedness is not sovereign good by presupposes it, 67. Blessedness is contentment or satisfaction of mind deriving from fact one possesses sovereign good, 67, cf. 72–73, 234. Sovereign good should be goal of our actions, 67. By end of our actions one can understand either blessedness or sovereign good, 67. Knowledge of one's duty suffices for one to perform it, but blessedness issues from such actions only because they afford pleasure, 72, cf. 28, 93, 249; cf. pleasure derived from exercise and tragedy, 111–12; cf. relation between pity, generosity, and compassion, P

CLXXXVII. Descartes discusses sovereign good on basis of reason, not faith, 47, 231–32. Opinions of Epicurus, Aristotle, and Zeno can be reconciled if favorably understood, 69, 233; cf. Epicurus and Zeno ordinarily taken as most difficult to reconcile, 233. Epicurus correct to identify blessedness, contentment, and pleasure, 72, cf. 234. Epicurus extended the word "pleasure" to all contentments of the mind, not just to the pleasures of the senses, 68. Epicurus admits blessedness requires virtue, [74]; cf. Epicurus' critics unfair, 68, [74]. (For difficulties in reconciling Epicurus' 'pleasure' with virtue, see Cicero, *Academica*, II, xlvi, and *Tusculanes*, III, xiii–xxi.) Blessedness, or pleasure, should be solid, that is, be based on one's genuine sovereign good, 72–73, 234. Sovereign good of all men together or of the most accomplished or men (as Aristotle treats) requires goods of fortune, not just things in our power, 69–70, 232. Sovereign good of each person in particular is a completely different thing and must be determined by reference to things in an individual's power, 232. Zeno of Citium correct to place individual's sovereign good in virtue, or honor, 69, 71, 232–33; cf. consequences of losing sight of what lies in one's power, 72, 79–81, 232–33. Zeno in error in deeming all vices equal, 71. (Stoics maintain all sins equal, Cicero, *Academica*, II, xliii.) Zeno in error in representing virtue as enemy of pleasure, 71. (Zeno says blessedness consists in virtue alone, Cicero, *Academica*, II, xliii.)

III. VIRTUE, OR THE SOVEREIGN GOOD

Virtue is steadfast attempt to judge well and do all reason advises, without letting one's passions mislead one, 52, 73, 232. Descartes first to explain virtue in this manner, 52; cf. attitude toward Seneca, 65. (Zeno, unlike predecessors, placed all the virtues in reason, Cicero, *Academica*, I, x.) Others have divided virtue into many kinds, 52. Office of reason is to evaluate the contentments produced by various goods and pleasures, 83. Virtues are habits: to judge well requires not only theoretical but practical knowledge of truth—that is, a firm habit of remembering and acquiescing in it, 89, 96, *P* CLXI; cf. virtue, sovereign good, and philosophy, 253–262; cf. role of examples, etc., *P* XLV. 'Virtue' false when not based on truth; for effects of ill-grounded virtue, *see* 54, 79–83, *P* XLIX; cf. false joys and self-deception, 105; cf. vice stems from ignorance, 233. Presumptuous to think one can know everything or avoid all mistakes, 53, 89, cf. 223, 232–33. All that lies within one's power is to follow advice of reason, 53; examine what seems good as much as morally possible, 233; limit vain desires or desires for things that do not depend on oneself, 53, *P* CXLIV-V; seek to know things most to one's advantage, 89, 255, *and see* IV. Truths Most to Our Advantage, or Truths Facilitating the Practice of Virtue. Contentment stems from interior testimony we have some perfection, 79. Virtue, or the correct use of one's power of free deciding, alone produces solid contentment, 72–73, 234, *P* CXLVIII. Virtuous soul realizes nobody properly praised or blamed except for the goods in his own person, that is, for the use of his free will, 29, 232–33, *P* CLII-IV. Virtuous soul is "generous"; for definition, cause, and effects of generosity, *see P* CXLV and *P* CLIII-XI; cf. generosity, pity, and compassion, *P* CLXXXVII. If desires are regulated according to reason, one can achieve contentment despite disgraces of fortune and despite fact one has fewer goods than others, 28, 49, 78. Good sense, or reason, can extract some good from everything, 42, cf. 142.

IV. TRUTHS MOST TO OUR ADVANTAGE, OR TRUTHS FACILITATING THE PRACTICE OF VIRTUE

Four principal truths concerning God, immortality, the vast extension of the universe, and the individual's relation to whole bear on all our actions, 90–94. Other truths concerning customs and the passions bear more particularly on our actions, 94–95.

A. Four Principal Truths

1. God

God exists and everything depends on him, 90, 201–02, cf. 64. God's infinity and human free will compatible, 119, [123], 131, [136], 141; cf. fortune, fate, and divine providence, P CXLV–VI; cf. fortune, divine providence, and free will, P CXLVI, 119, [123], 131, [136], 141. True object of rational love is a perfection, or good, 90, 196–97. We can love things below, equal, or above us, 204; cf. customs of language, 204. Rational love proportions itself to value of object, 205, 234. We can love God by sole force of our nature, or by natural light of reason alone, 195, 201. To attain rational love of God we must remember similarities and differences between God and men: God is a mind, 202; God's knowledge so elevated above ours we can never rival it or fathom all his designs, 201–02; Incarnation should not blind us to gulf between God and man or lead us to presume man the noblest creation, 201, 223. There can be a sensitive love of God by identifying with whole he created, 203, 223. Man most resembles God, not in knowledge, but in the power of free deciding, 201–02, 234, P CLII.

2. Immortality

Soul nobler than body and capable of infinity of contentments not found in this life, 91; cf. intellectual joy, sorrow, and desire, 196; cf. interior emotions, P CXLVII. Prospect of immortality helps prevent us from fearing death, and detaches us from things in fortune's power, 28, 91. Pure duty might demand we leave this life, 28, 93, 205. Natural reason allows favorable conjectures, but no assurance, concerning state of soul after death, 117, [124], 132. We should not fear death, but should not actively seek it, for life generally has more goods than evils, 117, [124], 132, [137], 142.

3. *Vast Extension of the Universe*

Helps us realize this life is not our best life and this dwelling not our principal dwelling, 92. By accentuating power of God, makes us realize his special providence extends even to men, [101], 118–19, [125], 133, 201–02, [214–15], 220–23. Warns us against impertinence of deeming ourselves the noblest, even in knowledge and virtue, of God's creations, 92, 223.

4. *Individual's Relation to the Whole*

We each have distinct interests, but are still parts of a whole including family, society, and state, 93. We should always prefer, with measure and discretion, interest of whole, 93; cf. rational love as proportioned identification with an object, 203–05. Recognition of importance of whole is source of heroic and generous actions, 93, 203–05; cf. generosity, *P* CXLV, *P* CLIII-XI; cf. thankfulness (*reconnoissance*), ingratitude, glory, shame, and impudence, *P* CXCIII-IV, *P* CCIV-V, *P* CCVII. Interrelation between love of God and love of whole, 93, 203, 223. Particular friendships should accord with obligations to whole, [218–19], 224. Measuring how far one should go for the whole, 93, [102], 120, [126], [138], 143. Self-interest, or prudence, accords with obligations to public, 93, [102], 120, [126], [138], 143. *See* V. Views Regarding Civil Affairs.

B. Truths Concerning Customs and Passions

Customs and sovereigns, 236. Philosophy vis-à-vis morals, 159, and 253–64, especially 260. Contentments issue from testimony we have some perfections, 79. Contentments stem from perfections of mind alone or from perfections of mind-body composite, 79. Pleasures of mind-body composite not so durable as those of mind alone, nor so great when one possesses them as when one looks forward to them, 94. Pleasures of mind alone not always good, 81; cf. interior emotions, P CXLVII; cf. intellectual joy, sorrow, etc., 196; cf. ingratitude and impudence, P CXCIV, P CCVII. Contentments stemming from mind-body composite depend on passions, P CCXII. Those with greatest passions, if they properly regulate them, can most enjoy this life, 28, P CCXII; cf. best minds have strongest passions, 42; cf. excess and the passions, 83, [86], [122], 129. Passions represent goods pertaining to mind-body composite as greater than they are, principally before one attains them, 79–81. If unevaluated, passions lead to error, repentance, regrets, etc., 79–81; cf. anger as example of passions, 80. If possible, avoid making judgments until passion is calmed, 1, 42, 94, P CCXI. Best procedure is to have acquired the virtues, that is, rules we can remember and apply during passions, 89, 96, P XLVIII-IX, P CCXI. If we must judge during harmful passions, we should divert imagination and senses from them, employ only understanding to consider them, and examine reasons contrary to those passion tends to exaggerate, 35, [39], P CCXI. Melancholy as effect of arresting attention on suggestions of a harmful passion, 27–29, [30–32], 36–37. Difficulties in diverting one's imagination, [57], 77. Strategies that help calm or prevent harmful passions: a firm determination to view everything in best light provided one is not deceiving oneself, 42, 106, 185; a firm realization of human finitude, 108, P CCXI, 156; cf. measuring one's obligations to whole, 93, [102], 120, [126], [138], 143. For discussion of metaphysical possibility of mind-body interaction, see [3–5], 6–12, [13–16], 17–26. For discussion of physical principles Descartes employs in reasoning about physiology, see [145], 152–53, cf. 197–200. Everything not action of soul is passion of soul, 113; cf. actions of soul are its volitions, *P* XVIII. Joy, sorrow, etc., inasmuch as they are not passions but reasonable thoughts or volitions, could be in soul even without body, 196. Passions defined as thoughts excited in soul by impressions in brain without any action of the soul, 113, cf. *P* XVII. Passions more properly defined as thoughts caused by some particular agitation of spirits, 113, *P* XXV. The six primitive passions are admiration, love, hate, desire, joy, and sorrow, *P* LXIX. Joy, love, hate, and sorrow only passions in us before our birth, 199–200. Passions as confused thoughts, *P* XXVIII, 200. Passions of soul called emotions of the soul because of agitation they cause, *P* XXVIII. Passions contrasted with interior and exterior sentiments, or feelings, 113; with ordinary humor or temperament of person, 113. Distinction between inclinations, or habits that dispose to a passion, and passion itself, 115. Difference between feelings of pain, pleasure or titillation, etc. and passions of sorrow, joy, etc., 114. Passions dispose to thoughts and to bodily movements, 80, 115, 197. Body can be disposed to a passion, such as love, even though soul has no worthy or suitable object, 197. Sometimes soul has an object but there is no bodily passion, 197. New thoughts can become associated with bodily movements characteristic of a passion, as in process of learning a language, 198, *P* L. Soul can act independently of the brain, as in purposive imagining, 113, 115, *P* XLV. Imagining something can occasionally cause the bodily movements that lay one open to a passion, 115. Attending to the reasons, and imagining objects, examples, etc., contrary to a harmful passion, often calms the passion, *P* XLV-VI; cf. indirect control of passions, *P* XLIV-V. Other things being equal, same thoughts will accompany same bodily movements and dispositions, and vice versa, 198. Certain bodily states (hunger, satiety, etc.) are associated prenatally with thoughts characteristic of primitive passions (sorrow, joy, etc.), and although we afterward acquire further objects of passion (of sorrow, joy, etc.) these same bodily states accompany these new thoughts, 199–200. As-

sociations between thoughts of sorrow, joy, etc. and bodily
states not same in all temperaments, [145], 153. Physiological states characteristic of primitive passions identified by
concomitant variation, [145], 152. Disordered love versus
disordered hate, 206–210; cf. physiological considerations
help us estimate relative strength of passions, 209; cf. inclination to particular friendships, [218], 224; cf. other aver-
sions and attractions, *P* CXXXVI.

V. VIEWS REGARDING CIVIL AFFAIRS

Machiavelli's *Prince* misleads by erecting general maxims
on basis of questionable particular actions, 162–65, [175–
78], 187. A prince should use legitimate means to establish
himself—as are nearly all means when he deems them
such, 165. Sovereigns and religion, 169. Justice among
sovereigns has other limits than among private individuals,
165. God gives right to those he gives force, 165; cf. 251.
Enemies defined, 166. Rights against, 166. Friends, or allies, defined, 167. Obligations to, 167. Sacredness of friendship and promises among sovereigns, 166–67. 'Subjects' include 'great' and 'people', 168. Great defined, 168. Prince's
right against great, 168. Importance of avoiding disdain of
people, 162, 168, 170. Prince not commonly envied by
people, 170. Sense of justice among people, 168, 170.

INDEX

Academy, statutes for Swedish xiii; at Upsala 232; at Groningen 128.

Accidents, and life 179.

Action, and blessedness xxi; mental 2; and generosity 27; causation of 28; of soul 106; and life 154; vs. passion 160–61; and doubt 247.

Admiration, primitive ' passion 3; exterior signs of 178; origin and effects 182.

Adolphus, Gustavus xiii.

Advantage, human 157.

Afterlife 104; see Immortality.

Albanus (Thomas White) 123.

Alexander VI, Pope 193.

Allies 188–89, 194.

Analogy 41; avoid being misled by 52, 55; and extension 55–56, 76–77.

Analysis, as species of demonstration 60–61; application of 61–63.

Anaxagoras 57.

Ancient philosophers, Descartes' use of their terminology xx–xxi; and virtue 37; Descartes' examination of 131; manner of explaining themselves 142, 194; Descartes' reconcilia-

tion of their opinions 139–41, 142, 228–29; and supernatural blessedness 228.

Angels 223.

Anger, and imagination 127; inclination to 144; effects of 146, 212, 226.

Animals, and mechanism 12; and instinct 43; and formation of the passions 159–60; treatise concerning 160, 235, 256.

Animal spirits 85–88, 181, 211, 238.

Antipathy 217.

Aristotle xx, xxi, 42, 62, 105, 140, 246, 247, 255.

Aristotelean 1.

Arminians 164.

Arminius, James 164.

Arnauld xiv.

Art xvi; and symbols 56.

Arts (applied) 14; sponsorship of 32; discovery in 49, 244, 255.

Assent (power of) 2, 64; see *Liberum arbitrium.*

Astrologers 226.

Astronomers 170, 223, 247.

Attribute 50.

Augustine xv, 36, 45.

Authority (political) 19, 23–31.

Axioms (moral) 96.

Balzac xiv.

Beasts 245; *see* Animals.

Beatitude 135, 142, 159; *see* Blessedness.

Behaviorists 58.

Being 65, 77, 108.

Benevolence, and criterion of good 15–18; and foundation of religion 21–23; and moral education 29–31; and moral motive 36–37; as species of love 205.

Biology, and physics xvii, xix, 49; and final causality 34.

Blessedness, term derived from ancients xx–xxi; Descartes' view of xxi; philosophical examination of 21; as related to fortune, the sovereign good, and virtue 35–38, 139, 228–30; as related to happiness 53, 132; causes of 132–134; Seneca's examination of 138; impediments to 143–45, 148–49; and self-deception 157; supernatural 228.

Blood, circulation of 124; and emotion 128; and formation of passions 180–83; and hate 211–12.

Body (human), how examined xvii; understanding of essential to morals xviii; affected by mind 2; passions dependent upon 4; understanding of and self-mastery 11; indirect control of 11; and physiological theory 58; united to soul 107–08, 114–15; distinct from soul 107–

08, 114–15; frailty of 121; cured with soul 122; affected by passions 127, 128; pleasures of 147, 153; and exercise 159; and formation of passions 159–62, 180–83, 202–05, 211–13, 223–24.

Borgia, Caesare 198.

Brain, and mind-body interaction 78; and determination of ideas 80; and passion 82; and acquired dispositions 96; and formation of passions 159–62; and admiration 182; and love 211–12, 223–24; and inclination to compose verse 238.

Brandenberg, Marie-Elenora of xiii.

Broachard, Jeanne xiii.

Catholicism xiii.

Catholic, Roman xiv, 19, 171, 173.

Cause, and biology 34; ideas about 50; meaning of term 52–53; of sense quality 62; and interaction of substances 64; and argument for God's existence 67–71; efficient 72, 73; and mind-body interaction 78; of contentment 145–46; of thoughts 161; universal and particular 162; and God 162–63; and dependence of free decision on God 166, 169; and first principles 244–46.

Certitude, pursuit of 43,

47; and method 48; about material things 61–64; about substantial distinction between mind and body 66; review of 72; retrieval from 73–80; concerning mind and body 117; and ancient philosophers 246–48.

Dreams 144.

Dualism, described xviii; topic of Descartes-Elisabeth correspondence xix; presupposed by Descartes' moral theory 39, 44; moral significance of 57–60; argument for 60–80.

Du Rier, M. 214, 219.

Duty, and training 37; and vice 84; and obligation to public 152; and virtue 229; and human industry 237–38.

Earth 216, 220, 223.

Education, and *Principles of Philosophy* vii, 13, *see* Erudition; moral and political 19–35.

Eloquence 232.

Emotion, and *Passions* xix; called passions 1; naturalness of 1; and physiology 39; and interior passions 84; examined 94–96; excited by nature 104; and sleep 128; and apprehension 130; and judgment 161; and imagination 161.

End, indecision about xix; means and 26; the ultimate 139; and blessedness 139; and sovereign good 139; and

pagan philosophers 139–41; *see Summum bonum.*

Enemies 17, 24, 188, 189, 198.

Envy 190–91, 222.

Epicurus xx, 135, 137, 139, 140, 142, 229, 247.

Epiphenomenalism 2–3.

Equality 30, 218, 224.

Error, and primitive notions 108; causes of 111; and pleasure 145; and ancient philosophers 246–48.

Erudition, treatise on 234–35; and *Principles* 235; *see* Education.

Evil, and passions 10; and mores 12; and Marxism 28; and sadness 84; and sensible pleasure 98; vs. good in life 172, 175–76; advantage to prince in doing 187; political maxims and 193; proper examination of 197; and divine decree 207; and hate 212.

Experience, vs. reason 183.

Extension, and sense quality 55–56; vs. thought 77; and soul 112, 115, 117; of universe 151; of universe and the belief in providence 155, 163, 167, 170, 215–16, 219–23.

Factions 20, 24, 25, 31, 191.

Faith, and reason xv, 21; and natural philosophy 144; and providence 154; and supernatural blessedness 162; and death 170; and sovereign good 245.

[276]

Falsity, and passions 94–95.
Fathers (of the Church) 194.
Favorinus 216.
Fear, passion of 161–62; and love 205.
Feeling vs. idea 50–51; as related to sensation, memory, and imagination 94; vs. volition 97; and passions 204.
Fermat xiv.
Fever 118, 121.
Force, and politics 240; and metaphysics xvii; and spiritual natures 58; and mind-body interaction 59–60; 108, cf. 77–78; and weight 109–10, cf. 59–60; and admiration 182.
Fortune xvi, xx, xxi, 3, 11, 12, 13, 23, 24, 35, 53, 118, 119, 120, 122, 129, 130, 132, 135, 144, 145, 146, 148, 151, 154, 173, 177, 193, 197, 228, 229, 239, 245.
Freedom, and the perception of values 2–3, 28; and blessedness 143; and the sovereign good 156; and contentment 229–30; the metaphysical argument for 60–80; esp. 79–80; its dependence on God 60–80, 154, 163–64, 166, 169, 170, 172, 174–75; see Assent, Liberum Arbitrium, Volonté, Voluntas.
Friendship, propriety of 32, 217–18, 223–24; and devotion to public 152; interior satisfaction from 159; conve-

niences from 177; and philosophical conception of love 208; demands of perfect 209; among political allies 188; and veracity among sovereigns 188–89; political advantage resulting from 240–41.
Fundamentals of Physics 256.

Generosity 19, 23, 27, 30, 32, 104, 155, 158.
Genesis, the Book of 221.
Genius 198.
Geometry 50, 54, 62–63, 64, 72.
Geometry 253.
Germany, the Peace of (Westphalia) 240.
God, and Descartes' metaphysics xviii; and values 3; intellectual love of 4, 201, 205–10; and moral obligation 22; and salvation 35; and virtue 35; and an infinite world 56, 151, 155, 163, 170, 215–16, 219–23; argument for the existence of 60–80; attributes of 106; idea of 111; knowledge of 115; and blessed life 138; and practice of virtue 150–52, 154–55, 162–64, 166–67, 169–70, 172, 174–75; and political power 188; and demons 211; as sovereign good 227; and esteem for various goods 229; free will renders us similar to 230; and perfect wisdom 244; and prin-

ciples 249; and metaphysics 252.

Good, reason can determine xviii; the sovereign xx, 138, 139–41, 142, 156–57, 228–30, 231–32, 236, 245; and the passions 9, 10, 84, 152–53, 168, 202–05; the public 24, 27; and Marxism 28; and virtue 37; and resentment 38; and experience 41; and blessedness 53; and symbols 56; and the nature of God 74–75; and pleasure 98, 153; and false virtue 134; and vengeance 146; the measuring of 148–49, 153, 155, 158–59, 169, 172, 175–76, 222, 230; and duty 152; and self-deception 156–57; and actions of princes 190; and political maxims 193; and intellectual love 201–02, 203; and hate 210–11; as property 65, 77.

Great (the politically) 24, 189.

Groningen, academy at 128, 129.

Habit 153, 161.

Hadrian, Emperor 216.

Happiness, and luck 53, 132; and passion 119; and conscience 120; and evils 122; and right use of reason 134; universally desired 144; and fortune 192.

Harangue 232.

Hate, reasonable and unrea-sonable 12; and nutrition 204; vs. love 200, 201, 210–13.

Health, and desire for philosophy xvi, 245; as consequence of philosophy 243–44; and rationality xvii; and Descartes' correspondence with Elisabeth xix; improvement of 19; strategies regarding 124; and tragedy 166; the conserving of 226; and daily life 237–38.

Heart, and formation of passions 180; and admiration 182; and exterior signs of passions 182–83; and love 203–04; and primitive passions 204–05.

Hegesias 163.

Hell 211.

Hercules 212.

Heresies 255.

Herford xiv.

Heroic actions 152.

Heydanus, M. 236.

Hippocrates 106, 110.

Hobbes xiv.

Holy Spirit 221.

Honor, and desire for philosophy xvi, 245; as virtue xx; abuse of 18; and Epicurus 142; and vengeance 146; and praise 229.

Hope, and love 181, 205; and disordered love 211.

Humanities 12–15.

Humility 4, 165.

[278]

Humors, as particles in body 85; and inclination to passion 144; and that which is natural to a person 160–61, 170, 176–77.

Huygens xiv.

Idea, not sense quality but in intellect 50–51, 54–55; and mind 63–64; causes of 68; and physiology 81; and perception 90–94; of mind-body interaction 111; and primitive notions 112–14; and free deciding 172.

Images 92, 94.

Imagination, and philosophy xvi; and passion 4–11; and recognition of values 12; and self-deception 38, 157; and prudence 43; role of 50; and ideas 81; corporeal 86; the physiology of 85–90; and truth 94–95; bounds of 108–09; and the understanding 113–14; and metaphysical meditation 115–16; need to divert 124, 127; and Seneca 142; and pleasure 145; and anger 146; and the brain 160; and love of God 205–08; and poetry 238.

Imitation xv, 28.

Immaterial things, mode of action of 106, 109–10, 111–12; principles of 249; and metaphysics 252.

Immortality, and contentment 119; and pleasures of soul 147; knowledge of 151;

knowledge of and death 155, 163, 166–67; 169–70, 172, 175–76.

Impossibility 53.

Impulsion, secret 217.

Incarnation, the mystery of 5, 167, 206, 216, 222.

Inclinations, secret 217, 223–24.

Individual, and acquisition of wisdom 13; rights of 16; respect for 17; and public 20; measuring worth of 155, 158–59, 164, 167, 172, 176; private 188.

Inertia xvii, 78.

'Information' 112.

Institutions 12, 18, 19, 36.

Intellect, and philosophy xvi; relation to other faculties of mind 43; and ideas 50–51, 64; and certitude 54–55; and physiology 81.

Intellectual virtues 42–56.

Interaction, mind-body xix, 58, 59–60, 77–78.

International trust and concord 19, 23–24.

Irrationality xv, 89, 90, 95, 96.

Ixion 206.

Jesus Christ 221.

Jonsson, Dr. 123, 126.

Joy, a primitive passion 3; and health 125; and the epicureans 142; and sovereign good 156; great vs. mediocre and transient 157; a passion, not a feeling 161; and love 178; movements pertaining

and self-mastery 11; and 'turning away from the senses' 52–56; as related to general concepts, general principles, and images 92–93; and language 93–94; and metaphysical reflection 111, 114; notions not requiring 245.

Meditations on First Philosophy 33, 66, 109, 117 (metaphysical meditations), 201, 253, 254.

Melancholy xix, 126, 140.

Memory, and 'turning away from sense' 52; importance of 55, 150; as related to meditation and language 93–94; abuse of 165; physiology of 85–87.

Metaphysics, as background to moral philosophy and psychology vii, xvii–iii, 50; and organization of introduction xxi; and possibility of volition 2–3; and moral foundation of religion 21–22; presuppositions concerning 39; quest for method and .40–42; and defense of reason 44; and 'turning away from senses' 52–56; and certitude 60, 66–67; and reflection upon mind-body relationship 113; principles of 115, 249; relation to other sciences 252; and Descartes' corpus 253–54.

Meteors 253.

Method, exercises powers of reason xvii; and the *Dis-*

course 39; intellectual virtues and 42; doubt and 48; and the role of mathematics 49–50.

Mind, passivity and activity of 8–9; powers of 50; nature of 50–52; proper description of 55; and reduction to matter 58–59; and interaction with body 58, 59–60; and steps in Descartes' demonstration 61–80

Ministers (political) 190, 193.

Morale xviii, xix, 44.

Morals, principles of 21; and dualism 57–60; axioms of 96; reflecting about 97; foundations of 186; and sovereigns 231; a perfect 252.

Mores xvii, 12, 13, 15, 16, 18, 19, 24, 30, 43, 210.

Motion 78, 106, 112.

Muscovites 241.

Natural, as related to actual and obligatory 15, 40; society as 16; ideal 42; light of reason 47; philosophy 144; blessedness 146; to a person 160; love and passions 165; light and love of God 201, 205; reason and sovereign good 245.

Naturalism, metaphysical 15.

Nature, tyranny of xv; and sovereign good xv, 138; development of human 17; of God 61; of a material thing, or substance 62; and emotions 104; and limits to de-

of 252; and other sciences 252; and Descartes' corpus 253–54; common 255; opinion of 256; and practice xvi, 14, 15; and morals xviii, xxi, 252; utility of 244; as sovereign good 13, 15, 245; and degrees of wisdom 245–46; among ancients 246–48, see Ancient philosophers; and doubt 44–50, 246–47; perception, general concepts, and 91–92; general concepts, general principles, images, meditation, and 92–93; meditation, language, and 93–94; and religion 21; rules of 136; and nature of evil 159; and man's dependence on God 162; of Hegesias 163; and contentment 163; Christina's understanding of 214.

Physics, and medicine xvii, xix, 252; and mathematics 49; and force 59; and passions 180; and morals 186, 252; and the foundations of Christianity 215; as treated in *Principles* 254.

Physiological theory, and *Passions* 1; and metaphysical possibility of volition, 2–3, 22, 39–40; the formation of passions, mental activity, volition, and 6–9, 84–90; and dualism 57–60; sensation, imagination, the passions, and 81; and perception 92.

Picot, Claude 243.
Pineal gland 78.
Plato xv, 23, 36, 42, 99, 197, 238, 246.
Pleasure, Epicurus' doctrine of xx–xxi, 139, 140, 142, 229; types of 145, 147; and knowledge of good 134, 145, 230; derived from doing good 230; and duty 152, 159; and passions 146, 153; feeling, passions, and 161; and imagination 146, 157; and measure 148; vs. evils in life 172; from doing evil 211; from loving 211.
Poetry xv, 94, 238.
Poets 206, 211.
Possibility 72.
Practice, and philosophy xvi, 15; as Descartes' aim xvii; virtue and xviii; and metaphysics xx; and religion 20; and meditation 52; and irresolution 153; and general maxims 194.
Predestination 22, 23, 72.
Prejudices 60, 64, 251. .
Prince, the 23.
Princes 24, 187, 188, 189, 190, 191, 193, 198.
Principles, first xv, 244; and structure of philosophy 252; limits of particular xvi; perception, general concepts, philosophy, and 91–92; general concepts, images, meditation, and 92–93; fruits of Descartes' 254–57.
Principles of Philosophy vii, xiv, 13, 151, 155, 185, 186,

225, 235, 236, 240, 243.
Probability, vs. knowledge
45–50; and the distinction between mind and matter
64; and practice 153; un-
satisfactoriness of 216.
Profession 172.
Progress 29, 30, 48.
Promises 189.
Properties, essential and inessential 65–66, 72, 75–77.
Prosperities 129, 134, 144,
148.
Protestant xiv, 19, 20.
Providence, and infinite universe 56, 155, 163, 167; and
free deciding 163, 172; trust
in 185; and our love of
God 206–07.
Prudence, native xv; and
self-interest 16, 36–38; and
Descartes' method 43–44;
of ruler 148; and manner of
regarding affairs 157; and
measuring obligations to
public 164, 167, 170, 172,
176–77; and political al-
liances 173–74; lacked by
certain ancient philosophers
247.
Psychology xviii, xxi, 1, 28,
35, 81.
Ptolemy 163.
Public, ministers 24; good
27, 31; governors of 148; individuals are parts of 152;
measuring obligations to
155, 164, 167.
Punishments 189.
Purgatory 166.
Pythagorean 57.

Qualities 109, 111, 115.

Rational, passions 201–02; investigation and method xvii.
Reason, and faith xv; Descartes' cultivation of xvii;
and the good xviii; phi-
losophy, sovereign good,
and 13, 245; scandals of
12; and duty to whole 16;
and human dignity 17; right
to cultivate 18; and values
35, 40; and determinism
44; able to attain truth 45;
natural light of 47; and
prejudices 48; and method
49; and mind-body distinction 55; and exploration of
ideas 91; and general principles 92; labors of 99; and
death 104, 170; and rules of
conduct 133; and mistake
134; Seneca's view of 138–
39; Descartes' vindication
of 143; the free use of 144;
and the measurement of
pleasure 145–46; true use
of 147; and quiet sentiment
149; and study 157, 165; and
measuring obligations to
public 164, 167; and control
of passions 166, 168–69; vs.
experience as regards civil affairs 183.
Reasoning ('correct' or 'right'),
as virtue xviii, xxi, 133, 134,
141, 194, 228; and ends xx,
96; and obligation 18, 36;
and vice 84.
Reduction, mind-body 59.
Reformation, the 20.

Regius 105, 236.

Regrets 133, 146, 153, 229.

Religion, and tyranny xv; and superstition 17; rightful claims of 19–23; and immortality 104; and extension of universe 170, 221; conversion to 173; forcing a change in 190; and demons 211; and the attributes of man 221.

Remarks on a Program 236.

Repentance 133, 136, 140, 146, 153, 158, 168.

Research, the organization of 32–35.

Resoluteness 134, 135.

"Response to Sixth Objections to *Meditations*" 109.

Revelation, divine 246.

Revenge 146.

Rhetoric 41.

Richelieu 13, 14.

Rights, human 18.

Roland 212.

Roman Emperors 191.

Rousseau 20.

Rules for the Direction of the Native Talents 69.

Rules 81, 94, 111.

Sadness, as cause of fever 118; happiness, compassion, and 120; inclination to 144; a passion, not a feeling 161; and tragedy 159, 166; movements characteristic of 181; and temperament of the blood 182; and health of body 197.

Sage 1, 218.

Satisfaction, and Epicurus xx; and correct reasoning xxi; and virtue 145.

Scholastics 117.

Schoockius 128.

School 153, 162, 217, 235, 252, 255.

Sciences, and philosophy xv, xvi; application of xvii, xviii; training in 12–15; at time of Descartes 18, 19; and cultural advancement 31; and research 32; and error 49; and Descartes' self-development 50.

Scripture, Holy 215, 223.

Security 23.

Self-assertion 29.

Self-deception xv, xvi, 37, 38.

Self-esteem 12, 18.

Self-interest 16, 17, 36.

Self-mastery 1.

Seneca 37, 131, 134, 135, 137, 138, 139, 141, 142, 143, 150, 154, 233.

Sensation 92, 94.

Sense, limits of xvi; 'turning away from' 43, 50–56, 61; as power of mind 50; experience and material substance 62; experience and geometry 63; quality and mind 76–77; and mind-body union 113, 117; respite of 114, 115–16; understanding, imagination, and 124; difficulty in turning from 127, 144; and formation of impressions 160;

love of metaphysical truth and detachment from 207; and the good 245; certitude and 247.

Sex 121.

Skepticism 21, 22, 45, 56.

Skinnerians 34.

Sleep 144.

Social contract 17, 18.

Society 12, 13, 16, 151, 164, 172.

Socrates xvi, 16, 23, 37, 57, 197, 238, 246.

Sorrow 202, 204, 205.

Soul, immateriality of 252; its manner of moving body 106, 107–10, 111–12, 112–15, 117, 180; and primitive notions 108, 109, 112–15; and force 109, 111, 226; and extension 112, 115, 117; and rational perception 201–02; as joined to body 202–05; and immortality 22, 147, 155, see Immortality; great vs. common 119; afflictions of 121; cure the body together with 122; and liberty 144, 183; and virtue 145; and self-deception 157; and self-esteem 158; pleasures of 159; goods of 228; and contentment 230, 245.

Sovereign 15, 17, 18, 23, 24, 25, 27, 30, 31, 32, 188, 231.

Sovereign good, and terminology of ancients xx; Descartes' definition of xxi; as philosophy 13, 15, 245; philosophy and 21; as related to fortune, virtue, and

blessedness 35–38; Seneca's treatment of 137–38, 150, 154; as related to blessedness and ultimate end of our actions 139; and opinions of ancient philosophers 139–40; Descartes reconciles ancient opinions about xx, 140–41, 142, 227–30; and self-deception 156–57; location of Descartes' views concerning 232–33; and Descartes' principles 249.

Sovereignty 24.

Spinoza 3, 32.

Spirits 85, 106, 112, 160, 161, 162, 166, see Animal spirits.

Spleen 121, 124, 211.

Stoic xx, 1, 36.

Stuart, Elisabeth xiv.

Substance, and Descartes' view of man xviii, 57–59, 64–67, 71–77.

Summum bonum 36; see End.

Superstition 17, 20, 190.

Symbol 4, 6, 41, 55–56.

Tartars 241.

Technology 13.

Theater 119, 159.

Theologians 164, 167, 170, 206, 225.

Theology 155, 163, 167.

Théophile 212.

Thirty Years War 19.

Thought, and volition 2; power of pure 4, 7; and values 12, 99; abuse of 18; and ideas 50; as action of soul 106; metaphysical

113; and meditation 114; and extension 117; and the restoration of health 125; and responsibility 158; and passions 11, 160; causes of 161; as determined by God 162; reasonable 202; and the mind-body connection 180–81, 203–04, 226.

Thrasymachus 23.

Thuillerie, M. de la 200.

Time 104, 158, 220.

Tragedy 37, 89, 159, 166, 239.

Truth, passion for 46; recognition of 47; and method 48; time and access to 49; metaphysical 50; and passions 94–95; and pleasures of soul 147; and judgment 150; and human action 152, 154, 155, 179, 183; and habit 153; and sovereign good 156; and study 158, 165; and principles 244; God as source of 249.

Understanding, and primitive notions 113; and study 114; and principles of metaphysics 115; and the contemplation of difficulties 124; distinguished from imagination or sense 124; and virtue 134, 141; means of fortifying 143, 150, 154; and death 176; and certitude 247, 249.

Unity, of consciousness 64; as property 65, 77.

Upsala, Academy at 232.

Utility 154, 176–77, 189, 194.

Utrecht 129.

Value, and *Discourse* xx; metaphysical justification of 3; and pure thoughts 4; and experience 9, 12–14; and mental joy and sorrow 10; and human nature 12; of the individual as related to good of whole 16; and action 27; and determinism 28, 39–40, 44; common source of 29; and final causality 34–35; science and 36; rational consideration of 96–97, 146, 230; and the process of moral evaluation 97–99.

Van Bergen, M. 117.

Vein, arterial 182.

Veins 180.

Vena cava 182.

Venal artery 183.

Vengeance 146.

Venice 177.

Verbal behavior 95.

Verisimilitude 46.

Verse 236, 238.

Vice 36, 83, 84, 140, 229.

Virtue, as correct, or right, reasoning xviii, xxi, 133, 134, 141, 194, 228; and *Passions* xix; terminology from ancients xx; etymology of 52; as sovereign good xxi; and study of the mind-body relation 1; special satisfaction of 16, 22; good-will, generosity, and 19; and immortality 22; fortune, the sovereign good, blessedness, and 35–38; and the pursuit of philosophy 41–43; volition, vice, and 83; passions caused by body, interior passions, and 83–84; and perception 91; and the sensuous realm 94; and values 96–99; force of 119; truths facilitating the practice of 136, 143, 150, 154; the ancients, the sovereign good, and 139–41, 142–43, 156, 228–29; and satisfaction 145, 156; and obligation to whole 152; and habit 153; Christian 159, 168; and political crimes 187; and envy 222.

Voetius, Epistle to 116.

Volition, and action xviii; and metaphysics 2; and interior passions 5; formation of passions, mental activity, and 6–9; will, virtue, and 15; and rules 81; and 'passion' 81–82; virtue, vice, and 83; passions caused by the body, the interior passions, virtue, and 83–84; and control of passions 89; and perception 91; vs. feeling 97.

Volonté 2, 79.

Voluntas 2, 79.

Weight 109–10, 111, 113, 115, 248.

White, Thomas 123.

Whole 16, 36, 151, 155, 201.

Will, limits of xvi; right use of 15; the good 18, 19; and power of assent 64; freedom of 79–80; and virtue 141; and sovereign good 228.

Wisdom 13, 45, 84, 138, 186, 243, 247.

Zeno of Citium xx, xxi, 139, 140, 229.